Zarathustra's Sister

Also by H. F. Peters

MY SISTER, MY SPOUSE: A Biography of Lou Andreas-Salomé
RAINER MARIA RILKE: Masks and the Man

ZARATHUSTRA'S

The Case of Elisabeth and
Friedrich Nietzsche

SISTER

H. F. PETERS

CROWN PUBLISHERS, INC.   NEW YORK

To the Miracle in My Life
My Wife
Mollie

Inquiries should be addressed to Crown Publishers, Inc., One Park Avenue, New York, N.Y. 10016.

Published simultaneously in Canada by General Publishing Company Limited

Printed in the United States of America

Library of Congress Cataloging in Publication Data

Peters, Heinz Frederick.
    Zarathustra's sister.

    "The writings of Elisabeth Förster-Nietzsche": p.
    Includes bibliographical references.
    1. Nietzsche, Friedrich Wilhelm, 1844-1900.
2. Förster-Nietzsche, Elisabeth, 1846-1935. I. Title.
B3316.P47 1976   193 [B]   76-18996
ISBN 0-517-52725-1

Contents

PART V
1900-1935

Introduction

NIETZSCHE DIED TWICE. Once in January 1889, a few months after his forty-fourth birthday, when he collapsed in a street in Turin, the victim of a stroke that left him with delusions of grandeur and reduced him gradually to a state of insanity. He died again in August 1900 when his body succumbed to the poison that had destroyed his brain. His steep, rocketlike ascent to fame occurred during the eleven-year interval between his mental and his physical death. Since "fame is nothing but the sum of all misunderstandings that gather around a new name," Nietzsche's fame—read: the vulgarization of his ideas—opened a Pandora's box of destructive drives that left the world in shambles.

Nietzsche had said "God is dead," and his followers tried to prove him right. Nietzsche had said "a good war hallows every cause," and his followers shouted approval. Nietzsche had said "this world is the will to power and nothing besides," and his followers acted accordingly. Intoxicated by the strong brew of his language, Nietzsche's followers claimed to be members of a super race who were destined to become "the lords of the earth." They tried twice and twice they failed—if the judgment of history in two world wars is proof of failure.

The transformation of ideas, beliefs, hopes, fears, wishes, and dreams into actions is a complex process and open to contradictory interpretations. It is easy to show that the French Revolution was influenced by Rousseau. Whether it would have occurred if Rousseau had not written a line is quite another question. Similarly, there is no doubt that the writings of Karl Marx exercised a profound influence on the mind of Lenin, who translated them into actions that wrought havoc with the lives of millions who had never heard of Marx. Marx would have been shocked if he had seen the use Stalin made of his ideas; nor would Rousseau have been pleased to find that one of his most devoted disciples was Robespierre. To blame Marx or Rousseau for the crimes committed in their names is of course absurd. But it is equally absurd to deny that the ideas they promulgated provided powerful intellectual weapons for revolutionaries and assassins. Nietzsche certainly was aware that his ideas were "dynamite." He was dismayed when the *Kreuzzeitung*, house organ of the Prussian Junkers, quoted him with approval, and was shocked when he discovered that he was on the mailing list of the most venomous anti-Semitic newssheet published in Wilhelminian Germany. "The thought frightens me that many people who are unauthorized and wrong-headed will cite me as an authority for their actions."

And yet, in Nietzsche's case the relationship between the ideological content of his writings and their political impact is particularly striking, and not by accident—he willed it so. He was not content with being a master diagnostician of the ills of man and society; he wanted to be a physician as well, for he insisted on prescribing a cure. He demanded action, including political action that called for a new Caesar to transform the world. "I know my fate," he proclaimed, "my name will be connected with the remembrance of something monstrous, a crisis, the like of which has never before occurred on earth. I am not a man. I am dynamite."

The irony of Nietzsche's case is that when he made these startling pronouncements, nobody took them seriously because nobody heard them. At the time of his collapse he was practically unknown. His numerous books and pamphlets had found so few readers that he had been forced to publish them at his own expense. And apart from a few esoteric spirits, such as Georg Brandes and August Strindberg, nobody paid any attention to his ideas. His professional colleagues had long since relegated him to oblivion. In the eyes of his friends he was a solitary eccentric, sick in body and, as some feared, in mind as well. They were alarmed by his frantic search for the ideal place and climate that would permit him to continue his self-imposed task of transvaluating all values. As for his relatives, his mother and sister, he was a prodigal who had forsaken the faith of his fathers. Being staunch Lutherans, they prayed for his soul.

Such was Nietzsche's position on that beautiful autumn day, October 15, 1888, when he buried his forty-fourth birthday and, looking back over his life, started to write an autobiographical essay in which he proclaimed his immortality. Taking his cue from the Bible—"Then came Jesus forth, wearing the crown of thorns, and the purple robe. And Pilate saith unto them: Ecce Homo (Behold the Man)!"—he called it *Ecce Homo*.

This amazing product of a mind taut to breaking point and trembling on the verge of insanity belongs among the sibylline books that cast flashes of lightning into the dark night of a soul in travail. Although meant as an exegesis of the gospel according to Nietzsche, it reduces the gospel to absurdity.

In a style scintillating with magnificent madness it portrays the prophet of Zarathustra as a practical joker who would far rather be a buffoon than a saint and who warns his followers not to be deceived by him. "I am going away alone now, my disciples! You, too, are going away alone. I will it thus. Go away from me and defend yourselves against Zarathustra. Or better still: be ashamed of him. Perhaps he deceived you."

Nobody paid any heed to Nietzsche's warning, for the crowning irony of his fate was that the world took notice of him only after he had gone mad. His ideas, ignored or scorned until then, now became topics of heated discussions in journals, magazines, and newspapers, and were bruited abroad by intellectual bohemians in the taverns and coffeehouses of Central Europe. Such Nietzschean expressions as "superman," "master race," "become hard," "live dangerously," "will to power," crept into the vocabulary of politicians and became party slogans almost overnight. Cheap editions of Nietzsche's works were published with commentaries exalting the militant spirit in a world weary of peace. Germany's intellectual elite, including poets like Stefan George and writers like Thomas Mann, saw in Nietzsche's "aristocratic radicalism" an answer to the decadent democratic ideals of the West. Fervent young men and women met for ritualistic readings from *Zarathustra*. Hymns were composed to celebrate the new religion, and by the time the body of the sick philosopher was finally put to rest, he was proclaimed a saint. What he had feared most had happened: "I am terrified that I shall be sanctified some day . . . I do not want to be a saint, rather a buffoon . . . perhaps I am a buffoon."

The high priestess of the Nietzsche cult, which spread far beyond the borders of Germany, was Nietzsche's sister Elisabeth. Two years younger than her brother, she was in Paraguay at the time of Nietzsche's collapse helping her husband, the notorious anti-Semite Bernhard Förster, in a colonizing venture that in 1889 ended in bankruptcy and Förster's suicide. Within six months Elisabeth lost the two men closest to her heart: her husband and her brother. Such a cruel double blow would have taxed the strength of most women, but Elisabeth spent little time mourning. Resolutely she picked up the pieces of the ill-fated colonizing venture and, leaving the colonists to fend for themselves, hurried back home. Her arrival coincided with the rapidly growing demand for Nietzsche's books, which had lain unread and unsold at the publishers. Elisabeth recognized their potential value at once, coerced her mother into surrendering to her the sole rights to her sick brother's literary estate, and administered it with such managerial skill and editorial ruthlessness that within a few years she made a fortune from it.

Volumes have been written about Nietzsche. He has been hailed as the herald of a new dawn of consciousness and cursed as the father of fascism. A legendary figure in his lifetime, he remains a legendary figure today largely because nobody has paid sufficient attention to the fateful role that Elisabeth played in creating the Nietzsche legend.

To be sure, Nietzsche scholars have known for a long time that the mistress of the Nietzsche Archives in Weimar was not a very reliable witness of her brother's life and work even before Karl Schlechta revealed the extent of her fraudulent activities. Most of Nietzsche's closest friends were offended by her ostentatious exploitation of her brother's fame and angered by her malicious tongue and pen. But even her enemies had to admit that she was an indefatigable propagator of Nietzsche's ideas, which she disseminated in books, articles, lectures, letters to the editors of literary journals, and in a number of widely advertised lawsuits claiming that her brother had authorized her to speak in his name and to interpret his philosophy. As the high priestess of the Nietzsche cult, "Zarathustra's Sister" played an active part in the literary and political life of Germany from Bismarck to Hitler. So much so that on three occasions—in 1908, 1911, and 1923—her name was proposed to the Swedish Academy for the Nobel prize in literature. When she died in 1935, almost ninety years old, the German press eulogized her as an undaunted exponent of the true German spirit. Hitler personally attended her funeral and laid a laurel wreath on her coffin.

The only account that exists of the life of this extraordinary and controversial woman is a hagiographical essay in German written by one of her friends under her supervision, entitled *Die Schwester*, in which she is portrayed as her famous brother's constant companion, counselor, and helpmate. While this picture, presenting Elisabeth as a woman of sweetness and light, which she certainly was not, is grossly overdrawn, it is true that the lives of Friedrich Nietzsche and his sister were so intimately intertwined that it is all but impossible to write about one without reference to the other. Despite Nietzsche's frequently expressed dislike for, indeed hatred of, Elisabeth, there existed a strong family bond between them, and if the flaws in Elisabeth's character are more apparent than the "human-all-too-human" failings of her brother, it is only because Elisabeth deliberately created the legend that Nietzsche was a noble "figure of light." In reality, he was a sick and tortured genius standing close to the pit of insanity into which he finally fell.

The reason why it has not been possible before now to show the interrelationship between Nietzsche and his sister is that as long as Elisabeth was alive nobody had access to her private papers, and even after her death they were kept under lock and key in the Nietzsche Archives, which was in control of her cousin, Major Max Oehler. The attempt to present the case of Elisabeth and Friedrich Nietzsche could only be made after the defeat of the Third Reich, and even then it took years before the rulers of the German Democratic Republic who inherited the Nietzsche Archives were willing to open that section that deals with Elisabeth. She had been an ardent Nazi, a friend of Hitler and Mussolini, and was consequently *persona non grata* in East Germany. For years her personal papers, correspondence, and diaries remained locked up in the newly organized complex of the "Nationale Forschungs—und Gedenkstätten der Klassischen Deutschen Literatur in Weimar."

My efforts to obtain access to these documents have extended over many ʼars and have included several visits to Weimar. In December 1969 I was ᴴally given permission to view them, to take extensive notes, and to order ᴼtostatic copies of entire documents. My request for some historic photographs, such as of Hitler and Elisabeth or of Hitler posing before Nietzsche's bust, was also granted. Therefore, I owe a great debt of gratitude to all the officials of the Weimar Research Center for the courtesy with which they met my numerous requests. If I single out Professor Dr. Karl-Heinz Hahn and Frau Anneliese Clauss I do so merely because they were most directly concerned with my work. I have tried to use the materials they put at my disposal with care and discretion, and I wish to apologize in advance for any possible misunderstanding concerning the use of these documents.

While Weimar provided the major source material for my study, it would have been incomplete and one-sided if I had not had access to the voluminous Nietzsche collection of the University of Basel. Thanks to a research grant from Portland State University I was able to acquire Xerox copies of the entire Nietzscheana deposited at the library of the University of Basel. They provided a necessary corrective to the picture that emerged from my studies at Weimar. Among other sources helpful to my work were documents at the Schiller-Archiv in Marbach, at the Thielska Galleriet, and the University of Stockholm.

I am also beholden to many professional colleagues both in this country and in Germany; in particular to Professor Karl Schlechta, who shared with me his personal recollections of Elisabeth Förster-Nietzsche, and to Professor Mazzino Montinari, co-editor of the definitive Nietzsche edition, who showed me several unpublished letters from Elisabeth to her mother.

In treating the encounter between Nietzsche and Lou Andreas-Salomé, née Louise von Salomé, I am closely following the account given in my book *My Sister, My Spouse: A Biography of Lou Andreas-Salomé,* W. W. Norton & Company, 1962; paper edition, Norton, 1974.

Finally, I am greatly indebted to my colleagues of the Portland State University library, Edmond Gnoza and Elmer Magnuson, for their professional help with many technical problems that arose during the preparation of the manuscript.

My purpose in writing this book was to present the case of Elisabeth and Friedrich Nietzsche as fully and completely as possible. I leave it to the reader to form his own judgment.

PART I
1846-1876

1·Pastoral Prelude

ON JULY 10, 1846, at the break of dawn the young wife of Pastor Ludwig Nietzsche gave birth to their second child, a daughter, in the parsonage of Röcken. It was an event of great significance to the three women who lived in the parsonage—Pastor Nietzsche's mother and his two unmarried sisters. As for the parson himself, tears of joy filled his eyes when the midwife handed him his newborn daughter. He noted in his diary: July 10 in the year of the Lord 1846—blessed be the Lord.

Röcken, a hamlet of a few hundred souls, lies in Prussian Saxony a few miles southwest of Leipzig and is so small that its name does not appear on most maps of central Germany. Its next-door neighbor, the village of Lützen, is not much larger but figures prominently in all books of German history. For there, on a gloomy November day in 1632, the Swedes, commanded by their king, Gustavus Adolphus, defeated the Imperialists, led by Wallenstein, and saved the protestant cause, although at the cost of the king's life. In commemoration of this historic battle the Gustavus Adolphus monument now towers over the flat fields of Lützen which became the scene of a second battle that raged from dawn to dusk on May 2, 1813, pitting the combined forces of Russia and Prussia against Napoleon. Although the French were outnumbered, the military genius of their emperor triumphed once again. But it was Napoleon's last victory. A few months later his army was routed and chased beyond the Rhine.

In the parsonage of Röcken these battles were often discussed. When Elisabeth's brother was asked where he was born, he used to say: "On the battlefield of Lützen." With a mixture of pride and bravado he informed the

Danish critic Georg Brandes that the first name he remembered was that of Gustavus Adolphus. His father, Pastor Nietzsche, was a passionate partisan of the Swedish king. That it was a king who had given up his life for the faith and not a mere monk like Luther, the pastor of Röcken considered particularly significant, for he venerated the nobility. Like many members of the clergy, he felt that kings were divinely ordained and must be revered accordingly. He himself owed his office to the favor of the Prussian king, Friedrich Wilhelm IV. Legend has it that the king granted him two personal audiences and was so favorably impressed with the young parson's piety, his patriotism, and his devotion to the royal family that he appointed him pastor of Röcken.

In his Sunday sermons Pastor Nietzsche extolled the virtues of loyalty to the Hohenzollern by reminding his peasant congregation that they owed as much obedience to their *Landesvater* as to their Father in Heaven. He considered it a particularly favorable omen that his son was born on October 15, the birthday of King Friedrich Wilhelm IV. As a token of his gratitude and in memory of his royal benefactor, he baptized the child Friedrich Wilhelm.

Two years later, when his daughter was born, Pastor Nietzsche felt again compelled to pay homage to a noble patron. Before he had assumed his duties at Röcken he had been tutor at the Court of Altenburg. His charges had been the three young princesses of the duke of Saxe-Altenburg: Elisabeth, Therese, and Alexandra. When he heard on that midsummer night that the Lord had given him a daughter, he decided to give her the names of all three princesses. The entry in the book of baptismal records kept in the vestry of the church at Röcken reads Elisabeth Therese Alexandra Nietzsche.

Both Elisabeth and her brother inherited their father's predilection for the aristocracy as well as his condescending attitude toward the people. All her life Elisabeth insisted that women of the upper classes should not devote themselves to the welfare of the people because "an abyss separates us from them; they are and remain common." And Bernoulli reports that Nietzsche used to become impatient when he heard the expression "rights of the people." "Nonsense," he said contemptuously, "they should be slaves." Like his father, he scorned the idea of a revolutionary reordering of society.

As far as Pastor Nietzsche was concerned, the revolution of 1848 was a calamity, an assault by criminals, malcontents, and infidels against the divinely established order. He hoped his king would deal with the revolutionaries as one deals with mad dogs—shoot them. He was alarmed when the king hesitated, and he was utterly dismayed when he read in the newspapers that Friedrich Wilhelm had bowed to the demands of the revolutionaries and worn their hated symbol, the black-red-and-gold cockade. This was too much for the loyal parson. He lapsed into a mood of bleak despair, wept uncontrollably, and locked himself into his study for hours in solitary grief. When he came out, he forbade his family ever to mention the dreadful scene that had taken place at the Royal Palace in Berlin.

A few months later his depression deepened. He suffered convulsions, a loss of memory, and could no longer fulfill his pastoral duties. His young wife tried valiantly but in vain to alleviate his suffering. His condition, finally diagnosed as "softening of the brain," worsened from day to day. For eleven months Pastor Nietzsche lived in a state of excruciating pain, gradually becoming a blind and incoherent invalid, until in 1849 death relieved him of his agony. He was thirty-six years old.

In 1893, when Elisabeth wrote her brother's life, he too was an invalid and had been for four years, the victim of a brain disease that left him insane at the age of forty-four. To be sure, Nietzsche's madness did not detract from his rapidly rising fame—quite the reverse. Many who had not bothered to read him while he was sane now rushed to buy the books of the "mad philosopher." But Elisabeth feared that if it became known that Nietzsche's father had died of a brain disease, her brother's illness might be considered hereditary and his ideas discredited as outpourings of a diseased mind. She was in Paraguay when her mother wrote her that Fritz had suffered a mental breakdown and that his friend Franz Overbeck had taken him to an asylum for the insane in Basel. Elisabeth was outraged. She was sure her brother was no lunatic. By committing him to an asylum Overbeck had cruelly betrayed his friend. In her letters from Paraguay, she warned her mother to be careful what she told people about the family, lest they would say madness was "a trait of the Oehler family." She added,

> Uncle Edmund was also very odd, and Uncle Theobald, Gustav Knieling, and poor Lieschen. . . . Defend yourself against such tales! The cause of Fritz's breakdown was overwork and that terrible sleeping medicine. And please don't talk such nonsense about poor Papa. If he had not fallen down those stone steps, he would probably still be alive today.

In her brother's biography Elisabeth repeated that her father had died as the result of a fall. This story has become the official version of Pastor Nietzsche's death.

Elisabeth was three years old when her mother had to leave the parsonage of Röcken, where she had spent six years of married life, leave the roomy, two-story house next to the church whose slate roof bulged with three dormer windows that peered upon the countryside like eyes watching fields, meadows, ponds, and the line of poplars along the road to Lützen. It was a sad leave-taking for the young widow and her two children, although life at the parsonage had not been easy for her because she had to share it with her husband's mother and his two unmarried sisters. Pastor Nietzsche had installed his relatives at the parsonage before he married Franziska Oehler, the young daughter of a fellow parson in next-door Pobles, and the three women remained with him after his marriage.

Franziska, or Fränzchen, as she was called, was only seventeen when she met Ludwig Nietzsche, who was just turning thirty. If it was not love at first sight she felt for him, it was certainly awe. For Pastor Nietzsche entered her young, happy-go-lucky life like a prince from the world of fairy tales. His serious and courtly manner, his elegantly tailored, black suits of finest English cloth, his polished conversation, and, not least, his accomplishments on the piano set him apart from the other men she knew. They were all peasants compared with Ludwig; she too felt more like a peasant girl than the daughter of a parson. Her home, the parsonage at Pobles, with its barns and stables, its horses, cows, chickens, with her father's interest in agriculture and hunting was indeed more like the home of a country squire than a country parson. It was filled to the brim with life, echoing with the screams and laughter of her ten brothers and sisters, healthy country children who enjoyed horseback riding and swimming in the summertime and sledding and skating in winter.

For seventeen years the parsonage at Pobles had been Fränzchen's home; all she knew about the world she had learned there. She had not gone to school. Her father, assisted by young candidates of theology who interned at Pobles, taught his children to read and write, introduced them to the world of numbers, and gave them a thorough knowledge of the word of God. His simple and steadfast faith left a deep impression on Fränzchen and remained her source of strength during all the vicissitudes of her long life. She was a bright child and learned easily, although book learning was not one of her favorite occupations. "In one ear, out the other," her father sighed when he reported Fränzchen's progress to the rest of the family. There was much good-humored teasing, but neither Pastor Oehler nor his wife lost their temper when their children neglected their homework or, in youthful ebullience, overstepped the unwritten rules of conduct.

Life at Pobles followed a natural rhythm; Fränzchen and her sisters helped their mother with the household chores, and her brothers spent part of their day in their father's study or roamed about in the fields. In the evenings, after dinner, the family often assembled around the piano; Pastor Oehler struck the mighty chords of his favorite hymn, Martin Luther's "A Mighty Fortress Is Our Lord," and his eleven children joined in so lustily that the rafters of the parsonage reverberated, and the peasants in the village below looked up and listened. On Sundays the whole family dressed up and followed their father to church. Pastor Oehler in clerical robes walked ahead, his family behind him at a respectful distance. After the service they ate a hearty Sunday dinner, grouped according to their ages around the large, oak dining room table, questioning their father about the sermon he had preached or poking fun at one another. They were lively, uninhibited children, rarely sick, and totally ignorant of those disturbances of the soul that cause neuroses and mental breakdowns. Once, during the time of Fränzchen's engagement to Ludwig Nietzsche, her fiancé told her that his sister Rosalie had been unable to come to the party because she was ill. When Fränzchen asked him what was wrong with Rosalie, he merely said, "Nerves." "I had never heard the word 'nerves' before," she confesses in an autobiographical sketch she wrote many years later, "and felt quite stupid that I didn't know what it was. When our guests had left I asked mother what 'nerves' were. Mother didn't know either, thought for a moment and said, 'I believe it is some sort of general weakness.' "

The world Franziska Oehler entered when she became Frau Pastor Nietzsche was so different from the world of her childhood that she could not bring herself to describe it in the autobiographical sketch she started to write almost half a century later. The long passage of time had not lessened the pain of those years. She recoiled from thinking of them and gave up her attempt to correct the idyllic picture of life at Röcken her daughter had drawn in her book on *The Young Nietzsche*, which had received much praise from reviewers. What good would it do if she, the mother, took public issue with her daughter? She knew her daughter. Elisabeth was quite capable of retorting that her mother's memory was failing. No, it was best to draw a curtain of silence over those years.

Even in retrospect Franziska shuddered when she remembered the morbid atmosphere of the parsonage at Röcken. She, who had never even heard the word "nerves," now encountered it in full force. There was her husband's mother, Erdmuthe, an old lady extremely sensitive to noise, interested in the affairs of high society and obviously ill at ease in the country; there was her husband's sister Rosalie, always ailing and fond of esoteric conversations about problems of theology; there was Augusta, her husband's other sister, a practical-minded spinster who was in charge of the household and supervised the work of Mina, the faithful family maid; and finally, there was her husband Ludwig, whom she loved. She loved sitting in his study, watching him work on his Sunday sermons or improvise on the piano, while she knitted baby things. It was a godsend that she had become pregnant soon after her marriage, for a baby would give meaning to her otherwise idle existence.

But even these hours of conjugal happiness were sometimes interrupted by frightening experiences. Franziska would notice that her husband suddenly stopped talking in the middle of a sentence, sat back in his chair and stared blankly into space. When she rushed over to him and shook him, he would wake up as from a sleep and look at her surprised. "What is the matter, Fränzchen?" he would ask her, quite oblivious that anything had happened. She mentioned these "spells" to Dr. Gutjahr, their family doctor, who prescribed rest. Pastor Nietzsche was a very high-strung person; his nervous system was easily upset. He needed plenty of rest. Here again was the dreaded word "nerves."

The birth of her son, a year and five days after her marriage, filled the void in Franziska's life. She assumed the chores of motherhood with such dedication that her baby hardly had to open his mouth before his wish was fulfilled. Fritz grew quickly and became a plump and healthy baby boy, but when he reached the age when most babies begin to talk, he remained obstinately silent. Franziska became worried and consulted her doctor, who told her that her excessive attention to her baby's needs interfered with his speech development. He advised that she stop watching Fritz's sign language so carefully. She did so and he soon learned to use words. She had no such problems with her daughter Elisabeth, born two years later. Indeed, if Fritz was a slow learner, Lieschen was fast, and while he was a quiet child, she was volatile and temperamental.

Taking care of her children occupied most of Franziska's time during the first four years of her marriage. Then came 1848 and her husband's illness, which coincided with the birth of a third child, a boy christened Josef in honor of Duke Josef of Altenburg. He seemed to be a healthy child, but a few months after her husband's death he developed difficulties while teething, suffered convulsions, and died.

Franziska was twenty-three years old, a widow with two small children, when she said good-bye to the parsonage of Röcken, leaving behind her brief married life and memories of happiness, anxiety, sorrow—and two fresh graves.

2·Growing Up in a Cathedral Town

*L*IFE IN THE parsonage of Röcken had not been easy for Franziska even while her husband was alive. Now that he was dead, she was faced with a new and formidable problem. She discovered that her widow's pension, amounting to some paltry thirty thalers a year, was not enough for her to live on, let alone to educate her children. Her husband's relatives were moderately well-to-do, largely because a stepbrother of Pastor Nietzsche's, who had amassed a fortune in England, had died childless and bequeathed his wealth to them. When her husband died, his share of the fortune went to his two children. Franziska, not being a blood relative, received nothing except the use of the interest until her children were of age. She was therefore more than ever at the mercy of her relatives. When they decided to set up housekeeping in neighboring Naumburg, she moved with them. Naumburg was chosen because her mother-in-law had many friends among the best families of that old cathedral town where her favorite brother had been pastor.

Naumburg, on the river Saale, had about fifteen thousand inhabitants in the middle of the nineteenth century. It was founded in the tenth century by Emperor Otto I, who established an episcopal seat there and built a fortress to protect Christian Europe from the intrusions of pagan Slavs. When Franziska and her relatives moved there in the mid-nineteenth century, it was still a walled town. Its five massive gates were locked and barred between ten o'clock at night and five in the morning. Dominated by the four towers of its medieval cathedral, Naumburg was also the seat of the provincial law courts and the court of appeals. Its leading citizens were high ecclesiastics, lawyers, and privy councillors. Elisabeth called Naumburg "a staunchly Christian, conservative, and royalist town, a pillar of throne and altar." And in one of the numerous autobiographical sketches that her brother wrote during his adolescence, he said:

9

Naumburg . . . made a very strange impression on me. The many new sights: churches, houses, squares, and streets astonished and confused me at first. I was also much impressed by its environment, its pretty hills, river valleys, palaces and castles which far surpassed the rural simplicity of my former home.

The Nietzsches rented a large apartment on the ground floor of the home of a railroad inspector. Franziska's mother-in-law occupied the front room, where she received her distinguished friends, such as the wives of privy councillors Wilhelm Pinder and Gustav Krug. Augusta and Rosalie moved into the adjoining rooms. Franziska and her children were relegated to two small rooms in the back of the apartment. Five years she endured this Cinderella existence. Cheerful and uncomplaining, she devoted her young life to the welfare of her children, who grew up in secret alliance against being dominated by women. They had no playmates, shared one room for play and sleep, and declared, much to the amusement of their mother and aunts, that they would become husband and wife when they were grown up.

Elisabeth worshiped her brother. "Fritz says so" was her standard reply when her mother or her aunts questioned her about something she had said or done. She knew her brother was right even if everybody else thought otherwise. Fritz, in turn, was devoted to his sister, although she startled him at times by violent fits of temper. On such occasions she would scream at him and pummel him with her small fists in uncontrolled rage; when he turned away in disgust, she would spit at him. That is why he gave her the nickname "Llama."

In her book on her brother Elisabeth says she was delighted when he called her "Llama" because the description of that animal, which he had found in a book on natural history, fitted her so well. "The llama," she quotes, "is a strange animal; voluntarily it carries the heaviest burdens, but if it is treated badly it refuses to eat and lies down to die." What she failed to quote was "when a llama does not want to go on, it turns its head round and discharges its saliva, which has an unpleasant odor, into the rider's face." Nietzsche knew very well why, to the end of his life, he called his sister "his faithful Llama."

He was touched all the same that she collected every scrap of paper on which he had written, every one of his youthful compositions, poems, essays as though they were priceless manuscripts. And although he made fun of Lisbeth's "treasure chest," as she called her hoard of his scribbles, her adoration flattered him. He felt she was the only one in his family who understood his literary ambitions. When he was ten years old, he told her that someday he would write a book and give it to her. Since she was younger than he was, and a girl besides, he considered it his duty to educate her. This was not always easy, for Lisbeth had a mind of her own. For example, she firmly believed that babies were brought by the stork. "Don't talk such nonsense about the stork," Fritz berated his seven-year-old sister, "man is a mammal and as such bears living young." To his intense annoyance his little sister shook her head vigorously and insisted that this time he was wrong. Mama had told her that the stork had brought her, and Aunt Rosalie had said so too. It was silly to think otherwise. Besides, they had both seen pictures of storks carrying babies. He shrugged his shoulders, said she was a "stupid goose," and walked away. Then and later his only defense against Elisabeth's willful ignorance was to walk away.

The question of schooling for her children was one of the problems Franziska had to face when they arrived in Naumburg. Her son was six years old. It was time that he received regular instruction. She herself had taught him to read, and Rosalie had taken care of his religious instruction in preparation for his future career. For there was no doubt in anyone's mind that Fritz would continue the long line of Protestant pastors founded by his forebears. There was no doubt in Fritz's mind either. He idealized his father, and everybody agreed that he had inherited Pastor Nietzsche's pious temperament as well as his love of music. It was preordained that Fritz would study theology, which meant that he would attend the *Domgymnasium* when he reached the age of ten. The question was where should he go to school until then?

Naumburg had a reputable elementary school for boys of the middle and lower classes; upper-class children attended private schools. After much discussion with her relatives, Franziska decided to send her son to the public school, not only because it was cheaper, but also because her mother-in-law believed that children of all classes should have common schooling up to the age of eight or ten. She thought that as a result of common schooling during those early years upper-class children would gain a better understanding of the mentality of the lower orders.

As it turned out, her theory did not work with her grandson. Fritz was very unhappy among those young ruffians, the sons of butchers, bakers, and candlestick makers who played tricks on him, laughed at his sedate manners, and scornfully called him "little pastor." There were only two kindred spirits in the entire school, the sons of privy councillors Pinder and Krug, and they were equally unhappy. Hence, the experiment in public education was abandoned after barely one year. In the spring of 1851 the three friends were entrusted to the care of a young Protestant clergyman who tutored small groups of boys in preparation of their entering the *Domgymnasium.*

They spent three years with him, studying the Bible under his expert guidance and learning the fundamentals of Greek and Latin grammar. For relaxation their young tutor took them on long hikes through the countryside, a form of exercise that Nietzsche continued all his life, and introduced them into the art of archery. It was a happy, carefree time and forged a strong bond of friendship between Nietzsche, Pinder, and Krug.

Elisabeth often participated in their games. Once, when she was eight years old, she was invited to act the part of Pallas Athena in a play jointly written by her brother and Wilhelm Pinder, entitled *The Gods in Olympus.* Everything went very well at first. The audience, including the parents of the little actors, were duly impressed with the stage presence of their offspring. They all looked forward to the play's climax, depicting the feasting of the gods. Franziska had prepared a large dish of vanilla pudding with raspberry sauce, which was to be eaten on stage. Alas, it proved the undoing of Pallas Athena. The young goddess, still wearing armor and helmet, got violently sick to her stomach and had to be led off the stage in tears. Her brother was torn between feeling sorry for his sister's plight and angry that she had spoiled his play. Girls, he concluded, could not be entrusted with serious tasks.

When the time came for Elisabeth to go to school, it was decided to send her to Fräulein von Pareskis's private school for young ladies, a high-class establishment, where she learned reading, writing, arithmetic, a little French, and a great deal of deportment. She was a bright pupil, quick in grasping new ideas, and she received good grades. The most striking feature of her pert little face, which was surrounded by blond locks, were her eyes. She had large blue eyes, but since she had inherited her father's myopia and refused to wear glasses, she had to make an effort to see distant objects and sometimes her eyes seemed slightly out of focus. Her friends whispered that Lieschen Nietzsche had a "*Silberblick*," an expression that infuriated her, for she certainly did not squint; she was merely nearsighted like her brother.

In any case, Elisabeth did not care what her friends said about her. She went to school to learn and to please her teachers. And in the latter art she excelled. "I have noticed," she confided to her brother, "that I can talk about anything without understanding much of it." She had a large circle of "bosom friends" but no really close confidante. Her quick temper and quick tongue intimidated most girls. They discovered that it was best not to quarrel with Lieschen Nietzsche, who was always right. If anybody doubted it she threw herself up to the full height of her five feet two inches and declared with finality: "Fritz says so too." There was no appeal against such authority.

Imperceptibly childhood merged into adolescence, and still the two children of Pastor Nietzsche were their own closest playmates. When Elisabeth was eleven years old, her grandmother died and her mother finally succeeded in setting up her own home for herself and her two children. She rented a small apartment in the house of a Naumburg friend, which was surrounded by a large old-fashioned garden. "Fritz and I lived in this garden from dawn to dusk, sailed in a swing to the highest treetops, played marvelous games, ate, drank and studied in deeply shadowed arbors, and told each other scary stories in the half darkness of ancient trees." The nostalgic lyricism of this passage, which Elisabeth included in her book on her brother, shows that this old garden was the paradise of their childhood.

They spent their vacations at their grandfather's large and rambling parsonage in Pobles, where they skated on the frozen village pond in the winter or went for long sleigh rides through the countryside. In summer they went swimming or helped with the harvest. It was a wonderful childhood, filled to the brim with secret joys, intimacies, and genuine love. The thought that someday they would be driven out of their paradise never occurred to them.

But then one day it happened, quite unexpectedly, in the form of a letter from the head of the famous boarding school Pforta who notified Franziska that her son had been awarded a full tuition scholarship to that ancient seat of learning, the alma mater of some of Germany's leading writers, poets, and scholars. Although Schulpforta was only an hour's journey by foot from Naumburg, Fritz would henceforth no longer live at home and Lieschen would lose her closest friend. Disconsolate, she wrote: "I, poor Llama, felt badly treated by fate, refused to eat, and lay down in the dust to die." Her brother, too, dreaded the separation, although he tried to be brave. He consoled his sister with the assurance that either he would come home every Sunday or they would meet in Almrich, a village halfway between Naumburg and Pforta. But in the depth of the night his courage failed him and he cried so bitterly that in the morning Franziska discovered his pillows moist with tears.

3·We Fools of Fate

*H*ER SON'S DEPARTURE for boarding school in October 1858 coincided with Franziska's move into a house of her own, her third home in Naumburg. The house on Weingarten 18, a comfortable two-story building with a large attic, had enough rooms for her own family on the second floor; on the ground floor were three two-room apartments that could be rented furnished to law students or young barristers, of whom there were many in Naumburg. Franziska was a practical woman; she knew that whatever income she could get from her gentlemen renters would be a welcome addition to her own meager widow's pension. What she could not have known, when she moved into the house on Weingarten, was that she would live in it for almost forty years, that here her son would write his philological essays that attracted the attention of his teachers and propelled him into a career so different from that which he had hoped for. Nor could she have known that her son would return to this same house thirty years later, a helpless invalid, and that here she would take care of him to the end of her life.

But even if she had known this tragic turn of fate, if she had known the bitter quarrels into which her daughter would embroil her here, she would not have despaired. Her faith in God was stronger than the vicissitudes of life. And as for her children, no matter how different their views were from hers, they were still her children. If they rejected God and if God rejected them, her love would shelter them. Her house would always be their refuge and their home.

The Royal Boarding School of Pforta, which Nietzsche attended for six years, had originally been a Cistercian abbey. Secularized in the sixteenth century, the *Monasterium Sancta Mariae de Porta*, was set apart from its rural environment by massive, twelve-foot-high brick walls and gave the impression of "a prison rather than an alma mater," Nietzsche told his mother and sister. Nor was this impression unfounded, for the two hundred boys at Pforta, ranging in age from ten to nineteen, were subjected to the rigorous discipline of a Prussian military academy. They lived by the clock, with every minute of the day patterned to a tight schedule that left little time for leisure. The school buildings—some dating back to the twelfth century with its cloisters, its Romanesque chapel, and its small dormitories that housed twelve or sixteen boys—exuded a heavily monastic air.

Every night at nine o'clock the dormitories were locked, the lights were turned off, and silence was enforced. At four in the morning the doors were unlocked and the dormitories had to be vacated by five in the summer and six in winter. If a boy overslept, he was roughly thrown out of bed by the dormitory supervisors, senior boys in charge of discipline. He was allowed ten minutes in the crowded bathroom and another ten for dressing. At five twenty-five the school bell rang for the first time, and it rang five minutes later again as a signal for the whole school to assemble in the prayer-room. There the dormitory supervisors kept order until a teacher, accompanied by an assistant, appeared. After a short organ prelude a hymn was sung, the teacher read a passage from the New Testament and closed the morning service with a final word from the Bible. Then the boys rushed to their rooms, where they drank glasses of warm milk and ate rolls. Lessons started punctually at six o'clock in the summer, at seven in the winter. Class instruction alternated with periods of review. At noon the entire school assembled in the cloisters according to class rank and marched into the dining room. One of the seniors said grace and the school replied with a response in Latin. Then they ate the main meal of the day, consisting of soup, meat, vegetable, and fruit. In addition, each boy received one-twelfth of a loaf of bread—an ancient custom commemorating the Last Supper. The meal ended with a prayer at twelve thirty. It was followed by a free period that lasted until ten to two o'clock during which the boys could play ball or walk about in the school grounds. They were not allowed to go up to their rooms. Afternoon classes started at two and lasted till four o'clock. Then came a fifteen-minute break for an afternoon snack, usually a piece of bread with plum jam. From quarter past four till five o'clock the seniors supervised a reading hour, during which Greek or Latin exercises or mathematical assignments were written. Another brief break at five o'clock was followed by supervised homework till seven. At seven o'clock sharp the evening meal began. It consisted of soup, bread and butter, cheese or herring or sausage, and it lasted three-quarters of an hour. Then the boys were allowed to play till eight thirty, when they had to assemble for evening prayer in the chapel. At nine o'clock everybody had to be in bed; the lights were turned off and the dormitory doors were locked. Such was the daily routine at Pforta.

For a shy and introverted boy like Nietzsche, who had known nothing but the warmth of family life in a circle of women, it must have been little short of hell to be thrust abruptly into such a militantly male environment. And hell it was, although he bore stoically what he later called the "uniformed co-ercion of life at Pforta." Only in his letters to his mother and sister did he pour out his heart and his homesickness. In letter after letter he urged them to meet him on Sunday in Almrich or he told them that he would come home. And he counted the weeks before each vacation. "Only two more weeks," he wrote early in December before his first Christmas vacation, "never has time passed so slowly as now, never have I wished more fervently that it had wings."

To cheer him up his mother wrote him frequently and dispatched a steady stream of packages and parcels in answer to his urgent requests. He needed underwear, handkerchiefs, shoes. "I am sending my black pants and must have them back before Sunday, please get them patched. They are torn. . . . You might also send me something to eat. I would love one of your home-made cakes. . . ." He complained about headaches and colds and asked his mother to keep him supplied with medicines. "I have no appetite, but I would eat an apple if I had money to buy one." These pleas did not go un-answered. Not only his mother and sister, but the whole family, uncles and aunts, tried to make life bearable for Fritz, who had brought honor to all of them by being admitted to Pforta.

Elisabeth, in particular, was very proud of her brother. She extolled his virtues on every occasion in school or during those afternoon kaffeeklatsches with her girl friends when they talked about boys. With ill-disguised conde-scension she listened to the stories her friends told about their brothers. It was absurd to compare Tom, Dick, and Harry with her beloved brother Fritz. He was incomparable. He was at the head of his class in Pforta; he wrote poet-ry and composed music—he was a genius. It was useless for her girl friends to remonstrate with her. Among the social circle in Naumburg where Elisabeth moved, her hero worship of her brother was proverbial. "You had to be care-ful in talking with Lisbeth Nietzsche," a young admirer of hers confessed, "she constantly quoted her brother as final authority which made you feel rather stupid."

Fritz too kept in close touch with his sister all the time he was in Pforta. He advised her what books to read, he sent her his compositions and told her how to play and sing them. When he heard that Lisbeth was to attend a finish-ing school in Dresden, he replied:

> I don't really like Dresden; it is not grandiose enough. Also its customs and dialect are too similar to ours in Thuringia. Now if she were to go to Hannover, for example, she would learn very different customs, habits, and dialect. It is good to be educated in different regions of one's country so that one does not become one-sided. However, as a small residential capital and art center, Dresden will offer sufficient stimulation for Elisabeth's mind and for that I envy her. . . . I am eager to learn how she

gets on in her new environment. A finishing school is always a risk, but I have full confidence in Elisabeth.

He did not have to wait long before he received an enthusiastic letter from his sister in Dresden. She wrote:

> Imagine that I am having dancing lessons with a Countess Ross, who is very friendly toward your little sister. Would you ever have guessed that I can get along very well with such high personages? I find it amusing myself. You will be surprised when I return home; your awkward teenage sister has become a debutante! But honestly, my dear Fritzchen, I have not changed much. Please think sometimes of your sister Elisabeth, who loves you dearly.

In a postscript she added that "it would be heavenly, marvelous, wonderful" if he would visit her in her Dresden *Pensionat* come Easter.

Fritz could not possibly turn down such an urgent request, and he spent two weeks of his Easter vacation in his sister's company. Arm in arm, they strolled through the Grosse Garten, visited the famous art gallery in the Zwinger, where they stood in awe before the Sistine Madonna, and took a boat ride on the Elbe to Pillnitz, the summer residence of the Saxon royal family. They made a handsome young couple: Nietzsche, stockily built but holding himself very erect and walking with the confident air of a Prussian officer, and his petite sister clinging to his arm and talking animatedly. Elisabeth introduced her brother proudly to the circle of her Dresden friends and beamed with joy when they commented on Fritz's good looks and noble bearing. All the young Saxon ladies agreed that he was a born gentleman, and they envied Elisabeth the company of her cavalier brother. Fritz was very gallant to his sister's friends but left no doubt that he preferred her company to that of any other girl.

All too quickly the two weeks passed and he had to return to his Spartan life in Pforta. From there he wrote her that the blossoming linden tree in front of his window reminded him of Dresden and the pleasant days he had spent there.

> But to be reminded of you, dear, dear Elisabeth, I do not need any such farfetched memory aids; on the contrary, I am thinking so frequently of you that I really think of you all the time, not excluding the time when I am asleep, for I dream often of you and of our last meeting.

Elisabeth was overjoyed to receive such assurances of brotherly love. It came therefore as a great shock to her when he told her that during his last year at Pforta he had fallen in love with the sister of one of his school friends, a pretty girl from Berlin, who was an accomplished pianist. He asked Elisabeth to send him a musical score, which he wanted to play as a duet with his Berlin sweetheart. Elisabeth felt hurt and betrayed. She told him that it was unbecoming to a senior at Pforta who was about to enter a university to be infatuated with a little girl. She did not send him the requested score. "I am sorry that I have upset you," her brother replied, "I promise I won't do it

Elisabeth Nietzsche, "Lieschen," as a teenager in Naumburg.

again, the more so since I must fear that horrified by the monstrosity of my letter, you completely forget its point—to wit, send the score." He concluded by saying that he was in no mood just now to answer more affectionately because he had just done his laundry and, calling her his "heart's Lieschen, sweetie pie, pussycat," signed himself "Frédéric."

The bantering tone of Nietzsche's letter is deceiving. He loved his sister and did not wish to hurt her. Her angry reaction to his confession that he was interested in another girl made him realize that Elisabeth's jealousy was easily aroused. He decided to forget the Berlin girl and he made no further mention of her.

Elisabeth returned to Naumburg with a sense of regret after her six-month stay in Dresden. She had enjoyed the elegant life, the opera, theaters, art galleries of the Saxon capital. Naumburg, by comparison, was dull and provincial. To her Naumburg friends she gave glowing accounts of her social activities in Dresden, of the glittering balls she had attended, of the witty and handsome students who had paid her court, of the wonderful picnics on the river, and of the hikes through the canyons of Saxon Switzerland.

It is doubtful whether these stories endeared Elisabeth to her friends. They knew that she had a vivid imagination and a fondness for high society. To judge from her tales she had been on intimate terms with counts and countesses and had been treated like a princess. There were no such high personages in Naumburg, and if Elisabeth Nietzsche preferred their company to that of the good burghers of her hometown, she had better go back to Dresden. Even such long-term friends as Sophie Pinder treated her noticeably less warmly and did not always invite her to her parties. Franziska worried about her daughter's growing isolation and told her son that Elisabeth was so unhappy in Naumburg that "she frequently has expressed the wish to leave it altogether." But where should she go and what should she do? Was it not expected that a young girl stay home until she had found a husband to take care of her? Remembering her own early marriage, Franziska became more and more alarmed as the years went by and her daughter remained single. She could not understand why Elisabeth seemed so unconcerned about the most important decision a young girl has to make. Lisbeth was pretty and vivacious, an efficient housekeeper, a good cook, and she was not without means. Her small inheritance would provide sufficient financial security during the first years of marriage for a struggling young lawyer or pastor. What prevented Elisabeth from finding a suitable husband?

Elisabeth herself treated the subject of marriage with studied indifference. She wrote her brother that on reading Schopenhauer's *Essays from the Parerga and Paralipomena* she had come across a passage that said that every human life moves in a causal chain: "should said chain end with me as an old maid—and I almost think it will because from inner necessity I have recently rejected three worthy suitors—then, my dear Fritz, do not think badly of me and love me also in my old age."

On another occasion Elisabeth informed her brother of the engagement of a young man, a distant cousin who had paid her court, to another girl. Somewhat wistfully she added:

> Mama behaves very amusingly; she considers it outrageous that I am happy about the engagement because I might have possessed Rudolf's heart, and that I scorned it. She says she will not eat today and will mourn and worry. But, good heavens, I had nothing to do with it and can't be blamed if Mama set her hopes on the wrong man. . . . But it is useless, she keeps on mumbling prophetically that by spurning the seed, I would be left with the chaff. And she is horrified when I add cheerfully "or perhaps with nobody."

Her brother did not pay much attention to such outpourings of feminine worries. He had other problems to worry about. The question of his future had to be decided. After completing his six years of rigorous schooling in Pforta he had gone to Bonn to study theology. That decision had been made long ago. His mother and all his relatives expected that he would prepare himself for the clergy, and to oblige them he had matriculated as a student of theology at the University of Bonn, although during his last years at Pforta doubts had already begun to assail him about the truth of the Christian faith, indeed of all faiths. During his first semester at Bonn he had tried to assuage these doubts by throwing himself wholeheartedly into the happy-go-lucky life of a student. He had joined the Frankonia, a dueling fraternity, had participated in nights of drunken revelry, had joined in swaggering parades through the sleepy villages on the Rhine dressed in the colorful uniform of the Frankonians, and had visited a brothel in Cologne. But his doubts had remained, and he had soon felt disgusted with fraternity life. It was vulgar and stupid. Worst of all, it was a waste of time. He had better things to do than spend his nights in smoke-filled taverns with a crowd of beer-soaked barbarians. He decided to give up theological speculations and enter a field that required rigorous mental discipline—classical philology. To make it easier for his mother to accept this change, he told her that he had met a great teacher, the renowned philologist Friedrich Ritschl, who had encouraged him in his decision. When Ritschl left Bonn and joined the faculty of the University of Leipzig, Nietzsche followed him. He was happy to be near his mother and sister again.

To Elisabeth he confided that the real reason for his turning away from theology was his loss of faith. He had come under the influence of Schopenhauer, who taught what he had suspected for some time, that the world was not the creation of a divine being but the working of a blind metaphysical will, a force without purpose or direction. Christianity, like all religions, concealed the truth that life on earth was meaningless by holding out the promise of a life to come under the protection of a heavenly father. A hope that, alas, was not founded on fact but on faith—blind faith. Once your eyes were opened to the reality of the human condition you could no longer accept the consolation of religion. You had to follow the commands of reason and of your own conscience.

These ideas disturbed Elisabeth, who went to church faithfully every Sunday, sang in the choir, helped in church socials, participated in collecting money for Christian missions abroad, and never once had questioned the tenets of her Protestant faith. But since she was used to accepting her brother's superior wisdom, she tried to follow him into the gloomy world he now revealed to her. Much to the surprise of her mother, she began to reflect a sad and mournful mien. Questioned by her mother why she was so depressed, she shrugged her shoulders and replied that Fritz had told her all life was suffering, an answer that no doubt puzzled the pious widow of Pastor Nietzsche who knew that her daughter had a naturally cheerful disposition. In her letters to her brother Elisabeth often referred to such misunderstandings between her and her mother.

Mama says that I have become too smart for my own good, but since I cannot forget my Llama nature, I am very confused and prefer not to think at all, because I am afraid all my thoughts are nonsense . . . however, one thing is certain: It is much easier not to believe than the reverse, and since what is difficult is probably true, I shall try my best.

Her brother took her to task for the latter statement. He wrote her that although he agreed with her in part, truth was always difficult: " . . . nonetheless, it is difficult to comprehend that two times two does not equal four—is it therefore true?" And he admonished her that while every true faith was infallible to the believer, it did not offer the least support "for establishing an objective truth. Here the paths of men divide. If you long for peace of mind and happiness, then have faith; if you want to be a disciple of truth, then search."

Elisabeth listened to these admonitions and promptly forgot them. The dismal picture of life that her brother, under Schopenhauer's influence, painted did not please her, and she recovered quickly from periods of pessimism. When life in Naumburg became too dull, she went to visit relatives in Plauen, took trips to Bohemia, or joined her brother for an evening at the theater in Leipzig. Fritz had rented a room on Luisenstrasse, Rue de Llama, he called it, and although he was working hard on a long essay about the Greek poet Theognis of Megara, which Ritschl had suggested he work on, and was an active member of the philological club, he was always happy to see his sister.

The outbreak of the war between Prussia and Austria in the summer of 1866 hardly interrupted life in either Naumburg or Leipzig. To be sure, Nietzsche, who was a Prussian by birth and proud to be a Prussian, found himself as an enemy alien in the Saxon city that was occupied by Prussian troops, but he seemed more amused than worried. While the future of Germany was being forged in the battle of Königsgrätz, he wrote letters home raving about a young actress, Hedwig Raabe, who was then the rage of Leipzig. Nietzsche called her a "blond angel" and told her in a fan letter that he hoped she would accept the dedication of a few of his songs as a sign of his gratitude for her moving performances. When martial law was declared for all of Saxony, he wrote home: "We are now living as on an island because all telegraph, post, and rail connections are continuously being interrupted." He hastened to add, however, that traffic to Naumburg was not affected since Naumburg was a Prussian town. And he invited his mother and sister to come and visit him in Leipzig. He felt sure his dear Llama would enjoy Leipzig now because the town was filled with handsome young Prussian officers. Nothing came of this invitation. An outbreak of cholera that summer made Leipzig unsafe, and at the end of the semester Nietzsche returned home.

Gradually a pattern of life evolved during the years that Nietzsche spent in Leipzig as a student. He cultivated his friendship with Professor Ritschl, worked hard on a number of scholarly projects, and when he was at home, he initiated his sister into his academic labors. He taught Elisabeth the rudiments of research and confided to her his hopes for an academic career. While other young girls dreamed of parties and marriageable men, Elisabeth remained her brother's companion and helpmate. When he was unexpectedly called up to serve in the cavalry—fortunately his regiment was stationed in Naumburg—she continued her services for him. And she helped to nurse him back to health after the painful injury he suffered when he hit his chest on the pommel of the saddle as he jumped on his horse. Whenever he had doubts about his future, Elisabeth would dispel them.

She was not surprised, therefore, when he confided to her that an astonishing event had occurred: Ritschl had proposed his name to the authorities of the University of Basel for the vacant chair of classical philology. He knew better than his sister that the odds against him receiving the appointment were very great. He had not yet finished his studies, and he did not have the doctorate, let alone the *venia legendi*, the traditional requirement for an academic position at a German or Swiss university. It was true he had published a few articles and that Ritschl thought the world of him, but it was foolish to pin one's hopes on such flimsy arguments. Elisabeth thought otherwise. She knew that her brother was a genius; obviously Ritschl thought so, too. All that was needed was for the people in Basel to accept Ritschl's judgment. When they did so, Elisabeth was transfigured with joy. Fritz, her beloved brother Fritz, a professor at twenty-four! It was a miracle. Let her friends try to catch husbands; she had pinned her faith on her brother and would follow his star.

Elisabeth would have been less jubilant had she known a secret her brother kept from her, a secret that he wished he could keep from himself: He had noticed a number of symptoms that made him wonder if he had caught a venereal disease. He had consulted a Leipzig physician who had treated him for syphilis. The treatment seemed successful and the symptoms disappeared, as they usually do in the primary phase of syphilis. But the fear that the poison remained in his body and would eventually destroy him must have been present in Nietzsche's subconscious, to judge by a mysterious biographical note he wrote at that time. "What I fear is not the terrifying shape behind my chair, but its voice; not the words so much as the horrifying, inarticulate and inhuman tone of that shape. If it only spoke as humans speak." Twenty years later Nietzsche's fears were realized.

Elisabeth was very close to her brother much of this time, though not as close as she later claimed. But she never knew and never accepted the truth of his illness.

4·Life with Brother

T HE NEWS OF her student son's miraculous elevation to a professorship came to Frau Pastor Nietzsche like a bolt out of the blue. She had been kept entirely in the dark during the negotiations that preceded the appointment. Only after it had been confirmed did her son send her a visiting card he had had printed for this occasion; it contained his name, his new title as professor of classical philology at the University of Basel, and the information that his salary was to be eight hundred thalers. Beside herself with joy, Franziska rushed into her daughter's room to tell her of Fritz's great honor. To her surprise Elisabeth laughed and told her that she had known it all along, but that Fritz had sworn her to secrecy until he had received a final word from Basel.

There was no holding back now. Mother and daughter made the rounds in Naumburg and informed all their friends and acquaintances of this extraordinary event. Incredulity at first, then joy, greeted their announcement. Elisabeth proudly wrote her brother:

All the Pinders, including old Mrs. Privy Councillor, danced a veritable adoration and jubilation dance in honor of the young god and professor. My ears are still ringing loudly, for I know that they are all talking about it in the *Ratskeller*. They will say: "How happy his mother must be, and his sister," and they are right, they are right, says your tenderly, ardently, eternally loving sister.

Nietzsche himself took this unexpected turn of the wheel of fortune calmly. "We are really fools of fate," he wrote his friend Rohde, "last week I was going to write you and propose that we study chemistry together and throw

Friedrich, the professor, 1872, in Basel.

philology where it belongs—on the rubbish heap. Now the devil 'fate' lures me with a philological professorship." His studied indifference did not, however, reflect his real feelings. He was a proud young man and had a high opinion of his own worth. When his friend Deussen could not conceal a feeling of envy in his congratulatory letter, Nietzsche replied with a curt note threatening to terminate their friendship. Let the academic philistines squirm with envy about his triumphant entry into the academic world, he would show them that being a professor at twenty-four was but the start of his real career.

The month of March 1869 was a high point in Elisabeth's life. Her famous brother had come home to prepare himself for his new role in life, which was to begin in May. His appointment had been confirmed in February with the understanding that he was to start teaching in the summer semester. An announcement to this effect had already been published in the bulletin of the University of Basel. He offered two seminars, one on Greek lyrical poetry, the other on Aeschylus. In addition, his contract required that he give Greek lessons to the senior class of the *Pädagogium*, a high school that had university professors on its faculty.

It was a heavy teaching load for one who had never taught before and one who had barely a month to prepare himself for it. To make things worse he had promised his Leipzig teacher and benefactor, Ritschl, that he would prepare an index for the twenty-four volumes of the *Rheinische Museum*, a scholarly journal in which his first articles had appeared. He knew that without his sister's help he could not possibly accomplish these tasks, but he also knew that he could always count on his "faithful Llama." After he had explained to Elisabeth the techniques of indexing, she carried on the work with zeal and precision, except that much to his amusement she took great liberty with the translation of Latin titles.

It was a month of concentrated work, but most of the time they were both in high spirits, with Elisabeth mimicking her brother's first encounter with his students by quoting from the student scene in *Faust* in which Mephisto plays the leading part. Sometimes, while Elisabeth worked with scissors and paste on the index, her brother would sit down at the piano and play with much feeling the *Meisterlied*, his favorite aria from his favorite opera. Then he took off his glasses, wiped his eyes, and told Elisabeth, with a voice choking with emotion, what a profound impression Richard Wagner had made on him when he had recently met him in Leipzig.

Everything about that meeting was shrouded in mystery. Wagner had decided on the spur of the moment to pay a secret visit to his sister Ottilie, the wife of the orientalist Hermann Brockhaus, who taught at the University of Leipzig. Only a few intimates knew that he was in town. The newspapers reported that he was at work on a new opera in his home in Switzerland. During his brief stay in Leipzig Wagner learned that a young student was a fervent admirer of his music. His curiosity aroused, he expressed the wish to meet the young man, provided that a meeting could be arranged without endangering Wagner's incognito. The Brockhauses decided to invite Nietzsche to their home; they told him that Richard Wagner wanted to meet him but swore him to secrecy. Nietzsche was dumbfounded. Like everybody else, he was unaware that Wagner was in Leipzig. While waiting for the appointed hour, he walked around as in a dream. Was it true that he would meet the man whose music intoxicated the world? "You must admit," he wrote his friend Rohde, "that the beginning of this acquaintance borders on the fairy tale."

To his eagerly listening sister, Nietzsche confided that in the course of a long conversation he had discovered that Wagner was not only a great musician but a great man. He told her that Wagner knew Schopenhauer by heart and that they had talked for hours about music and philosophy. It was friendship at first sight. When they had parted late at night, Wagner had asked his young friend to pay him a visit at his home in Triebschen on Lake Lucerne.

Although Elisabeth had heard this story before, including the amusing anecdote of her brother's struggle with an obstinate Leipzig tailor who refused to let him keep the new suit he wanted to wear in Wagner's honor, until he had paid for it, her brother's enthusiasm proved infectious. He was right. It was a fairy tale, with Wagner playing the role of a prince of music. Elisabeth knew how unapproachable Wagner was and how quickly he could get rid of unwanted visitors. That he had spent hours with her brother was another sign of Fritz's rising star. The good burghers of Naumburg would be surprised if they knew in what famous circle her brother moved. Well, she would make sure that they heard of it.

For the rest, she was determined not to be left behind her brother in his rise to fame. She too wanted to rise in the world, with her brother's help if possible, if not, on her own. Her restless energy did not permit her to sit at home and wait for something to happen. Now that Fritz was leaving his native town for good, she too had to get away from Naumburg as often as possible, even if her mother did not approve of young ladies traveling unchaperoned. She insisted that she could take care of herself. After all she was twenty-three years old and, by virtue of her inheritance, financially less dependent than her mother.

During the often heated arguments between his mother and his sister about Elisabeth's future, Nietzsche usually took his sister's side. It was he who suggested that she ought to improve her mind by enrolling as a student at the University of Leipzig, an unusual suggestion in view of Nietzsche's often-expressed contempt for "intellectual women." In any case, soon after he left Naumburg to take up his duties in Basel, Elisabeth went to Leipzig where she "happily played the role of a female student."

She stayed with the family of Professor Biedermann, attended lectures at the university, took English lessons from an English lady, paid social calls on her brother's former teachers, and spent most of her evenings in theaters, at concerts, or at the opera. She wrote her brother that she was getting thoroughly familiar with his Leipzig past, a remark that must have made him wince, for there were aspects of his past that nobody knew—furtive nightly visits to prostitutes, anxious moments in doctors' consulting rooms. It was just as well that his faithful Llama would never know this part of his past.

Elisabeth had to cut short her stay in Leipzig because she developed a violent dislike for her hostess. Mrs. Biedermann was too pedestrian for her taste; she lacked class. Her brother tried to console her by inviting her to come to Basel. She would have loved to accept his invitation, but her mother insisted that she needed her at home. Franziska worried about her daughter's wanderlust; it was unbecoming to an unmarried woman—besides, it was too expensive. She had to remonstrate constantly with both her children about their extravagance with money. Fritz too spent much more money than he should have. He seemed unable to live on his Basel salary, although he earned far more than she had at her disposal. She had to send him the interest from his inheritance, and he even wanted to touch the capital. It hurt her when Fritz put Elisabeth in charge of his finances.

Elisabeth gladly took on a chore her brother hated but one that she felt she could handle better than her mother. Her mother simply did not understand the function of money; she thought it had to be saved. The truth, of course, was that money has to be spent. Elisabeth was willing to help her brother spend his money. Eagerly she undertook the commissions he entrusted her with, mainly to buy presents for his friends in Triebschen. Toys for Wagner's children, a portrait of an uncle of Wagner's, a coat of arms for the maestro. She was flattered when her brother told her that Wagner's friend Cosima von Bülow had asked him to thank her "most kindly for her willingness to help with the matter of the portrait, but especially for her kind disposition toward me."

Fritz had been very discreet about the relationship between Wagner and Cosima, the wife of Wagner's friend Hans von Bülow, although by 1869 it was no secret that Wagner and Cosima were lovers. That the family idyll of Triebschen, which Fritz described in such glowing colors, was based on an illicit love affair deeply offended his mother. In Elisabeth it aroused a titillating curiosity. She was determined to meet the woman who dared to violate so blatantly the sacred bonds of matrimony. As usual, her determination bore fruit, but she had to wait almost a year.

She wanted to join her brother in Switzerland in the hope that he would take her to Triebschen; however, Fritz decided to spend his vacation in Naumburg, finish his work on the index, and prepare his lectures for the coming winter semester. He told his mother and sister that he could not come home for Christmas because he had only six free days during the holidays; besides, Wagner and Cosima had invited him to spend Christmas with them. Franziska shook her head sadly when she heard this news. She understood that he could not travel from Basel to Naumburg for such a short period, but that he should want to spend this holy occasion in the company of a couple who openly violated the Ten Commandments dismayed her. And she began to worry about her son's faith. Elisabeth reminded her that Fritz was old enough to form his own judgment about the company he kept. Her mother should be proud that Fritz had become an intimate of such a celebrity as Wagner; she, Elisabeth, certainly was. She was even prouder when her brother sent her, as a Christmas present, the bound copy of his inaugural address, "The Personality of Homer," bearing the printed dedication to "my dear and only sister Elisabeth, faithful co-worker in the stubble fields of philology." So he had kept the promise he had made when they were children: He had written a book and dedicated it to her. Impatiently she awaited the coming of spring when he had invited her and her mother to visit him in Basel. He wanted to introduce his relatives to his colleagues and his Basel acquaintances; about Wagner he was silent.

On the day before Franziska and her daughter left Naumburg for Basel they received a brief note from Fritz informing them that he had just been promoted to full professor. Within a year he had risen to the highest academic rank, the cherished goal of most scholars twice his age—the professor *ordinarius*. It was unnecessary for him to ask them to spread the news among their friends. Before they left Naumburg, the whole town knew that at the age of twenty-five and a half Nietzsche had reached the pinnacle of his profession. His well-wishers predicted that he would be a privy councillor before he reached thirty.

Their reunion in Basel was a very happy event; their spirits were high and so were their hopes for the future. Franziska was proud of her children. It pleased her motherly heart that Fritz and Lieschen were such good companions, although they often talked about things she did not understand. She was impressed with her son's dignified bearing; he looked every inch the Herr Professor and seemed in excellent health, except that he complained about overwork. Since he did not want to spend his entire vacation in Basel, he took his mother and sister to the small, beautifully situated resort Clarens au Basset on Lake Geneva. There, where everything was "blue blue blue warm warm warm from dawn to dusk," they loafed in the sun, swam in the lake, enjoyed gourmet food and one another's company.

In the midst of this idyllic existence, the news reached them that Franziska's sister, Ida, had fallen seriously ill. Without hesitating a moment, Franziska cut short her vacation and returned home. Elisabeth remained with her brother who had wrenched his left foot and was forced to stay in bed. She took care of him in his Basel home. In the middle of July he received an urgent summons from Wagner to come to Triebschen at once; this message was coupled with the request that he bring a few pounds of Dutch herrings. Elisabeth was not invited. Since Nietzsche did not want her to stay alone in Basel, he asked the wife of a colleague, who had met Elisabeth and who liked her, to offer her hospitality for a few days. The arrangement was the more satisfactory since his colleague's villa, which was situated on Lake Lucerne opposite Triebschen, permitted Elisabeth to watch the goings-on at the Wagners' through a telescope. One day she noticed her brother and another gentleman approaching in a rowboat. Her heart beat faster. Was she finally going to meet the famous couple? Her brother and a friend had indeed come across the lake to take her to meet Wagner. Could she do so without offending her hostess, who strongly disapproved of Wagner's conduct. She decided to ask the old lady and was much relieved to hear her say: "Dear Elisabeth, in the company of your brother you may go anywhere."

At the boat landing of their home Cosima and Wagner greeted "Fräulein Nietzsche," the sister of their dear young friend, very warmly. Elisabeth was embarrassed and a little bewildered because she had not expected "Wagner to be so short and Cosima so tall." Cosima was dressed in "a pink cashmere gown with broad revers of real lace which reached down to the hem of her garment; on her arm hung a large Florentine hat trimmed with a garland of pink roses." Wagner wore "a Flemish painter's costume—a black velvet coat, black satin knee-breeches, black silk stockings, a light-blue satin cravat tied in many folds, showing his fine linen and lace shirt, and a painter's beret on his head, which was covered with luxuriant brown hair." The small procession led by Cosima, with Elisabeth in tow and Wagner and Nietzsche behind, wended its way through the garden up to the old country house, which blended harmoniously with its surroundings. Once inside, Elisabeth was disappointed because "the house was not furnished in a manner befitting its style, but according to the taste of the Parisian furnishing firm which had been unpleasantly lavish with pink satin and Cupids." She did not stay long on that occasion; however, she established cordial relations with Cosima, whom she admired and envied. There was something unmistakably aristocratic about Cosima's life-style, a poise and self-assuredness that Elisabeth wished she could acquire herself.

Elisabeth and her brother had barely returned to Basel when an event occurred that was to change the face of Europe: the outbreak of the Franco-Prussian War. Nietzsche was deeply troubled. He had become a Swiss citizen by virtue of his Basel professorship, but he felt he could not possibly remain neutral in a war that involved the fate of his fatherland. "I am sad to be a Swiss now," he wrote his mother; "our culture is at stake. And there is no sacrifice too great. That cursed French tiger!" He decided to request a leave of absence from his academic duties and to volunteer for medical service with a Prussian regiment. Elisabeth accompanied him to Erlangen, where he underwent a brief course in first aid, then she returned home to Naumburg.

As it turned out, her brother's tour of duty was very brief. He was sent to Metz and ordered to accompany a transport of badly wounded soldiers back to Germany. Some of his charges suffered from dysentery and diphtheria. When the transport reached Karlsruhe, it was discovered that Nietzsche himself had contracted both diseases and had to be hospitalized. He asked to be sent home for convalescence. Lovingly cared for by mother and sister, he quickly recovered and returned to his post in Basel.

For Elisabeth, who remained in Naumburg, the war meant excitement and a chance to offer her services at the home front. French prisoners of war and wounded German soldiers filled the town and had to be taken care of. Elisabeth devoted herself to this task with considerable energy. She cooked and sewed for the wounded, helped with their laundry, sang in the church choir, played Santa Claus at the veterans hospital, and practiced her French with imprisoned French officers. Franziska was proud of her daughter's patriotic zeal and told her relatives: "Lieschen is happy that she does not have to go to any parties this winter." The times were too serious, there was too much suffering. Everybody hoped the war would end soon. When Fritz wrote from Basel that the reason for the prolongation of the war was Prussia's demand for Alsace-Lorraine and that he was rapidly getting disenchanted with this "German war of conquest," Elisabeth gently rebuked him. "Surely, you must admit that it is not the fault of our dear king, he would love to make peace, but it cannot be done without Alsace-Lorraine. Oh, these obstinate French!"

While Nietzsche scoffed at such expressions of political naïveté, he was in no mood to argue with his sister. He needed her. Life in his bachelor quarters was dull and uncomfortable. To be sure, Franz Overbeck, a colleague who taught theology and who occupied an apartment in the same house —Baumann's cave, they called it with joking reference to the owner's name—had become a good friend of his, but Nietzsche missed the familiar atmosphere of his Naumburg home. When Overbeck married, Nietzsche contemplated marriage, too, but somehow he never found the right woman. The women he liked were either already married or not interested in him. Thank God, there was his sister. Elisabeth was only too willing to keep house for her brother. "If I may wish anything for the New Year," she wrote him late in December 1870, "my wish has but two words: To Basel!" Trying to make her wish more appealing to him, she added: "I'll bring my cooking utensils and cook for you in your pretty little kitchen—oh, how cozy it will be—besides, it will be much cheaper than eating in restaurants."

The year 1871 was barely a month old when Elisabeth received a telegram from her brother asking her to come to Basel at once. He was in very poor health and was plagued by painful hemorrhoids, terrible headaches, and insomnia. His nights were awful. He could not go to sleep even with the help of the strongest sleeping medicines. His doctor had advised him to take a vacation at Lake Lugano, and he wanted Elisabeth to accompany him. The telegram caused worry in Naumburg. Franziska could not understand this sudden deterioration in her son's health. When she had met him in the spring, he had looked well. He had probably overworked himself. Elisabeth was eager to accept her brother's invitation, but travel in the middle of winter was difficult—there were rumors that snowslides blocked the alpine passes. Franziska felt it would be unwise to risk her daughter's safety, the more so since Fritz had told her in a letter she received after his telegram—although the letter was written before the telegram—that he could manage alone if for some reason Elisabeth could not join him. She telegraphed that Elisabeth would stay home, although Elisabeth had already told him that she wanted to come. Fritz was outraged. "I am in no mood for such jokes," he wrote his mother. "I trembled and had to vomit when I received your telegram."

There was no holding her back now. Elisabeth rushed to her brother's side and spent six months with him. She met him in Lugano, stayed with him at the *Hôtel du Parc*, and accompanied him back to Basel. She was shocked when she saw him, both by his physical and his mental state of health. The reason for his mental depression was his growing awareness that he was in a profession totally unsuited to him. He was not cut out to be a philologist. Poring over ancient manuscripts in search of hidden meanings or interpreting classical authors to immature minds was a pedestrian occupation. He had always been interested in broad philosophical problems. His present position had been thrust upon him by accident.

He confided to his sister that he had petitioned the administration of the university to appoint him to the chair of philosophy that had just become vacant. He proposed his friend Rohde as his successor in classical philology, should his request be granted. It was an audacious proposition, coming, as it did, from the youngest member of the faculty, and the Swiss did not accept it. They had just promoted him to professor of philology and saw no reason for a change. Besides, he had no credentials as a philosopher; all his publications had been in the field of philology.

Nietzsche was deeply disappointed. He told his sister that he would give up his position in Basel and join Wagner in his campaign to raise funds for the Bayreuth festival theater. He would travel through Germany giving public lectures about Wagner and Bayreuth in all the major towns and trying to arouse public support for a rebirth of German culture. Such talk dismayed Elisabeth. Her brother's academic position reflected glory on her as well. What would people say if he quit his job? And she could not see him as a crusader and money raiser for Wagner's project, quite apart from the fact that he was in no condition to undertake such a strenuous task. His health was far too fragile. What he needed was a home of his own, plenty of rest, and a good companion. In a word: He needed her.

To obtain her mother's permission to spend at least part of the year with her brother in Basel, she argued that if she did not take care of Fritz, he might be forced to give up his position and lose his livelihood. This argument proved convincing. Franziska agreed that Elisabeth could keep house for her brother until he had found a wife. She could not understand why neither of her children who, she thought, had more to offer than most, had been able to find suitable mates. With her mother's blessing, Elisabeth commuted between Naumburg and Basel, spending approximately six months of the year with her brother and the remainder of the year at home. This arrangement suited both of them.

Nietzsche wrote his friend Gersdorff:

> I have set up house with my sister's help, and it works out very well. At long last, for the first time since my thirteenth year, I am once again in familiar surroundings. . . . Because of my sister's cheerful disposition, which suits my temperament excellently, I am probably more fortunate than many others.

Elisabeth loved keeping house for her brother and felt flattered by the attention she received from the leading families of Basel. She did not know that there was good-natured gossip about the "Nietzsche ménage" and that people smiled about her social ambitions. In the eyes of the Basel patricians she was a small-town girl with the pretensions of a grande dame. When she heard that the wife of her brother's colleague Overbeck had made some slighting remarks about her, she became furious and warned her brother to be on guard against both Overbecks.

Much to her chagrin, her brother's health did not permit an active social life, and she had to decline many invitations she would have liked to accept. She consoled herself with the thought that Fritz needed her not only as a housekeeper but also as a sounding board for his ideas. He read her the draft of a long essay he was writing concerning the Dionysian world view of the Greeks, which was to become his first major work— *The Birth of Tragedy from the Spirit of Music.* She rejoiced with him when the book was hailed as a masterpiece by Wagner, who had inspired much of it and who shared her brother's contempt for those pedants among his professional colleagues who found it wanting in scholarship. She applauded his decision to give a series of public lectures on subjects of general interest. The more people he reached, the better known he would become. The road to fame did not lead through the classroom. Nietzsche agreed. While his sister was in Naumburg, he delivered a series of lectures on "The Future of Our Educational Institutions," which attracted considerable attention. Proudly he informed Elisabeth and his mother that hundreds of people had come to hear him and that his ideas had provoked animated discussions among students and his colleagues. Elisabeth regretted that she had not been present at her brother's triumph but was delighted that he sent her a copy of the *Grenzpost* with the "amusing" review of his lectures. He was becoming well known in Basel and among the elite of Europe's intelligentsia. Her only worry was whether his health would permit him to continue on his road to fame.

As the years went by, Elisabeth realized more and more that her brother suffered from a mysterious disease. There were times when he was radiant and bursting with energy, but there were others, and they seemed to increase, when he was forced to spend days and nights prostrate in a darkened room tormented by migraine headaches and stomach cramps, swallowing medicines and vomiting bile. On such occasions she would sit by his bedside watching over him in "deadly fear that something might happen to him." To keep herself occupied, she did the ironing or repaired his underwear. She was afraid that if the people in Basel knew the full extent of her brother's illness they might question his ability to hold his position. That must be avoided at all costs. Hence she kept her fears to herself. Only to her mother did she confide that she feared Fritz would go blind someday or suffer a stroke. She told her that she was terrified by "strange fits of a kind of paralysis he suffers for brief periods," which left him unconscious.

During those dreadful nightly vigils Elisabeth had plenty of time to take stock of her own life. She had always thought of it in terms of her brother's and had never given any serious thought to a life without him. For none of the young men she had met had she felt the same love and affection as she did for her brother. She had idolized him from childhood on, and she idolized him still. But she was beginning to have doubts about the future. What should she do if something happened to him? It took several years before she found an answer to that question, an answer that so deeply offended her brother that he called it a betrayal.

5·*Discord in Bayreuth*

URING THE TIMES that Elisabeth spent with her brother in Basel the magic word that dominated most conversations was Bayreuth, the small town in upper Franconia chosen by Wagner for the realization of his long-cherished dream to present to the world the four great operas that constitute the *Ring of the Nibelung.* Years before the tetralogy was completed Wagner had become obsessed with the idea that the existing opera houses were unsuited for this work, which was not an opera, in the traditional sense of the word, but a music drama, a new and higher art form combining poetry and music on a stage and in a theater specially designed for total effect. Even the traditional audiences were unfit to hear his *Ring*, Wagner insisted, and he planned to invite the musical elite to come to Bayreuth for this occasion. It was a grandiose concept, awe-inspiring to those among Wagner's compatriots who longed for a rebirth of the German spirit now that Germany under Bismarck had risen to political prominence. They embraced the Bayreuth festival project with the ardor of neophytes eager to be initiated into a new cult that wedded the ancient Teutonic gods of the *Nibelung* saga to the intoxicating sounds of Wagner's music.

Wagner's more practical-minded compatriots looked upon the Bayreuth enterprise with considerable skepticism. They questioned the wisdom of locating a musical festival that claimed to represent the German national spirit in a small Bavarian town. Why had Wagner rejected invitations from such established cosmopolitan art centers as Vienna, Berlin, or Munich? Wagner replied that it was precisely the cosmopolitan aspect of these cities that he detested. He had formed passionate prejudices against journalists, bankers, professors, businessmen, music critics and their ilk who flourished in big cities. Many of them, he said, were Jews and corrupted the pure German spirit. By locating his festival in a small town he was returning to the roots of genuine Germanism.

Concerning the financial support needed for such a costly undertaking as building and maintaining an opera house, not to mention the expense of the performances: orchestra, singers, stagehands, and stage sets, Wagner counted on his patron, King Ludwig of Bavaria. And he was not disappointed. However, even the king's largesse proved insufficient; more than a thousand wealthy supporters had to be found to help finance the Bayreuth festival. Although neither Elisabeth nor her brother were wealthy, both rushed to purchase patronage vouchers at three hundred thalers apiece—more than one-third of Nietzsche's annual Basel salary. To their frugal mother, this was further proof of the financial irresponsibility of her children. Elisabeth, too, secretly wondered if it had been wise to invest that much money in an enterprise that at times seemed destined to fail. For neither the German nobility nor the wealthy bourgeoisie responded to the fervent pleas of Wagner and his friends to support with hard cash the building of a German cultural shrine in Bayreuth. They were either indifferent to it or openly scornful. With the theater half built and no funds in sight to complete it, Wagner decided to take his case directly to the German people by addressing an appeal to them to support him. He asked Nietzsche to draw up the appeal. Nietzsche obliged by reminding his countrymen in a stern and moving *Mahnruf* that it was a matter of their national honor to bring to fruition the Bayreuth work of art, brainchild of that "great, brave and indomitable champion of German culture: Richard Wagner." He sent a copy of it to his sister in Naumburg, who was so stirred that she was about to broadcast it among her Naumburg friends when, to her utter surprise, her brother informed her that Wagner had not accepted his draft. The finance committee of the Bayreuth festival felt that it was written in far-too-esoteric language and that it was not likely to have the desired effect. Outwardly Nietzsche took the rebuff calmly, but Elisabeth was certainly wrong when she later said that her brother was relieved that his appeal was rejected. On the contrary, Nietzsche's pride of authorship was badly hurt, for he had proposed to Wagner that his appeal be published simultaneously in French, Italian, and English translations.

Her brother's friendship with Wagner was important to Elisabeth because it paved the way for her own entry into the inner circle of Bayreuth and the haut monde of music lovers. Not because of the music—Elisabeth had a pretty voice, but she was not particularly musical—but because she enjoyed the company of Wagner's distinguished friends, especially if they were of noble birth, such as Malwida von Meysenbug, or had to be addressed as "excellency." All her life she had a weakness for "excellencies." When the University of Jena awarded her an honorary doctorate on her seventy-fifth birthday, she whispered to a friend that she would have preferred the title *Exzellenz*. Wagner and Cosima had introduced her into a world she dreamed about as a child. She was determined not to be excluded from it. There was no danger of that as long as her brother was Wagner's friend, and she had not noticed any cooling in that friendship as far as Fritz was concerned. Quite the reverse. He was working on a long, laudatory essay entitled *Richard Wagner in Bayreuth*, which he wanted to present to the maestro as a sign of his love and admiration on the opening of the Bayreuth festival in July 1876.

What worried Elisabeth was not the relationship between her brother and Wagner but her brother's health. It had been deteriorating so rapidly that in May 1876 he was forced to request a year's leave of absence from his duties in Basel because he needed a complete rest, preferably in a climate milder than Switzerland. He decided to spend it in southern Italy. Elisabeth declined to accompany him because she had reached the conclusion that she must start to build a life of her own. She would supervise the dismantling of their Basel home, the storing of their furniture, china, and books, and would join him at the Bayreuth festival a week after the rehearsals, which, as a special favor, Wagner had asked Nietzsche to attend. But then she would go home to Naumburg. When he returned to Basel after his year in Italy, she would again gladly keep house for him, provided he still needed her. However, the best solution for both of them would be if he found a "good but wealthy wife" who would take care of him. They both treated the subject of his marriage with humor by drawing up lists of eligible ladies who fitted this description, because they both knew that it was very unlikely he would find such a person. But the future would take care of that. The more immediate question was whether her brother's health would permit him to attend the festival at all. As Wagner's intimate, Nietzsche had been privileged to watch the development of the festival idea from the start. He had supported it enthusiastically with both his pen and his purse, he had been present on the historic occasion in 1872 when Wagner, in the company of his closest friends, had laid the foundation stone of the festival theater, and he had just published a moving tribute to Wagner, the man and the musician. Would fate now play him such a dirty trick as to prevent him from participating in the musical feast to which he had been looking forward all these years? At times it almost seemed so. Elisabeth shuddered when she recalled the violent attack he had suffered on Christmas day 1875. Amidst spasms of vomiting that had been preceded by days of terrible headaches, which had caused such a severe strain on his eyes that he was forced to keep them closed, he had collapsed and he seemed to be on the brink of death. When he had regained consciousness he had told her that he was certain now that the real cause of his illness was a brain disease that affected his stomach and his eyes. He reminded her that their father had died of a brain tumor at the age of thirty-six. Quite possibly he would die even younger.

Modern medical science confirms Nietzsche's diagnosis, except that his illness was not caused by a brain tumor but by the onset of the tertiary phase of cerebral syphilis, which twelve years later climaxed in a paralytic stroke. Patients who suffer from progressive paralysis experience periods of such acute pain that they wish to die, alternating with others of a euphoric well-being, when they feel on top of the world, like dancing stars. The erratic course of Nietzsche's life is symptomatic of both extremes.

Elisabeth, who did not suspect the cause of her brother's illness, was shaken by the severity of the attack and torn between feeling pity for her brother and worry about her own future. She would take stock of her life during the year her brother spent in Italy. Her decision not to accompany him was reinforced by his morose behavior when he was sick. She was appalled by the cynical remarks he made then, his cantankerousness, and his totally negative attitude. He seemed to take a perverse delight in tearing down all ideals, including those that he himself cherished. There must be some connection between his illness and his mind. Perhaps a long rest and a change of climate would restore his health and his cheerfulness. She knew he admired Wagner and loved Wagner's music, and she was happy when he told her that he felt well enough to travel to Bayreuth. He had often said that music was medicine for his soul. She thought of that when she saw him off at the Basel railroad station late in July 1876 on his way to Bayreuth.

But if Elisabeth really hoped that a musical miracle would cure her brother, she was mistaken. He had no sooner arrived in Bayreuth than he wrote her that he was sorry he had come. He felt absolutely awful. "Head-aches from noon on Sunday till Monday night, today such fatigue that I cannot write." And the rehearsals were disappointing, just as the weather was—hot, sultry, thunderstorms. He would probably have to leave. Three days later she received another letter that sounded much more cheerful. He felt better, he said, mainly because Malwida von Meysenbug was taking good care of him. He could sit in her garden, drink lots of milk, go for swims in the river, and enjoy his food. He also liked the music better. "I have now seen and heard the *Götterdämmerung* in toto; it is good to get used to it; now I am really in my element." He also informed his sister that King Ludwig was expected this very evening, and he added proudly that he had received a congratulatory telegram from the king about his essay *Richard Wagner in Bayreuth*. Both Wagners had been very kind to him, and the children wanted to know when Aunt Elisabeth would arrive in Bayreuth. He concluded his letter by repeating that his health was improving greatly and that he felt much more cheerful. He urged her to come soon. "Farewell, my good Lisbeth; come soon, dear little Llama."

Elisabeth read this letter with a deep sigh of relief and thanked God for Malwida and for Wagner's music. But her joy was short-lived. Barely four days later her brother wrote again. This time in a mood of bleak despair.

> . . . It's hopeless for me, I realize that now. Continuous headaches and fatigue. I could listen to the *Walküre* only in a darkroom yesterday; seeing is impossible! I am longing to get away from here, it is madness if I stay. Every one of these long art evenings makes me sick. . . .

Racked with pain and feeling irritable, he was becoming fed up with the whole festival—the turmoil of it all, the banal conversations of the Teutonic

Wagnerians, their patriotic platitudes, their vanities, their petty jealousies. He hated crowds even when he felt well. And there was such confusion on the stage during rehearsals. That ridiculous scene with the London-built dragon that appeared with its head and tail only because its body had been sent to Beirut by mistake. A grotesque caricature but, alas, a telling reflection on the entire festival. And Wagner strutting like a peacock amidst a crowd of fawning admirers. This was not the great artist he had eulogized. No, he was through with it all. He would flee from the vanity fair of Bayreuth into the solitude of the Fichtel Mountains. He begged his sister to be his eyes and ears in Bayreuth and to take care of such practical matters as selling his tickets. They were expensive; they had cost one hundred thalers. Then there was the question of what should be done with the apartment he had rented for the four-week duration of the festival at such an exorbitant price. He hoped Elisabeth could sublet it. In any case, he would not be in Bayreuth when she arrived, nor would he return to Bayreuth on his way to Italy. "Perhaps we will not see each other again this year," he added sadly. "How strange life is. I must gather all my strength together to endure the terrible disappointment of this summer. I shall not see my friends either. Everything is now harmful and poisonous for me."

Elisabeth wept when she read this letter, and she was in tears when she arrived in Bayreuth. It was very inconsiderate of Fritz to leave without giving her a chance to talk with him. What was she to tell their friends? Wagner must feel terribly hurt by his sudden disappearance. And where was she to stay if she sublet the apartment? She poured out her heart to Malwida, who tried to console her by reminding her that everybody understood her brother's need for a rest from the exhaustions of the past week. They knew that he was a sick man, and the rehearsals had been very trying for everybody because Wagner was such a perfectionist. Malwida too felt weary; she assured Elisabeth that there was no need to worry about Wagner's reaction to her brother's leaving Bayreuth. Wagner had quite other worries. He expected King Ludwig for the dress rehearsal and was determined that nothing should go wrong then.

Cheered up by Malwida, Elisabeth threw herself wholeheartedly into the festival. She paid her compliments to Wagner and Cosima, spent some time with their children, and met a number of very distinguished visitors. In Malwida's company she attended the dress rehearsals and was among the few privileged persons who were permitted to attend a performance of the *Rheingold* given exclusively for the king. As an intimate member of Wagner's court, she really felt in her element. It was the kind of life she wanted to live. If it did not suit her brother, that was his affair. She made up her mind in Bayreuth, if not before, that she would no longer play the role of her brother's little sister.

While Nietzsche was giving vent to his ill humor in bitter aphorisms that he scribbled down in his notebook during solitary walks in the woods of the Fichtel Mountains, Elisabeth had a gala time in Bayreuth. She was the center

of attention of earnest young Wagnerians who were attracted to her by her
cheerful temperament, her pretty face, and, not least, by the fact that she
belonged to the master's inner circle. Among the men who paid her court was
one of the most ardent Wagnerians, Dr. Bernhard Förster, whose patriotic
zeal stirred her heart. He told her that her brother's book on *Wagner in
Bayreuth* was his Bible and that he had to meet the sister of the man who had
paid such a moving tribute to the greatest living German artist. In long conversations he explained to Elisabeth his own far-reaching plans for a rebirth
of the German spirit.

Under the impact of such experiences Elisabeth wrote enthusiastic letters
to her brother, informing him how much he was missing now that the
Bayreuth festival was really under way. Even the old emperor had made an
appearance. Everybody who was anybody was present in Bayreuth. It was a
great pity that he was not. These letters had the desired effect. Despite his ill-
health and his ill-humor, Nietzsche felt he could not stay away from Bayreuth
after all. He returned, grudgingly he said, and attended the first cycle of the
Ring. Then he left for a year's stay in Italy. Elisabeth returned to Naumburg,
where she gave glowing accounts of Wagner's triumph in Bayreuth.

PART II
1877-1885

6·Turning Point

URING THE YEAR her brother spent in Italy Elisabeth kept herself resolutely busy in Naumburg. She was not content to stay at home and help her mother with the chores of the household because her mother's way of keeping house irritated her. It was far too slow for her taste. Her mother simply did not know how to organize her work, and she spent too much time picking up after her old servant Alwine, whom she should have dismissed long ago. To escape the inevitable arguments at home, Elisabeth occupied herself with her own circle of friends. She took drawing lessons and a course in French conversation; she tried her hand at short story writing— "hatching out novella eggs" her brother called it—and took a leading part in establishing the Naumburg Wagner Society, of which she later became president.

Among Elisabeth's visitors was Bernhard Förster. It was fortuitous that Förster's mother lived in Naumburg and, being the widow of a Protestant parson, moved in the same circle as the Nietzches. Elisabeth enjoyed the company of this handsome and energetic man who was about her brother's age and whose facial features, in particular his bushy eyebrows and mustache, reminded her of her brother. Like her brother, Förster was a teacher. He taught at the Friedrich's Gymnasium in Berlin and, again like her brother, was an enthusiastic disciple of Wagner. What attracted Förster to Wagner was not primarily Wagner's music but his political and racial views. Förster applauded when Wagner told his royal patron, King Ludwig of Bavaria, that "the Jewish race is the born enemy of pure humanity and everything that is noble in it." The Jews, Förster told Elisabeth, were responsible for the rapid decline of the ancient German virtues—respect for honest work, authority, and discipline. As worshipers of the "golden calf," they were founders of capitalism, that most heartless system of human exploitation; at the same time it was a Jew, Karl Marx, who propagated the abolition of private property and the establishment of a communist utopia. Capitalism, communism, democracy—these were the forces that were corrupting the German spirit, and international Jewry was responsible for them. Elisabeth's latent anti-Semitism was stirred by such talk. She was pleased to hear that Förster and his Berlin friends knew and admired her brother's writings. They considered him an authentic voice in the struggle, led by Wagner, for the rebirth of German culture.

In a letter written in January 1877, Elisabeth told her brother of Förster's visit.

> The widow of Superintendent Förster, accompanied by her son, Dr. Förster (it is not the one you know but his brother), paid us a visit quite unexpectedly the day after I had written you. They wanted to pay their respects because they admire you, and Dr. Förster spoke very highly of your writings. It was a great joy for me to talk with someone who shares all your ideas, who bitterly regrets the decline of German style, who honors Jakob Burckhardt and Gottfried Keller as writers and stylists and who knows all or almost all those we love: Burckhardt, Gersdorff, Overbeck, Rohde, as well as a number of people from Basel. Förster considers Basel a very attractive town and understands why you love to live there. In short, it was really a feast for me to listen to someone who talks our language.

Because Elisabeth feared that her brother might hear adverse comments about Förster from Rohde or Gersdorff, who had met him and found him unsympathetic, she hastened to add that at first sight Förster was not a very likeable person; "besides he resembles them [Rohde and Gersdorff] too much, or perhaps they mistook him for his brother." She knew that Fritz had met Förster's brother, who had not made a favorable impression, and was at pains to clarify the relationship. For she liked Förster and was pleased that he liked her as well, since "he returned the following day and we talked and talked like two books. He promised to return to Naumburg at Easter and at Whitsun also, if you are here then."

It is doubtful that Nietzsche shared his sister's enthusiasm for her new friend. For one thing, he was not in a very enthusiastic mood. He had fled from Basel to Sorrento in the hope of regaining his health, but so far his hope had proved illusionary. Apart from brief periods of well-being he was in such acute pain most of the time that he could neither read nor write; he lamented that he was living "in the entrance hall of hell." Fortunately, he was cared for with tenderness and motherly love by Malwida von Meysenbug, who had invited him to join her in Sorrento, where she had rented the comfortable and beautifully located Villa Rubinacci. And even more fortunately, a former student and ardent admirer of his, Dr. Paul Rée, had also been invited and was willing to serve as his famulus. Rée's caustic humor, his philosophic skepticism, and his utterly disillusioned world view suited Nietzsche's present mood very well. He was sick and tired of the world, sick of the sham, the pretense, the hypocrisy of the human race. He shared Rée's contempt for idealistic do-gooders, trumpeters of Christian morality, and patriotic zealots, and took a Mephistophelian delight in unmasking their "human all-too-human" frailties in a number of poignant epigrams. Rée, too, was jotting down notes for a book in which he wanted to trace the origin of morals, when he was not occupied with reading aloud from the works of Voltaire or writing letters to Elisabeth about her brother's condition.

Elisabeth had mixed feelings about Rée. Although she was glad that Fritz had found a companion who was willing to devote his time to reading to him and helping him with his correspondence, she was sorry that it was Rée. His critical attitude toward all ideals she cherished annoyed her. She had read a slender volume of Rée's entitled *Psychological Observations* and was outraged by what he said about women. She told him so in reply to a letter Rée had written her from Sorrento. Rée answered by thanking her profusely, tongue in cheek, for her remarks concerning the chapter on women in his book. "You are quite right, it is one-sided. Alas, moralists are terrible people; they rejoice about everything bad they find in man and then express it as sharply and pointedly as possible, merely to show how clever they are."

Elisabeth was stung by the irony of Rée's response, and since, under Förster's tutelage, she had learned that irony was a tool used by Jewish intellectuals to undermine German ideals, she was the more upset because she knew that Rée was a Jew. It was most unfortunate that her poor sick brother, who needed to be cheered up, was in Rée's company. According to her, Wagner, who also spent a few weeks in Sorrento, was equally disturbed about Rée's presence and warned Nietzsche to be on guard.

But Nietzsche was in no mood to listen to such warnings. He enjoyed Rée's wry humor and was partly amused, partly impressed, by the young man's coldly analytical intellect. He called it Rée's Réealism. "I must tell you," he wrote him when they had parted, "that in my whole life I have never gained as much from a friendship as I did with you this year, not to mention what I have learned from you." Rée was moved by these words, for although he was only five years younger than Nietzsche, he looked up to his sick friend with profound admiration. It was a tragedy, Rée felt, that this brilliant man had to suffer the tortures of the damned from a disease that baffled all medical authorities. For Nietzsche's sake Rée endured Elisabeth's suspicions and even paid her a visit in Naumburg on his way home from Sorrento. He told her that her brother had been examined by the leading eye specialist of the medical faculty of the University of Naples, Professor Schrön, who held out hope for an eventual recovery.

Her brother wrote her in the same vein. At long last he now knew the cause of his illness. It was more serious than a chronic head cold, as had been suggested. There was no chance for a quick improvement, but he had complete confidence in Schrön's treatment. Time would tell. In any case he was making plans for the future. Quite possibly he would not return to Basel. His academic duties were too much of a burden and did not leave him enough time for his own work. Besides, he had found that the climate of southern Italy suited him much better. He had discussed with Malwida a favorite idea of his with which Elisabeth was familiar: the establishment of a school of his own. In his lectures on the future of educational institutions he had warned his listeners against two tendencies in modern education that he considered detrimental to the future of mankind: the tendency toward mass education and the tendency toward specialization. To counteract them, he proposed the establishment of special schools, where students of all ages and both sexes could live and learn together, communities of humanists dedicated to the cultivation of their minds without any ulterior motives. Malwida, who was easily moved by idealistic projects, especially if they included the education of women, thought it was a great idea. She knew many young women who were starved for intellectual nourishment and would eagerly join such an ideal community. Rée, too, was in favor or at least pretended to be, and he volunteered his services as a teacher. "The School for Scholars [also called Modern Convent, Ideal Colony, Université libre] lies in the air," Nietzsche wrote his sister. "Who knows what will come of it. We have already appointed you in spirit to be in charge of all domestic matters of our institution of some forty people. Above all, you must learn Italian."

Elisabeth was excited by her brother's proposal. She was eager to find an outlet for her energies, which, she felt, were wasted in Naumburg. Being a practical woman, she wondered where the money for such an enterprise would come from. But she knew that Malwida had many wealthy friends. It should be possible to arouse sufficient interest among Europe's educated elite to support a "free university" headed by her brother. Malwida had helped Wagner to find patrons for Bayreuth and Fritz's school would be far less expensive than the Bayreuth festival theater. She wrote and told him that she would be glad to assume the position they had in mind for her; she even offered to invest her own small capital in the venture. Much to her dismay, the whole idea had to be dropped a few weeks later because her brother's health had taken a turn for the worse. It had become so bad in fact that in May 1877 he informed his friend Overbeck that he could not possibly think of taking up his teaching duties in the fall and that he considered resigning his professorship. "Please help and tell me to whom [under what title] I must address my letter of resignation. Don't mention it to anyone for the time being. It has been a very difficult decision, but Miss von Meysenbug considers it absolutely necessary. I must be prepared to endure my sufferings, perhaps for years."

In Naumburg, Fritz's intention to resign caused worry and alarm. The question his mother and sister asked themselves immediately was—what would he live on? His small inheritance was totally insufficient. And would the Swiss grant him a pension when he had taught less than ten years? They urged him not to act hastily and encouraged him instead to try to find a wealthy young woman and to propose marriage. Once he was settled and no longer forced to work for a living, his health might improve. Malwida agreed. She knew many girls of well-to-do families who would feel flattered if they were asked to become the wife of a university professor.

Half in jest, half seriously, Nietzsche went along with the scheme. He wrote his sister:

> This is the plan which Miss Meysenbug believes we must keep steadily before our eyes and with which you must help me. We convince ourselves that in the long run my university existence in Basel is impossible. . . . Unfortunately, I will have to endure it this coming winter. But I shall resign at Easter 1878, if the other part of the plan is successful: my marriage to a suitable but necessarily wealthy woman with whom I would live the next few years in Rome. . . . This project will be promoted this summer in Switzerland, so that I shall return to Basel in autumn as a married man.

He signed his letter: "In old brotherliness, your Fritz. In future a Roman (if I am still alive in a year)."

Elisabeth was relieved to hear that her brother, aided and abetted by Malwida, was actively pursuing a plan to marry, although it remained to be seen how she would react emotionally if another woman were to enter her brother's life. At the moment she felt it would be easier for her to arrange her own life once Fritz was settled. Through letters from Naumburg she participated in the marriage game that was being played in Sorrento by submitting lists of suitable partners for her brother. She favored a young Swiss girl, the daughter of a rich Geneva banker. She suggested that her brother spend a few weeks in Geneva and seek out the girl's company. "If you get to know Miss K. well in July, you will perhaps become engaged and marry in autumn."

Whether Elisabeth seriously believed that there was a chance of her brother's getting married that quickly is questionable. It is quite possible that she secretly hoped he would not.

As it turned out, the summer passed and Fritz returned to Basel without a wife. Once again he called on her to keep house for him, once again she did so, and once again she was shocked by the rapid changes in his health and his moods. There were weeks when he seemed perfectly well, felt on top of the world, and was cheerful, happy, and confident. But then came days when all color was drained from his face, when he walked around slowly, like an old man, complaining of head and stomach pains and acting so strangely that Elisabeth confided to Mrs. Overbeck, who did not believe her ears, that she feared her brother would end up in an "insane asylum."

But her brother's health was not the only reason why Elisabeth found living with him the fall and winter of 1877—1878 such a strain. He had brought back from Sorrento a manuscript filled with almost illegibly scribbled notes on all sorts of subjects, which he was transcribing with the help of Heinrich Köselitz, a former student and budding musician whom he called Peter Gast. The original title of the book, *The Plowshare*, was changed to the more suggestive one, *Human All-Too-Human.* The subtitle read, "A book for freethinkers," and it was dedicated to the memory of Voltaire. It consisted of six hundred thirty-eight aphorisms, varying in length from one line to several pages, in which Nietzsche took issue with all aspects of life and culture. Assuming the role of a thinker who dissects the motives of human behavior coldly and analytically, like a scientist vivisecting animals, Nietzsche concluded that man always acted from ignorance, folly, or greed, and that even actions springing from such apparently selfless emotions as mother love, compassion, or mercy turned out, upon close examination, to be either self-illusions or weaknesses. Following the example of his mentor, Voltaire, Nietzsche directed some of his most poignant aphorisms at religion, especially Christianity. He asked:

> Is it possible that the church bells we hear ringing on a Sunday morning are meant for a Jew who was crucified two thousand years ago and who claimed to be the son of God? All proof for such a claim is missing . . . a God who has children by a mortal woman; a sage who calls upon man not to work anymore, not to judge anymore, but to wait for signs of the coming millennium . . . someone who asks his disciples to drink his blood. . . . How gruesome all this is. Is it believable that such things are still believed?

The more Elisabeth heard of her brother's views as expressed in his latest book, the more disturbed she became. What he said about Christianity was bad enough; the sneering tone in which he said it was intolerable. She remonstrated with him by reminding him that it was a slap in the face of his family and that it would hurt his mother deeply. Love and compassion were genuine virtues. It was absurd to deny that. In short, the book was mistitled. These views were not human at all, they were inhuman. What had caused her kind and gentle brother to espouse them? Clearly Rée's influence was to blame. He was the real culprit. Her poor sick brother had merely been Rée's mouthpiece.

She pleaded with Fritz not to publish the book because she was sure it would offend all his friends. Or if he must publish it, not to publish it under his own name. Moved by his sister's arguments and also by the thought that his book would be reviewed more objectively if it were not known that he was the author, Nietzsche considered publishing it under the pseudonym of Bernhard Cron. But his publisher objected. Being concerned about sales, he informed Nietzsche that "a pseudonym would be all right for a small book, but in the case of a book so comprehensive and expensive the author's name alone guarantees buyers."

Over the protests of his sister, *Human All-Too-Human* appeared in May 1878 under Nietzsche's name. A quarter of a century later, when Elisabeth was writing her brother's biography, she still felt that it was a mistake and that the book should have appeared anonymously, for "much would have been spared my brother if it had."

Actually, what upset Elisabeth at the time was not so much what the book might do to her brother's reputation, but how it would affect her own relations with her friends, especially her friends in Bayreuth. She was on intimate terms with the Wagner family, Cosima addressed her with the familiar *Du*, and the children called her Aunt Elisabeth. And she enjoyed the pomp and glitter that surrounded the life of the famous musician. Wahnfried, the house that Wagner had built as a monument to his genius, embodied all the features that Elisabeth revered: grandeur, dignity, decorum. It thrilled her that she could share, if only vicariously, the life-style of Europe's most-talked-about couple. Besides, her chances of meeting a suitable husband were far better in Bayreuth than in Naumburg.

She feared that all this was in jeopardy now that her brother had publicly denounced Wagner's ideals. It was not likely that the old master would take kindly to the innuendo of some aphorisms on art and artists in her brother's book. And how would her newly found friend Förster, who was a staunch Wagnerian, react to Fritz's apostasy? He knew how close she was to her brother. She had told him only recently that she shared all her brother's ideas and ideals. What would Förster think of her when he read *Human All-Too-Human*? Would he not assume that she was party to her brother's defection from Bayreuth?

As the months passed and *Human All-Too-Human* reached Nietzsche's friends, Elisabeth's fears proved justified. The book was read with shocked disbelief. Even Rohde, Nietzsche's oldest friend, shook his head sadly and found no other explanation for the book's "frigid content" than that it reflected the pernicious influence of Rée. Wagner did not even acknowledge it; instead, without mentioning the book's author or its title, he wrote a scathing article in the August issue of the *Bayreuther Blätter*, ridiculing those German professors who, by confusing aesthetics with chemistry, delude themselves that they can thereby achieve "illimitable progress in the art of criticizing all things human and inhuman."

Elisabeth had already left Basel when Wagner's article appeared. After frequent and often tearful arguments between her and her brother, she had decided that it would be best for both of them, and certainly for her, if they stopped living together. She had dissolved their household, helped her brother find bachelor quarters on the outskirts of Basel, and had returned home.

Since some of their friends thought that Elisabeth had left him because she felt insulted by his treatment of women in *Human All-Too-Human*, Nietzsche took pains to explain that this was not the case. His sister had taken no offense at anything he had written. And as for conjectures that "the unusual circumstances that made us decide to live together for a time and which nobody needs to know in detail" had influenced his thinking about women and marriage, they were completely unfounded and had nothing to do with their decision to part company.

To her mother Elisabeth confided that she had come home because she could not live with Fritz anymore. He had changed too much and his ideals and hers were now diametrically opposed. Franziska's motherly heart ached when she heard this news. She refused to believe that her son had changed and felt sure that whatever was wrong with him it could be cured if he came home, too. She implored him to spend a few weeks with her in Naumburg before he had to face a solitary winter in Basel.

After his sister's departure, Nietzsche had decided to spend his vacation in the Bernese Alps. He hoped that mountain air and high altitude would make his suffering bearable. But the dread disease that was slowly eating into his cerebral cortex would not be appeased. It followed him wherever he went. "I feel utterly miserable," he wrote Overbeck, "it is as though I were on a flight from myself and hardly know where to lay my head." In despair he told his mother that he would come home because he was at the end of his rope.

Franziska was shocked when she saw him. He looked awful, hollow-cheeked and emaciated. He was obviously not getting the right food. She also blamed his poor health on his constant use of pain-killing medicines. No wonder that he was sick—he was traveling with a chest of poisonous tinctures, sleeping pills, and drugs. Her recipe for good health was fresh air, plenty of exercise, cold water ablutions, and rest. Reading and writing were absolutely forbidden. For almost a month she took care of her sick son, cheerfully and without being offended by his morose moods. She was happy to notice that whatever had happened between Fritz and Lieschen they still seemed to be good friends.

What Franziska did not know was that her son's bad humor was caused not only by his illness but also by his deep disappointment with Wagner. Day after day he hoped to get word from Bayreuth assuring him that, even though Wagner disapproved of the ideas in *Human All-Too-Human*, he still valued their friendship. It was Wagner's total silence that unnerved Nietzsche. Since he could not penetrate it, he asked his sister to do it for him. She could approach Cosima and tell her that he had meant no offense when he wrote his book. It was an objective critique of modern culture, not a personal attack on any individual.

Elisabeth had reasons of her own to approach Cosima. She wanted to know whether Wagner's displeasure with her brother had affected Cosima's attitude toward her. In long letters to Cosima she deplored the misunderstandings that had arisen between them and caused the unhappy state of affairs. She blamed the malicious gossip of third parties for it. At heart her brother loved and revered the master as he always had; surely there was nothing in his latest work that could be interpreted as unfriendly to Wagner or his music. But her pleas fell on deaf ears. While Cosima assured Elisabeth that nothing had changed in the warm affection she felt for her, she was very blunt in her contempt for *Human All-Too-Human*.

I know your brother was ill when he wrote these intellectually so insignificant, morally so regrettable aphorisms. . . . I wish he had been well enough not to publish this sad testimony of his illness. . . . Why, the author of *Schopenhauer as an Educator* is pouring scorn on Christianity in the sneering tone so common today. Let us not talk about it anymore. I do not know the author of this work, but I know and love your brother who has given us so many magnificent books.

This was plain language and secretly Elisabeth agreed with much of it. She too was appalled by her brother's blatant anti-Christian sentiments. But she made one more attempt to mediate between her brother and Bayreuth. She insisted that *Human All-Too-Human* was not the product of a sick mind. On the contrary, it showed that her brother had overcome his illness; otherwise he could not have written so many penetrating and even witty passages.

This time Cosima answered at great length, asking Elisabeth to accept her letter as a sign of her deep and enduring friendship. "When I said that the author wrote the book we are discussing during his illness, I did not mean that he was critically ill, merely that he was in a generally poor state of health." It was no accident that Cosima remained adamant in her conviction that Nietzsche would not have written *Human All-Too-Human* if he had been well. She had seen some correspondence between Wagner and Nietzsche's Frankfurt physician, Dr. Otto Eiser, who regarded *Human All-Too-Human* "as marking the beginning of mental derangement." Cosima argued that if Nietzsche had been well, he would not have written a book in such poor style and taste. She mentioned several specific passages in which she found both the style and content appalling. She felt personally offended by an aphorism in which Nietzsche compared the wives of famous men with lightning conductors. Nietzsche had written:

> The wives of famous men often sacrifice themselves by assuming full responsibility for their husbands' follies. Their contemporaries will forgive a great man even acts of gross injustice if they find someone else they can blame for them. Not infrequently it is a woman's ambition to offer herself for such a sacrifice; in such a case a man can call himself lucky if he is enough of an egoist to permit near him such a voluntary lightning, storm, or rain conductor.

Referring to that aphorism, Cosima asked Elisabeth which example the author had in mind. "Pericles, Cromwell, Frederick the Great, Albrecht Dürer, Sebastian Bach, Titian, Montaigne, Alexander the Great? I considered all possible men and finally asked myself: 'Should the author really have gained from his visits to Triebschen no other than that malicious image?'" Elisabeth chuckled when she read these words. She remembered how struck she had been, when she had first met Cosima and Wagner, by the difference in their heights. Next to Wagner, Cosima seemed indeed like a lightning conductor. But for the rest, there was nothing to laugh about. Her brother was right when he felt that he was banished from Bayreuth. Thank God, she was not. She still loved her brother and felt sorry for him, but she was unwilling to sacrifice her friends for his sake.

In May 1879 an urgent summons from Overbeck called her back to Basel once more. Her brother's illness had finally reached the point when he could no longer carry on his teaching duties and was forced to resign. Once again Elisabeth supervised the breakup of her brother's household, a specially sad occasion, for it meant that henceforth he would no longer have a home of his own. But he did not care. He was so weary of life that he did not care what happened to him or where he went. Home, that was his first thought, home to Naumburg so that his mother could take care of him. He asked her to rent a small room in the tower of the town wall, which bordered on a large garden where he could spend his time gardening. The idea of becoming a gardener appealed to him, not only because he hoped that outdoor exercise would benefit his health, but also because gardening was an occupation worthy of a sage. Had not Voltaire summed it up by saying that man's ultimate wisdom is "*cultivons notre jardin.*" "I have ten fruit trees, roses, lilies, carnations, strawberries, gooseberries, and red currants. My work will start in the spring," he told his friend Peter Gast, who shook his artist's mane in amazement.

Elisabeth did not accompany her sick brother back from Basel. She remained in Switzerland as the companion of a wealthy elderly lady who had taken a liking to her. "Unless it is absolutely necessary, I have no intention of returning to Naumburg this winter," she told him. "The sight of an unmarried, aging daughter is not very cheerful for a mother and, frankly, one person more causes more work and, what is worse, two nurses are too many for one patient."

But even his mother's devoted care was no match for Nietzsche's illness. At Christmas he was once again on the threshold of death. For three days he vomited, then he collapsed in a dead faint. "The most terrible year of my life is drawing to a close," he wrote his sister. He knew now that there was no help and no cure for him. Alone and unaided, he had to endure his excruciating pain to the end. He fled south in search of a climate and a place where his sufferings were at least bearable. Supported by a small pension the Swiss had granted him, he checked in and out of second-rate hotels and boarding houses in Stresa, Venice, Marienbad, Genoa, a fugitive from the disease he could not shake but which was entering a new phase during 1880-1881, a phase that bore some resemblance to the final phase of his life before his collapse in Turin.

He now experienced moments of visionary bliss during which he was overwhelmed by such profound insights into the riddle of life that he wept with joy. Surely, no other mortal had ever experienced such blinding flashes of beauty and terror. Fate had chosen him, Friedrich Nietzsche, *fugitivus errans*, a sick German professor, to proclaim to the world the coming of a new man, a superman who would regenerate mankind. *Amor fati:* Must he not love his fate, no matter how grim it was?

During that crucial period in her brother's life Elisabeth saw him only rarely. She watched his peripatetic course from Naumburg, where she had returned after he had left and where she remained most of the time, restless and discontent and still trying to find an outlet for her energies. Her friend, Bernhard Förster, was in Berlin teaching high school or lecturing to the Berlin Wagner Society, when he was not occupied with promoting the cause of anti-Semitism. He had become obsessed with the idea that German life and art were threatened by the increasing activities of Jews in the press, in business, and in politics. His anti-Semitism was so fierce that in 1880 he had become involved in a public scandal by provoking Jewish passengers in a Berlin streetcar through pointed anti-Semitic remarks that led to an exchange of blows. During the investigation of the incident at a police station, Förster retorted, when he was asked to state his name: "My name is Dr. Bernhard Förster and I have an Aryan father." Since his accuser could not make such a claim, he felt completely vindicated.

Not content with such direct actions, Förster and his anti-Semitic Berlin friends prepared a petition that they addressed to Bismarck, in which they requested that the German Chancellor take steps to cleanse German society of Jewish pollution. They petitioned Bismarck to curtail Jewish immigration from eastern Europe, to control Jewish influence in the stock exchange, in banks, and in the press, and to exclude Jews from positions in the civil service.

In order to impress upon Bismarck that this was not the request of a few extremists but the overwhelming opinion of the German people, the signatures of thousands of Germans from all walks of life were to be appended to the petition. Förster appealed to his friends to help him get signatures. Elisabeth received a letter from him in May 1880 with the request that she collect signatures from among her Naumburg friends and acquaintances. "I remember that you have declared yourself to be a follower of our movement," Förster wrote her. Elisabeth rejoiced. An agitator by temperament, she had finally found a cause that she could embrace wholeheartedly and with a good Christian conscience.

7·Lou: A Melodrama in Four Acts

Act One

The outstanding cultural and social event of 1882 was the world premiere of *Parsifal*. For years Wagner had been at work on this, his last opera. He called it a "Stage Dedication Play," but the closer he came to finishing it, the more he dreaded the thought that it would be performed in the traditional setting of an opera. To his king and benefactor, Ludwig of Bavaria, who urged the production of *Parsifal*, Wagner complained: "How can a drama in which the sublimest mysteries of the Christian faith are shown upon the stage be produced in theaters such as ours, as part of an operatic repertoire such as ours?" He pointed out that the authorities of the Church were entitled to protest against the stage representation "of the Holiest of Mysteries, complacently sandwiched between the frivolity of yesterday and the frivolity of tomorrow, before a public attracted solely by frivolity. I must have a dedicated stage for it, and this can only be my theater in Bayreuth. There alone should *Parsifal* ever be produced."

As usual, Wagner had his way. He announced that *Parsifal* would be performed at Bayreuth in July and August 1882 before an invited public, the patrons of his art. Musical circles all over the world hailed the event as the crowning glory of the master's career, and members of Europe's high society made preparations for yet another pilgrimage to Bayreuth. Elisabeth was among those most eager to be present on that occasion. Since she did not hold a patronage voucher and could not attend without one, she asked her brother to let her use his, for she knew that in spite of his breach with Wagner Nietzsche had continued his contributions to the society of patrons of Bayreuth. She also knew that he smarted under Wagner's banishment and

Louise von Salomé, "Lou," 1882. Lebensrückblick

would want her to be in Bayreuth if for no other reason than to remind Wagner of his existence.

Elisabeth was right. Her brother did want her to go to Bayreuth, but for a totally different reason, a reason that puzzled her at first and filled her with passionate hatred when she discovered what it was. Unknown to her, Fritz had made the acquaintance of a young Russian girl in Rome, who was to play a brief but poignant part in his life. He wanted Elisabeth to meet her and persuade her to spend her summer vacation with him in a small Thuringian forest retreat.

Louise von Salomé, or Lou as she was called, was the twenty-one-year-old daughter of a Russian general of Baltic-German and Huguenot extraction. She had grown up in the cosmopolitan atmosphere of St. Petersburg, an unusually gifted, willful young woman, endowed with a vivid imagination and a marked bent for religious speculation. After an intensely emotional encounter with a minister of the Dutch Reformed Church in Petersburg, which left her mentally and emotionally exhausted, she had gone abroad with her mother in search of better health and deeper knowledge. For a time she had

attended lectures on comparative religion and philosophy at the University of
Zürich, where she was among a small group of emancipated young women
who fought for and obtained the right to enroll at institutions of higher learning. But the Swiss climate had not agreed with her. She was constantly running a temperature, and when she started to cough blood, her mother, on
medical advice, decided to take her to Italy.

The two women had arrived in Rome in March 1882 with an introduction
to Malwida von Meysenbug, whose book *Memoirs of an Idealist* had made a
deep impression on Lou. She saw in Malwida a kindred spirit, a woman who
had liberated herself from the shackles that traditionally kept a woman within
the narrow confines of home and family. Although almost half a century
older than Lou, Malwida, who in her youth had defied her aristocratic family
by making common cause with the revolutionaries of 1848, embodied Lou's
ideal of the emancipated woman. Malwida, in turn, was reminded of her own
youthful rebellion by Lou's struggle for independence. She welcomed the
young Russian with open arms to her home and her circle of friends. Lou
noted in her diary:

> One March evening in Rome, a few friends were sitting in Malwida von
> Meysenbug's salon when the bell rang and Malwida's faithful servant Tri-
> na came rushing in. She whispered something into her mistress's ear,
> whereupon Malwida stepped quickly over to her bureau, took out some
> money and left the room. She laughed when she returned, but the fine
> silken kerchief on her head fluttered from excitement. At her side stood
> young Paul Rée, an old friend of hers, whom she loved like a son. He had
> just come, head over heels, from Monte Carlo and was in a hurry to return
> the fare he had borrowed from a waiter after he had gambled away every-
> thing he possessed, literally everything.

Rée's dramatic entrance had amused and impressed Lou. He seemed like a
real daredevil, a bold adventurer who had suddenly stepped into her life out
of a Roman night. Rée, in turn, had been pleasantly surprised to see a new
face among the dignified countenances of Malwida's visitors. A young, handsome face, pale but with the interesting pallor of a high-strung, intellectually
active temperament. Meeting Lou had been a welcome change for Rée who
had just spent a few weeks with Nietzsche in Genoa. His friend had seemed
in much better health than he remembered and was eager to talk about his
discoveries in the realm of morals, during long walks they took along the
crest of the hills overlooking the ancient seaport. What had puzzled Rée was
Nietzsche's strangely exalted mood. There was something uncanny about his
friend's mysterious references to the world-shaking impact of his ideas. And
the imperial manner in which he had received him, pretending to be Prince
Doria, the sixteenth-century ruler of the Republic of Genoa, had certainly
been weird. Was Nietzsche serious or was he pulling his leg? Rée could not
tell. Mystified, he had persuaded Nietzsche to accompany him to Monte Car-
lo, where he had tried his luck at the roulette wheel, and lost. Then he fled to
Rome, leaving Nietzsche in Genoa in solitary pursuit of further cosmic mysteries.

Rée and Lou had been drawn to each other from the start. They had spent hours arguing whether there was a divinity that shapes our ends, as Lou believed, or whether life was an illusion, as Rée thought. And they had scandalized both Lou's mother and Malwida by escaping unchaperoned from the sanctuary of Malwida's salon into the nightly streets of Rome. Her daughter's unconcern about the conduct proper for a young lady so dismayed her mother that Madame von Salomé had decided to take Lou back to Russia. But Lou protested violently. She insisted that life was just opening up for her and that she had finally met the partner who could satisfy her intellectual curiosity. When Malwida warned her that Paul was falling in love with her, she became indignant. She told Malwida that she had made it very clear to Rée on their first meeting that the chapter of love was closed in her life. Hendrik Gillot, the Dutch minister who had confirmed her, had been her great and only love. She had not left Russia in search of a lover but in search of the truth. Paul, too, was in search of the truth. And that is what they had in common. They were friends, close and intimate friends. To say that there was anything else between them was a lie, a malicious lie.

The vehemence of Lou's denial of a love affair had startled Malwida and reaffirmed her first impression that the young Russian was an extraordinary creature. As for Rée, he respected Lou's wishes, although he was indeed falling in love with her. His most immediate concern was to prevent Lou's mother from taking her daughter back to Russia. Lou wanted to spend a year in his company in some university town—they talked of Paris or Vienna—but that was obviously impossible unless a chaperon could be found to accompany them. Lou asked Malwida, but Malwida said she had already made other plans. Rée thought at first of his mother, although he doubted that she would want to exchange her pleasant rural home for a year in a big city. Then he thought of Nietzsche. The presence of a retired university professor would lend respectability to their study plan.

Rée had often mentioned Nietzsche during his nightly discussions with Lou. He had told her that his friend was a provocative thinker and interested in the same subjects they were: the question of the existence of God, the problem of evil, the origin of morals. He had also told Lou that his friend's health was very poor, although during his recent visit he had seemed surprisingly well. Rée did not know, indeed nobody knew, that the demon of Nietzsche's disease had propelled him into a state of mental and physical euphoria. He looked ten years younger and felt like a new Columbus about to embark on a voyage of discovery to the furthermost reaches of the human mind.

Laughter and tears shook him as he contemplated his fate. There he was in Genoa, alone and unknown but possessed of a secret that would shake the earth. There he was, *il santo tedesco*, about to depart to the end of the world, to that "rim of the earth" where, according to Homer, happiness dwells. He felt like dancing in the streets and sometimes, when he looked at himself in the mirror, his face twitched and twisted in anticipation of things to come. He laughed and cried and grimaced and felt like shouting from all the rooftops who he was, for if they only knew, those good citizens of Genoa, what dynamite he was carrying in his head, they would fall down on their knees and worship him.

Such was Nietzsche's mood when he received a letter from Rée with the news that Rée had made the acquaintance of a fascinating Russian girl. We do not know what Rée said about Lou, but we have Nietzsche's reply from Genoa dated March 21, 1882. It reads in part:·"Greet this Russian from me if you think it does any good. I am greedy for her kind of souls. In the near future I am going to rape one. Marriage is a very different chapter. At most I could agree to a two-year marriage, and even that only because of what I have to do in the next ten years."

Rée, who was deeply in love with Lou by the time he received Nietzsche's letter, must have wondered about these lines. Very likely he dismissed them as merely another instance of his friend's eccentricity. He would hardly have done so if he had known the state of Nietzsche's mind. Overwhelmed by blinding flashes of insight, Nietzsche felt that it was his mission to revalue all values and to proclaim the coming of "the great, distant human-kingdom, the Zarathustra kingdom of a thousand years." To accomplish this mission he needed help, he needed a disciple to work with him, a witness to his visions. "I need a young person near me," he confided to his friend Overbeck, "who is intelligent and educated enough to work with me. I would even enter into a two-year marriage for that purpose, in which case a few other conditions would have to be considered of course." Quite possibly Rée's description of Lou fitted Nietzsche's picture of the needed disciple and merged in his mind, the moment he heard of her, with the vision he had of himself as the new Columbus. However, he was in no hurry to go to Rome to meet Lou. On the spur of the moment he decided to follow the example of the great Genoese explorer and embark on a small freighter bound for Messina. In letters that contained mysterious allusions to his fate, he told his friends that "this Messina is made for me, and the people here are so polite and accommodating that the strangest thoughts occur to me. Perhaps somebody is traveling ahead of me, bribing them in my favor?" Seven years later, a few weeks before his collapse in Turin, he wrote similar letters hinting that he was a prince traveling incognito among his people.

While Lou and Rée were anxiously waiting in Rome for an answer from Nietzsche, the new Columbus remained silent in Messina where he planned to spend the summer. He was in high spirits, wrote cheerful verses, frivolously playing on the theme of love, and felt that the long crisis of his life was over. He had crossed the tropic and his sun was rising while that of his archrival, Richard Wagner, was going down. His Mediterranean sun would dissipate the foggy realm of the Nibelungs.

In the midst of this state of euphoria Nietzsche received yet another and more urgent letter from Rée. His friend told him that the young Russian had planned to travel to Genoa to meet him and was greatly vexed to hear that he had gone so far away. Rée added that the reason for Lou's eagerness was "her desire to spend a year in the company of interesting people. She thinks that you and I and an elderly lady like Miss Meysenbug are necessary for such a project. But Miss Meysenbug does not want to join us."

This proposal aroused memories in Nietzsche's mind of the winter he had spent with Rée and Malwida in Sorrento. They were pleasant memories, although his present mood was very different from his former skepticism. The idea of spending a year in the company of two young friends appealed to him, especially since one of them was that mysterious Russian. He had planned to spend the summer in Messina, but after a few weeks there he realized that it was impossible. Sicily was far too hot for comfort, and when the sirocco started to blow, he suffered another fierce attack of nausea, which made life miserable. Barely three weeks after he had set foot on his "island of happiness" he fled from it in pain and disappointment. He went straight to Rome, met Lou, and, like all men, was immediately captivated by her. During the weeks that followed, Nietzsche and Rée courted Lou like medieval knights vying for the favors of a young princess. Nietzsche paid his respects to Madame von Salomé and pleaded with her to let her daughter spend a year in his and Rée's company. He told her that Lou was unusually talented and should be given a chance to develop her mind. Since he had some experience in tutoring young people, he volunteered to assume that role for her daughter. In any case he assured Madame von Salomé that there was no cause for anxiety about the propriety of Lou's plans to study with him and Rée. As mature and responsible men, they were both above suspicion.

It is unlikely that Nietzsche's assurances calmed Madame von Salomé's misgivings. Indeed, secretly Nietzsche himself shared them. He was afraid that if it became known that Lou wanted to share living quarters with him and Rée, as she did, there would be a scandal. The obvious solution was for Lou to marry either him or Rée. He had been toying with the idea of marriage lately, even a two-year trial marriage would be better than his miserable boarding-house existence.

In her memoirs Lou says that Nietzsche made two marriage proposals to her, one by using Rée as his intermediary and one in person. Since by now Rée was deeply in love with Lou and wanted to marry her, it is not very likely that he exerted himself on his friend's behalf. He probably told Lou that, quite apart from anything else, Nietzsche was financially in no position to support a wife. He had probably made his proposal in the mistaken belief that Lou was wealthy. Lou used this argument to turn down Nietzsche's proposals. She was determined to remain free, but she was equally determined to carry out their joint study project, which they jokingly called their "Holy Trinity," although in reality it was quickly becoming an unholy triangle. Neither Rée nor Nietzsche trusted each other's intentions toward Lou.

As for Lou, she was supremely confident that she could handle the situation despite the warnings she received from all sides. Malwida thought the whole idea was preposterous, a slap in the face of respectability. And Gillot, the Dutch minister and Lou's youthful idol, advised her from Petersburg to forget the project because it was unrealistic. She was in no position to judge men like Rée and Nietzsche, who were so much older than she was and so much more experienced. She must not forget that she was a woman and owed certain obligations to her sex and to society. Such admonitions annoyed Lou; if anything, they strengthened her in her conviction that she was right. She would prove to the world that it was possible for a woman to have men as friends, and not only as lovers or husbands.

Nietzsche admired this "heroic trait" in Lou but had by no means given up hope of winning her. What he needed was a chance to be alone with her. Rée's presence prevented him from getting to know her as intimately as he wished. He had been alone with her only once during an unforgettable afternoon that he and Lou had spent on Monte Sacro, while Rée had entertained Madame von Salomé on the lakeshore of Orta. It had been an intensely emotional experience, a spiritual union, that made him tremble even in retrospect. When he wanted to remind Lou of that afternoon, he said he was experiencing "Orta weather." Lou's feelings too had been aroused. Many years later, when she wrote her memoirs, she wondered whether she had kissed Nietzsche on Monte Sacro. She mentions that Rée had been jealous and her mother had been annoyed that she and Nietzsche had tarried so long on the sacred mountain.

This experience had convinced Nietzsche that he might win Lou if he proposed in person rather than through Rée. But first he had to confide in someone, had to share with someone his great good fortune, and nobody was closer to him at that time than his Basel colleague and friend Franz Overbeck and Overbeck's wife, Ida. Hence, after that glorious day in Orta, while Lou, her mother and Rée traveled to Lucerne, Nietzsche made a quick trip to Basel. He surprised his friends by his extraordinary cheerfulness. They had never seen him so animated. He talked incessantly, mostly about Lou, improvised on the piano, and revealed to the Overbecks his plan to spend a year with Lou and Rée in Paris or Vienna. Bewildered by Nietzsche's obvious infatuation with Lou, the Overbecks wondered what kind of girl she was. She seemed to have bewitched him. But Nietzsche assured them that there was no need for alarm. Although Lou was young, she was very strong-willed and knew exactly what she wanted. He suggested that the Overbecks form their own opinion of her. He would ask Lou to come to Basel and pay them a visit. When he left, he told them that he had arranged to meet Lou in Lucerne for a very personal reason.

The meeting in Lucerne had taken place as planned, but while Nietzsche had still been in his exuberant Orta mood, Lou had been calm and reserved. She had turned down his proposal, again insisting that she did not want to get married. Much to her relief, Nietzsche had acquiesced quickly, but he urged her to visit his friends, the Overbecks, to find out what manner of man he was. Lou had promised to do that.   .

Before leaving Lucerne they decided to have their picture taken together, to celebrate their trinity. Nietzsche knew just the right person to take the picture, Jules Bonnet, one of the best-known photographers in Switzerland.

Among the props in M. Bonnet's studio was a small farm wagon that came in handy for rural scenes. Nietzsche ordered it placed in the center of the stage and asked Lou to kneel in it—a rather awkward position, Bonnet thought, and not at all suitable for a young lady. But his protests went unheeded. Then Nietzsche asked him for a piece of rope, which was to be tied to his and Rée's arms and held by Lou as if it were reins. Thus the two men were harnessed to the wagon in which Lou knelt. Over Rée's protests Nietzsche claimed that no other pose could more fittingly represent their relationship. Lou, who felt rather cramped in her half-kneeling position, told them to hurry. But Nietzsche was not satisfied yet. As their driver, Lou must have a means to enforce her authority. A small stick was found, a piece of rope tied to it, and thus a whip fashioned. Nietzsche gave it to Lou. As a finishing touch, he tied a sprig of lilac to it. A second later the camera clicked and the picture was taken. It turned out well. M. Bonnet's camera caught the rapt ecstasy on Nietzsche's face. It remains a grotesque reflection of the way his mind worked, a mind that a few months later, when his dream for Lou was shattered and he was alone once more, would coin the savage phrase: "You go to women? Don't forget the whip!"

After a brief excursion to Wagner's former home in Triebschen, where Nietzsche had sadly reminisced about his lost friendship, the trio had separated. Their winter plan was settled. They would meet again in September to live and study in some university town, either Paris or Vienna. The question was what should Lou do between May and September, since she was determined not to return home to Russia with her mother. Upon Malwida's suggestion it had been agreed that Lou would spend the last week of July in Bayreuth to attend the premiere of *Parsifal*, although she confessed she did not have an ear for music. Rée had prevailed upon his mother to invite Lou to spend part of the summer with them in their family home in Stibbe, West Prussia. Nietzsche, who also wanted to spend some time alone with Lou, decided to turn to his sister and ask her to act as chaperon. On his way home to Naumburg he paid another brief visit to the Overbecks, who urged him to use discretion when he talked about Lou to his relatives because they might misunderstand her motives. But there was no need for such advice. Nietzsche realized that any mention of the trinity project would outrage the Naumburg concept of feminine virtue. He would keep silent about it. Before leaving Basel, he told Mrs. Overbeck that Lou would visit her in a few days, and he asked her to speak to the young girl with "complete frankness" about him. No third person should be present on that occasion, not even her husband. Since he sensed that Mrs. Overbeck was puzzled by this request, he wrote her a few days later from Naumburg: "I was too excited during our last meeting and left you and friend Overbeck worried and disturbed. There was no reason for that, quite the reverse. Fate always turns out to be my good fortune, at least my good fortune in wisdom—why then should I be afraid of my fate, particularly if it comes to me in the completely unexpected person of Lou?"

In the same letter he assured Mrs. Overbeck that he had said nothing about Lou to his mother or sister, adding, however, that in the long run his silence was impossible because his sister and Mrs. Rée were in correspondence. Thus began the comedy of errors.

Act Two

Elisabeth was pleased and puzzled by her brother's unexpected arrival in Naumburg. Pleased because he looked so well and was in such high spirits; puzzled by his mysterious allusions to a young Russian girl he had met in Rome. She says that she first learned about Lou in a letter her brother wrote her from Rome at the end of April. It reads in part: "Don't faint with surprise. This letter is by me and from Rome. I have asked Miss von Meysenbug to write the address and in addition 'private' on it so that the letter gets into your hands only. You will understand why. . . . '' Elisabeth did understand. She and her brother loved to keep their mother in the dark about what they were doing. She was more surprised to hear that he was in Rome. She thought he was still in Messina. With artful diplomacy Nietzsche told her that "her wish had come true." She had always wished he would find a young assistant who could help him with his work. Now Miss Meysenbug, or rather Dr. Rée, had found such a person. Alas, it was not a man, it was a young woman. He had come to Rome to meet her, urged to do so by both Malwida and Rée. But he was already disappointed for "up to now I have been able to observe only that the young girl has a good head and has learned much from Rée. In order to form a real judgment of her I would have to see her without Rée. He prompts her constantly so much that I have been unable to discover one single thought of her own. Could you not come to Switzerland and invite the young lady? This is Malwida's suggestion." He went on to say that Lou was twenty-four years old—actually she was only twenty-one—and not pretty. "But like all plain girls she has cultivated her mind to become attractive." In a postscript he added: "This letter has been delayed. In the meantime Malwida has told me that the young girl has confided to her that she has striven for knowledge from her earliest childhood and has sacrificed everything to that end. I was profoundly moved. Malwida had tears in her eyes and told me she thinks Miss Salomé is deeply akin to me." The authenticity of this letter, which Elisabeth published in the chapter of her book that deals with her brother's "Lou Affair," has been questioned because no original exists. And in view of Elisabeth's grossly distorted account of the episode, caution is indicated. However, what would have been her purpose in forging this letter? Sooner or later she was bound to hear about Lou either through Malwida or Mrs. Rée because she was corresponding with both. And even though she may have edited the letter, its general tone sounds genuine enough. There is no doubt that her brother wanted to get to know Lou without Rée being present. But without a chaperon that was not possible. And it is quite likely that Malwida suggested Elisabeth for that role. What does seem strange is that in his letters to Lou, Rée, and the Overbecks, Nietzsche insisted that he had made no mention of Lou to his relatives. More than a week after his arrival in Naumburg Rée informed Lou that "Nietzsche thinks it is best to hide your existence entirely from his mother and sister." The explanation of this apparent contradiction is that Nietzsche had in fact told Elisabeth soon after his arrival in Rome that he had met Lou, his protestations to the contrary notwithstanding, but that he kept Elisabeth in the dark about his winter plan. He knew she would be shocked if he told her that Lou had proposed they all three live together. He was uneasy himself and suspected that in the eyes of the world their "trinity" would appear as a "*ménage à trois.*" What had seemed attractive in Rome and might be possible in Paris or Vienna was clearly unmentionable in Naumburg. He was afraid that his mother or sister might hear about it accidentally, hence his repeated requests to Lou and Rée not to broadcast their winter project. "I urge you to remain silent toward everyone concerning our winter plan. One should remain silent about all things to come. The moment they are divulged prematurely opponents arise, and counter plans. The danger is not slight," he warned Rée in a letter from Naumburg.

Her brother's arrival offered Elisabeth welcome relief from her humdrum existence in her native town. She had been trying to keep herself busy by writing short stories—a solitary occupation that did not suit her active temperament. Moreover, she had received bad news concerning her friend Förster in Berlin. He had become so deeply embroiled in anti-Semitic agitation that some Berlin papers had begun to demand that action be taken against high school teachers who carried on anti-Semitic propaganda in the classroom. To defend himself against these accusations, Förster had founded a "German People's Party" and urged the suspension of the Berlin magistrate because "conditions in the Berlin City Hall were not kosher." He had charged corruption and even theft of public property. These charges had led to a number of lawsuits that Förster had lost. As a result, his position at the Friedrich's Gymnasium had become untenable and he was forced to resign. When Bismarck rejected his anti-Semitic petition, although he had succeeded in obtaining almost a quarter of a million signatures, Förster decided that the only way to save his Aryan ideal was to found a "New Germany" overseas. He planned to leave his "stepfatherland" in search of a suitable home for German patriots who shared his conviction that a regeneration of the ancient German virtues could only be accomplished on a soil unadulterated by Jewish influences.

Förster's departure saddened Elisabeth and she too longed for a change of her environment. Naumburg was too confining and life at home was becoming difficult because she sensed that her mother pitied her for not finding a husband. After talking it over with her brother, she decided to spend the winter in Genoa and later in Rome. Nietzsche encouraged her to do this, although he did not tell her that his main concern was that her winter plan did not interfere with his. As for the summer, he suggested that Elisabeth, who was eager to meet that mysterious Russian, accompany Lou to Bayreuth. That would give her a chance to get to know Lou and, since Malwida would undoubtedly introduce Lou to Wagner and Cosima, provide a good excuse for a visit to Wahnfried. Concerning the period after Bayreuth he proposed that Elisabeth invite Lou to spend a few weeks with both of them in Tautenburg, a forest resort in Thuringia where he planned to spend the summer.

Much to her later regret Elisabeth agreed to both suggestions. She formed the impression from her brother's descriptions that Lou was a very charming and talented young woman. That she was the daughter of a Russian general and of noble birth was proof once more that Fritz moved in far more distinguished circles than she did in Naumburg.

Elisabeth was also very happy that the manuscript her brother had brought with him was much more cheerful in tone than *Human All-Too-Human.* Even its title—*Gay Science*—appealed to her. She gladly helped him get it ready for the printer by dictating the almost illegible manuscript in her brother's presence to an old unemployed merchant who had been hired as a scribe.

It was like old times. They were in high spirits, cheerful and animated, and amused their mother by mystifying allusions to a comedy that was very popular at the time: *Somebody Must Marry.* Franziska did not know what her two grown-up children referred to. But whatever it was, nothing would have pleased her more than to see both Fritz and Lieschen finally getting married.

For Elisabeth the moment of truth came when she met Lou, as agreed, at the Leipzig railroad station. Her first impression was favorable. There was something unmistakably aristocratic about the slender young girl in the elegant tailor-made suit who walked up to her, greeted her cordially, and immediately engaged her in lively conversation. The candor of Lou's remarks, her shy boyish smile, were disarming. Elisabeth was moved when Lou told her how ill she had been in Switzerland. She listened attentively to Lou's account of her meeting Malwida and Rée in Rome and was amused when Lou told her that she and Nietzsche had first met in St. Peter's Cathedral. Her brother had been very solemn on that occasion, Lou added quietly.

Malwida loomed in the background of all these events, a great woman, Lou said, and a good friend to all of them. She was looking forward to seeing her again in Bayreuth, and she asked Elisabeth what Cosima and Wagner were like. Elisabeth seized the chance to tell Lou all she knew about the famous couple, boasting of her close friendship with Cosima and minimizing her brother's quarrel with Wagner. Great men sometimes disagree, but at heart they remain friends. While exchanging confidences with Lou, Elisabeth hoped the young Russian might facilitate her own reentry into the small circle of Wagner's intimate friends. That was the main reason for her going to Bayreuth. Fortunately, Lou did not seem to know or care much about the unhappy events that had led to her brother's estrangement from Wahnfried. With Lou as an ally, who expressed great respect for Fritz, Elisabeth thought she might even reconcile Wagner and her brother. Before they arrived in Bayreuth, Elisabeth suggested to her "younger sister," as she called Lou, that as a sign of their friendship they use the familiar *Du*. Lou readily agreed. Her frank admission that she and Rée were on equally intimate terms startled Elisabeth. Since the train was pulling into the station, there was no time for her to enlighten her young friend about the impropriety of a young lady's using the familiar *Du* with a young man unless he was her brother or her fiancé. Elisabeth's disenchantment with Lou grew rapidly during the Bayreuth festival. As Malwida's protégé, Lou was introduced to Wagner's intimate circle and very quickly became a favorite member of the master's entourage, especially among the men. She was often seen in the company of the gifted young Russian painter and stage designer Count Paul von Joukowsky, one of Wagner's long-time friends, who had been entrusted with the task of designing the sets for *Parsifal*. It rankled Elisabeth to see the two Russians frolicking so closely to the master's throne, while she, because of her brother's stupid feud with Wagner, had to keep at a certain distance. And the stories she heard about the girl! It was rumored that Lou had taken off her dress in public and had permitted Joukowsky, who was also a noted dress designer, to design a dress right on her body. She was also said to have attended nightly séances as the only lady present. God knows what went on there. It was not hard to imagine what kind of girl Lou was.

What really incensed Elisabeth was Lou's boast that she would spend the winter with Rée and Nietzsche in Paris. That was something her brother had not told her. It showed what a liar Lou was. She spread the story from a perverse desire to appear daring and unconventional. But when Elisabeth complained to Malwida about it, she heard to her horror that the story was true. Her brother had agreed to share an apartment with Lou and Rée in Paris and attend lectures at the university. It was incredible. Elisabeth was furious that Fritz had kept her in the dark about this nefarious scheme.

Malwida assured her that she had tried to discourage Lou from going ahead with this plan, not only because a living arrangement with two men was improper for a lady but because it was bound to destroy the friendship between Nietzsche and Rée. She advised Elisabeth to talk to her brother and tell him that he—being the oldest member of the trio—should put a stop to the unwise project.

There was no need for Malwida's advice. Elisabeth could hardly wait to tell her brother in plain language what she thought of him. She wept bitterly when she saw the Lucerne photo showing her brother and Rée hitched to Lou's wagon. This was too much! By flaunting this wicked picture in public, Lou was compromising her brother. She must hurry home to tell Fritz to break with Lou at once.

This she did. When she said good-bye to Lou, who wanted to stay a few more days in Bayreuth, Elisabeth concealed her outraged feelings. On the surface they parted as friends. But the moment Elisabeth arrived in Naumburg she enlightened her deluded brother about the true character of that terrible Russian. She told him that Lou was not at all interested in serious studies. All she wanted was to amuse herself. It was disgraceful how she had behaved in Bayreuth. By displaying the Lucerne photo she had ridiculed him and his philosophy. What serious thinker would let a girl with a whip direct his course! That stung. Nietzsche could bear hostility, but ridicule, especially ridicule in Bayreuth, was unbearable. To indicate his displeasure, he sent Lou a telegram informing her that he had left Tautenburg because of bad weather and was therefore not able to meet her, as they had planned. Lou was disappointed, but not knowing the real reason for Nietzsche's abrupt change of plans, she suggested that they meet in Jena instead, where they could surely find pleasant quarters. They could wait there for the weather to clear and later enjoy the forest peace of Tautenburg. Torn between his love for Lou and his sister's angry denunciations of her, Nietzsche hesitated. "One day a bird flew by me," he wrote his friend Peter Gast, "and I, superstitious like all lonely people who stand at the crossroads of their lives, thought I saw an eagle. Now everybody tries to prove to me that I was mistaken. It has caused a pretty European tattle. Who is the more fortunate, I wonder? I, who have been deceived as they say; I, who have lived all summer in a higher world of hope because of this bird omen—or they who 'cannot be deceived'?"

And to Lou he wrote, much to Elisabeth's displeasure, "Please come."

Act Three

Since her brother was unwilling to break with Lou, Elisabeth decided to do it for him by telling her to her face what she thought of her. She had not been able to do that in Bayreuth, but now she had a chance. Her brother had asked her to meet Lou in Jena and bring her to Tautenburg, to which he had returned when the weather improved. The confrontation between Lou and Elisabeth occurred in the home of Professor Heinrich Gelzer, a former colleague of Nietzsche's in Basel. It started innocently enough. Elisabeth took Lou aside and told her "younger sister" that a girl's most precious possession is her reputation. Alas, it was easily damaged and hard to repair. Then she sighed and said that Lou was perhaps too young to understand how careful a girl had to be—an incautious gesture, a glance, a rash word, and everything was lost. Everything. At this point Lou burst into laughter. She told her "older sister" that there was no need to go on, for if Elisabeth was right, then indeed everything was lost. However, Lou had no regrets. She said she had enjoyed every minute of it.

Elisabeth reprimanded her sternly. It was not proper for a young lady to talk like this. In fact, she considered it her duty to tell Lou that she had been shocked by Lou's behavior in Bayreuth. The way Lou had flirted with Joukowsky had been a public scandal. Everybody had said so. Malwida had told her in confidence that she was sorry now that she had introduced Lou to her Bayreuth friends. And she, Elisabeth, had felt terribly embarrassed when people had asked her if it was true that Lou was going to join her brother in Tautenburg. Did Lou realize who her brother was? Did she know that he was one of the greatest living thinkers, a man of the highest principles, almost a saint? Did she not feel cheap for having publicly associated with his enemies?

Lou was startled. She knew that there had been talk about her and Joukowsky, even Rée in faraway Stibbe had heard of it and written that he was jealous. But she had paid no attention to it. She considered it beneath contempt to take notice of gossip. What she did with her life was nobody's business. As for taking sides in Nietzsche's quarrel with Wagner, it had never occurred to her. Rather pointedly she said that nobody could have cared less about Nietzsche than Joukowsky. He never even mentioned his name.

Elisabeth was stung by Lou's remarks. Joukowsky was Wagner's favorite. It was a bitter blow to be told that her brother's name was not even mentioned in Wagner's circle anymore. As far as Wagner was concerned, Nietzsche was dead. Vehemently she replied that Joukowsky was a charlatan who did not deserve to be mentioned in the same breath with her brother. Lou obviously did not know the difference between a genius and an impostor. And since they were talking so frankly she might as well tell Lou that her proposition to share an apartment with her brother and Rée was downright indecent. Among Russians such an arrangement, masquerading as friendship, might be possible. But not among civilized people. To suggest it to her brother was an insult.

This was too much for Lou. Her blue eyes flashing in anger, she shouted: "Don't get the idea that I am interested in your brother or in love with him. I could spend a whole night with him in one room without getting excited. It was your brother who first soiled our study plan with the lowest intentions. He only started to talk about friendship when he realized that he could not have me for anything else. It was your brother who first proposed 'free love'. . . . Pooh to platonic friendships anyway. What all men wanted was to go to bed with women." Lou knew what she was talking about; she had already been caught twice in such a relationship.

Elisabeth did not trust her ears. Never in her life had she heard such indecent talk. It was unbelievable that a twenty-one-year-old girl dared to say such things about men in general and her brother in particular. If it became known that Fritz associated with such a creature, he risked losing not only the respect of his friends but also his Swiss pension. The Swiss were not legally bound to pay him anything. They would hardly continue paying a pension to a retired professor who cohabits with an amoral woman. She must warn Fritz that if this kind of talk became known in Basel, he might be left penniless. He must get rid of the Russian monster at once.

Such were Elisabeth's thoughts as she and Lou arrived at Dorndorf station, where her brother met them. He was in high spirits. Lou's arrival meant that his Monte Sacro dream had come back. Gallantly he helped her from the train, kissed her hand and bade her welcome in his Thuringian forest retreat. His eyes sparkled, he smiled and chatted happily and passed on the latest local gossip. Utterly disgusted by the sight of her brother "madly in love with

Lou," Elisabeth took him aside at the first opportunity and told him what Lou had said in Jena. The girl was obviously making a fool of him. She was not a serious student at all; she was a common adventuress and had already done great harm to his reputation. He must send her away at once.

His sister's moral indignation upset Nietzsche. While he could not help but admire Lou's contempt for bourgeois morality, he deplored her indiscretion. It was perfectly all right for a freethinker to pour scorn on the moral taboos of society, but it was stupid to flaunt his personal indiscretions in public. He would talk to Lou about that. Elisabeth was not present when her brother took Lou to task about her imprudent behavior in Bayreuth and Jena. He told Lou that it hurt him to think that she had made fun of him in front of his Bayreuth enemies, particularly in view of the fact that she had accepted his invitation. During the scene that followed Lou suddenly felt that Nietzsche treated her as though she owed him a special loyalty.

"Strangely enough," Rée wrote, after having read Lou's diary, "Nietzsche seems to have looked upon you as his bride the moment you consented to come to Tautenburg and he reproached you for the Bayreuth stories in his capacity as your fiancé." Elisabeth would have been outraged if she had seen Lou's Tautenburg diary. She would have said it was another proof that Lou was a liar. Fritz was infatuated with the girl, that was unfortunately true, so infatuated that he disregarded her, Elisabeth's, advice to send Lou packing. But it was a lie that he proposed to her. When she later described the "Lou Affair," Elisabeth flatly denied that her brother ever harbored any feelings for Lou other than those of a teacher toward a gifted student. At the time, her feelings were very different. She was angry that her brother permitted Lou to spend almost a month with him in Tautenburg and shocked when she overheard their conversations: "What was a lie? Nothing. What a breach of confidence? Nothing. What the most shameless talk about the most delicate subjects? Nothing. What was loyalty? Folly. . . . What was pity? Contemptible . . . I have never seen my brother and his whole philosophy in such a miserable light. And since Lou always boasts of her evil nature (she says that evil is a greater source of strength than good), poor Fritz pretends to be as evil as possible. This is how Lou explained her indecent outburst in Jena: Good heavens, she said, she had not thought I held such old-fashioned views. What was wrong with free love? Surely, it was nothing degrading since she and Fritz were above morality. There was nothing degrading in what she had said, nor had she meant it as such."

While Lou and her brother deported themselves in such a shameless manner, Elisabeth withdrew more and more into her wounded self. "I withdrew completely from their company and then Fritz would come and flatter me to my face, while I knew very well what he meant. I wept the bitterest tears over my poor deluded brother. He had never been like that before, so insincere and deceitful. He blamed me behind my back for writing short stories: it was unworthy of him, he said, when he knows very well that I started to write only to give him a share of my royalties."

The month of August 1882 was one of the bitterest in Elisabeth's life. Alienated from her beloved brother by a young girl he loved and she detested, and without anyone to comfort her, she felt betrayed and insulted. When the day of Lou's departure came, she could hardly bring herself to bid her a civil good-bye. She reproached her brother bitterly for the way he had behaved toward her and she refused to go home to Naumburg with him. If she were a Catholic, she cried, she would bury herself in a convent to atone for his sins. Nietzsche called her a stupid goose and went home alone. Asked by his mother why Lieschen had stayed behind, he dropped hints about differences between him and his sister concerning a young lady. Franziska, who had been kept in the dark about Lou, became suspicious and began to ask questions. Nietzsche tried to explain but succeeded merely in upsetting his mother more and more. When she heard from her daughter what had happened in Tautenburg and what Fritz, infatuated with an immoral woman, was planning to do, her Lutheran conscience rose up in righteous indignation. She severely reprimanded her thirty-eight-year-old son and told him that his behavior had been unpardonable. His pious father would turn in his grave for shame. This was too much. Nietzsche packed his bags angrily and left his mother's home, vowing that he would never return. He went to Leipzig, rented a small room, and waited for Lou and Rée, who had agreed to meet him there later in the month. He was desperately lonely. He wrote Overbeck:

> My talks with Lou were the most profitable occupation I had all summer. Our tastes and minds are deeply akin, and yet there are so many differences that we are the most instructive object and subject for mutual observation. Rée wrote me yesterday: "Lou has definitely grown several inches in Tautenburg"—Well, perhaps I have too. Tautenburg has given Lou a goal. She left me a moving poem "Prayer to Life". . . . Unfortunately my sister has become Lou's deadly enemy, she was full of moral indignation from beginning to end and claims to know now what my philosophy means. She wrote my mother that she had seen my philosophy come to life in Tautenburg and was horrified: I love evil but she loves the good. . . . In short, I have the Naumburg virtue against me. There is a real breach between us—even my mother forgot herself once so much that I packed my suitcases and left for Leipzig early in the morning. My sister, who refused to come to Naumburg as long as I was there, commented ironically: "Thus began Zarathustra's downfall." In truth it is a new beginning.

During Nietzsche's solitary vigil in Leipzig his mother, pondering the fate of her wayward son, told her daughter that Fritz now had three choices: "he either marries the girl, shoots himself, or goes mad." One gets the impression that the first of these options was the least acceptable to the pious old lady. But Elisabeth knew better: "The Russian doesn't want to marry Fritz, she only wants to become famous through him. She wants to marry a rich man because she needs much money and has none." In long and bitter diatribes directed against both her brother and Lou, Elisabeth told her mother the wrongs she had suffered and vowed to revenge herself. She would tell the world what a despicable creature Lou was. She would inform the Prussian police of Lou's immoral way of life and see to it that she was sent back to Russia where she belonged.

Act Four

While Elisabeth started her poison-pen campaign against Lou in Naumburg, her brother was impatiently waiting for Lou's return in Leipzig. She had gone back to Stibbe, where she and "brother Rée," as she called him, had such a marvelous time that they were in no hurry to join Nietzsche in Leipzig, despite his urgent pleas. He pursued them with letters, told them that the malice in his sister's nature, which she ordinarily vented against her mother, was now directed against him, and insisted that, since he had lost a natural sister, he deserved a supernatural one—"our dear Lou—my sister." He counted the days until he would see her again. When Lou and Rée arrived in Leipzig at the beginning of October, Nietzsche tried in vain to reestablish the intimate relationship with Lou that had existed, or that he felt had existed, in Tautenburg. Rée's presence prevented that. Although they still talked about their trinity and attended plays and concerts together, Nietzsche began to feel more and more like an outsider. Lou was obviously much closer to Rée than to him. His efforts to alienate Rée from Lou by making caustic remarks about his friend's "sterile pessimism" had the opposite effect. They irritated Lou and made her wonder about the wisdom of their winter plan. The more she hesitated the more insistent Nietzsche became. He reminded her of Orta and of his pledge to share with her the great discoveries of his new philosophy. How could she hesitate? He offered her a chance to mature, a chance to participate in the deepest mysteries of the age. Mistaking Lou's surprise for emotion, he became more and more lyrical. He began to allude to his love in sensuous images. And again Lou was perturbed. She noted in her diary:

> Just as Christian mysticism (indeed all mysticism) at the point of its highest ecstasy returns to crude religious sensuousness, so too the most ideal love can become sensuous again, precisely because of its emotional intensification of the ideal. It is an unpleasant fact this revenge of the body. I do not like circular feelings that return from whence they came, for that is the point of false pathos, of lost honesty and truth of feeling. Is it this perhaps which alienates me from Nietzsche?

Rée watched Lou's growing disenchantment with satisfaction. He had suspected for some time that there was something wrong with Nietzsche. The less people took him seriously the more he tried to shock them. His entire philosophy was aimed at shock effect. By alternately issuing imperious commands in the name of a future philosophy, or making hushed allusions to the wheel of eternal recurrence, he tried to impress them. It was pathetic and absurd. Nietzsche was obviously not in a suitable mental state to be their study companion.

To avoid an open break with their friend in Leipzig, Rée suggested to Lou that they leave him under the impression that they would join him later in Paris as agreed, although they actually planned to spend the winter in Berlin with Rée's mother acting as chaperon.

It was a sad Sunday, the first Sunday in November, when Nietzsche said good-bye to his friends at the Leipzig railroad station. Many unspoken thoughts lay between them, although outwardly everything seemed the same. They would soon meet again and live together, as they has planned, in the perfect harmony of their "holy trinity." But Nietzsche was not sure. Grave doubts filled his mind as he watched his friends depart: Lou cheerful and relaxed as always, Rée reticent and serious.

During the weeks that followed Lou's departure Nietzsche's mood vacillated between bitter self-irony and deepest despair. In letters and especially drafts of letters jotted down on the spur of the moment, the depth of his anguish is starkly revealed. Calling Lou his "dear heart," he begged her to lift the cloud of suspicion from his mind:

> A solitary suffers terribly from suspecting the few people he loves, particularly if he suspects that they harbor a suspicion of his whole being. Why was there never any cheerfulness in our relationship? Because I had to use too much restraint—I am talking obscurely? Once I have your confidence you will see that I find the right words.

When Nietzsche finally realized that his Orta dream had vanished and would not return, he fled to Italy, hurt to the quick and at war with himself and the world. His friends were frightened by the desperate tone of his letters. He talked of suicide, called himself a madman, and boasted of taking overdoses of opium.

> My dears, Lou and Rée, do not worry too much about these outbreaks of my paranoia, or my hurt vanity. Even if, perchance, in some fit of despondency, I should take my own life, there would not be much cause for mourning. What do you care about my fantasies—you did not even care for my truths. I want you both to consider that I am, after all, nothing but a semi-lunatic, tortured by headaches, who has been completely unhinged by his long solitude. I have arrived at this, I think, reasonable insight into my situation after taking an enormous dose of opium from desperation. But instead of thereby losing my mind, it finally seems to have come. Besides, I have really been sick for weeks, and if I say that I have had Orta weather for twenty days, I don't need to say anymore—please, friend Rée, ask Lou to forgive everything. She will perhaps give me an opportunity to forgive her. For so far I have not forgiven her. It is much harder to forgive one's friends than one's enemies.

Elisabeth knew nothing of her brother's ordeal. She did not even know where he was much of the time, for he refused to answer her letters. "I cannot bring myself to open a letter from Naumburg," he jotted down in a fit of anger, "and I do not see how you can ever repair the wrong you have done me last summer." So far from suspecting the depth of her brother's despair over the loss of Lou, Elisabeth feared that he was living in sin with her in Paris and she was all the more determined to break up the affair. To gain allies for her anti-Lou campaign, she wrote long and accusing letters to Nietzsche's closest friends: Peter Gast, Malwida, and the Overbecks, although she disliked Ida Overbeck and was angry that Ida did not share her violent denunciations of the Russian adventuress. "Is this terrible creature perhaps with Fritz?" she asked. "Please write me the truth. But otherwise, please, don't try to pass judgment, for it seems to me that you know nothing of the whole story or have an entirely false impression from the poor, blind lamb of my brother, who believes Miss Salomé's lies or pretends to do so."

Since the Overbecks knew how grievously Nietzsche suffered from his disappointed love and suspected that Elisabeth's hatred had influenced Lou's decision to withdraw, they watched her continuing campaign with undisguised dismay. The worst that could happen to their sick friend, now that the unfortunate episode was over, was to be reminded again and again by Elisabeth's vituperations. To protect Nietzsche, they acceded to his request not to tell his relatives where he was. Elisabeth was furious: "The only thing we want to know is if Fritz is well and still in Santa Margherita. Why don't you tell us that?" In a long and tearful letter she informed the Overbecks how much she had suffered in Tautenburg, not only because of the breach between her and her brother, but because it hurt her to see him in the power of that "low, sensuous, cruel and dirty creature." She continued, saying that Miss Salomé's behavior in Leipzig, "where she lived with Rée," was even more outrageous. There were rumors among their friends "that Fritz and Rée had brought a mistress from Italy and took turns in sleeping with her."

She trembled at the thought that these rumors would reach Basel and said she would do all she could to quash them, for she still loved her brother and was certain the time would come when he would thank her for having fought with all her might against a creature so harmful to him. But by then, she added sadly, she would be dead:

> The thread of my life is running out this year. I have become so strangely visionary, and after many terrifying visions I have had this blessed one. Since then I am filled with a gentle serenity and all these strange events seem to lie far behind me. But I have written them down and I warn Miss Salomé to watch out. If she should ever dare again to come near Fritz alone with Rée or quite alone without her mother or some other worthy chaperon and ruin poor Fritz's reputation by her compromising presence — but I will say nothing more. . . .

The Overbecks, who knew Nietzsche's respect for Lou, were aghast by such language. They felt that if anyone was ruining his reputation, it was his sister. And they advised Gast, who had also been bombarded with letters from Elisabeth, not to furnish her ammunition for her calumnious campaign. Gast heeded Overbeck's advice and merely told Elisabeth that to the best of his knowledge her brother and Lou had parted company. Elisabeth was jubilant and wrote back at once: "I cannot tell you how happy we are to get this news." Then she went on to tell Gast that she had lately been deeply submerged in Wagnerian ideas.

> A friend of ours, Dr. B. Förster, now lives here. He is filled with a magnificent enthusiasm for Wagner's efforts to regenerate our country. We feast on compassion, heroic self-denial, Christianity, vegetarianism, Aryanism, southern colonies. I find all this so sympathetic and feel so much at home in it. You understand that, don't you? Dr. Förster is at the moment writing an excellent article on "National Education," which will appear in the first quarterly issue of the *Bayreuther Blätter.* Please read it, even though it represents a different point of view.

Elisabeth's enthusiasm for the ideas of her new friend amused Gast. It showed the gulf that separated her from her brother. For precisely at this time Nietzsche told Gast that he had risen above his despair and written the first part of *Thus Spoke Zarathustra.* He called it his testament. It presented his philosophy in poetic form and heralded the coming of a new man, a superman, who would sanctify the earth and not wait with fear and trembling for a nonexisting heaven or hell. "God is dead," said Nietzsche's alter ego Zarathustra; "man is a rope stretched between the animal and the superman—a rope over an abyss. Man is something that has to be overcome. But behold I teach you the superman." Such were her brother's thoughts, while Elisabeth, in the company of her friend Förster, luxuriated in Wagnerian music and Christian sentimentality.

Her only regret was that Förster was about to leave Germany in search of a new field of activity. After his dismissal from his Berlin teaching post because of his anti-Semitic agitation and his failure to enlist Bismarck's support, Förster had become convinced that there was no future in Germany for a man of his convictions. He had to find a new home for himself and those of his countrymen who shared his views. North America was not the proper place to go, he told Elisabeth, because the Germans could not retain their national identity among the Yankees. "Southern Russia, the lands of the lower Danube and the Balkans, is the most natural region for German colonization . . . but in view of the terrible condition of the Russian Empire, where Jews and Nihilists work systematically, and as it seems successfully, for the destruction of the existing order, German emigration is hardly desirable." He decided to investigate the chances for an Aryan colony in South America and picked Paraguay as the most promising country.

Förster's departure in February 1883 saddened Elisabeth and left a void in her life. She had been secretly hoping that he would ask her to come with him as his wife. But although they had been very close and she had given him every chance to propose, Förster had not done so. He had always withdrawn at the last moment by saying that his heart had died as the result of an unhappy love affair. But he thanked Elisabeth warmly for having made his last painful months in Germany so pleasant and promised to keep her informed of the results of his travels.

When Förster had left, Elisabeth decided to escape the tedium at home by doing some traveling herself. She planned to visit the Wagners in Venice and spend some time with Malwida in Rome. Malwida had suggested that she and her brother try a reconciliation now that Lou was out of the picture. But Elisabeth told Gast that she was not enchanted with this idea, "for the road that lies ahead of me, the road toward my own ideals, is a hard one and I must not be exposed too soon to other influences." But she soon changed her mind and thought that a friendly brother-sister relationship might still be established despite the difference in their ideals. When Nietzsche, who had also been invited by Malwida to come to Rome, heard that his sister was planning to be there, he abruptly changed his plans. "I don't want to see anyone at present," he confided to Overbeck. "It displeases me to hear my sister's voice. I have always been sick when I was with her." And to Malwida he wrote that with Zarathustra he had crossed the Rubicon. "I have taken my decisive step. Everything is right now. Do you want a new name for me? The church has one: I am—the Antichrist."

When Elisabeth saw this letter, she indignantly wrote her mother:

Antichrist, it is terrible. I cannot help myself, but I find Fritz's views more and more unsympathetic. I do not see who could benefit from them in the slightest. Do you understand now why I wish Fritz shared Förster's views? Förster has ideals that will make people better and happier if they are promoted and carried out. I laugh at the uproar he causes among stupid people. You will see that someday Förster will be praised as one of the best Germans and a benefactor of his people.

In long and confidential talks Elisabeth told Malwida how greatly she admired her friend. Förster was a man of principle and courage. Unlike his critics, he was genuinely concerned about the future of his fatherland and determined to build a New Germany in the virgin forests of Paraguay. If she were a man, she would join him at once and help him found his ideal colony. Compared with Förster's practical idealism, her brother's philosophy was not only alien to her—she had come to abhor it after she saw the kind of disciples it attracted. Miss Salomé's behavior had been outrageous. She was flagrantly violating all the laws of decency right now by openly cohabiting with Rée in Berlin. When Malwida suggested that Lou and Rée might get married and reminded Elisabeth that Cosima and Wagner had also lived together before becoming married, Elisabeth protested: "Cosima had indeed violated traditional morality," she said, "but she had done so as a sacrificial offering to genius, and such an act is honorable and quite unlike Miss Salomé's, who does it in a frivolous mood of adventure, which is contemptible."

Malwida was upset by Elisabeth's violent denunciations of Lou. She had been very fond of the young girl, whose independent spirit reminded her of her own youthful struggles. Perhaps Rée was responsible for Lou's unconventional life-style. Elisabeth could not care less. She had never liked Rée and detested Lou. Thank God her brother was rid of them both.

Upon Malwida's suggestion Elisabeth wrote a conciliatory letter to her brother, urging him to come to Rome and talk things over with her. Much to her relief, her brother answered by return mail:

> My dear sister—it was a pure coincidence that your letter reached me, for I do no longer go to the post office. But in the hope that it was a *good* coincidence, I am answering at once. I am very glad that you do not wish to make war on your brother anymore. Indeed, I have now reached the point when you must not make war on me anymore if you are wise and my sister.

He referred to Lou only briefly in the context of speaking of his typewriter, which had been damaged in transport from Naumburg to Genoa. Rée, who had been in charge of the transport, was hardly to blame for the damage, but Nietzsche wrote his sister: "The typewriter is damaged, like everything that people of weak character have in their hands for a time, whether machines, problems or Lous." For the rest, Nietzsche insisted that his "son" Zarathustra was all that mattered now—for him or for Elisabeth. Their reunion in Rome was a success, at least outwardly. Nietzsche demanded that no mention be made of the unfortunate events last summer. He told his sister that whatever she thought of Lou, he still considered her an unusually gifted young woman. Although Elisabeth would have liked to rub salt into her brother's wounds in the hope of making him share her contempt for Lou, she kept her tongue. "Fritz has been here in Rome for weeks," she wrote her friend Förster in Paraguay, "and we are again as good friends as before, perhaps even better, although our thoughts differ in many respects. He has just published a new book, *Thus Spoke Zarathustra*. It is moving and magnificent. I shall send you a copy as soon as I am back in Germany."

Nietzsche was pleased by Elisabeth's enthusiasm for *Zarathustra* and forgave her the animosity she had displayed in Tautenburg. And although he felt that Rome was hardly a proper place for the author of *Zarathustra* and self-proclaimed Antichrist, he liked Malwida's company and enjoyed his sister's cheerfulness. In the middle of June, when it became too hot in the Eternal City, he and Elisabeth left and traveled to Milan together, where they parted, after having spent some time sightseeing. Nietzsche returned to his Swiss mountain retreat, Sils Maria, where the vision of *Zarathustra* had burst upon him like a flash of lightning in August 1881. Elisabeth visited friends in Basel before returning to Naumburg.

A few days after Nietzsche's arrival in Sils Maria, in another burst of creative energy, he wrote the second part of *Zarathustra*. It took him only ten days, from June 26 to July 6.

His triumph over his despair was complete. But his mood of exhilaration was rudely interrupted a few days later by a letter his sister had written to Rée's mother, apparently on Malwida's request, in an effort to enlist Mrs. Rée's support to have Lou sent back to Russia. To inform her brother what she had told Mrs. Rée, Elisabeth sent him a copy of her letter. Nietzsche liked it and called it "her literary masterpiece." But it opened the old wounds once more. Nietzsche now felt that Rée was responsible for the slanderous remarks that, according to Elisabeth, Lou had made about him in Bayreuth. Once again he became embroiled in a hellish circle of self-pity and suspicion. The thought tormented him that Rée had betrayed their friendship by ridiculing his philosophy and turning Lou against him. He toyed with the idea of challenging Rée to a duel, called Lou the mouthpiece, the very dirty mouthpiece, of Rée's ideas, and told the Overbecks, who begged him not to listen to his sister's tirades, that she was perfectly justified in trying to have Lou sent back to Russia.

Sensing that Nietzsche was once again in a suicidal mood, Overbeck went to see him and pleaded with him to wipe the unfortunate episode from his mind. Nietzsche, who was angry because of Rée's betrayal and angry that his sister had not told him about it last summer, confided to Overbeck that he

> hated his sister who for a year now has cheated me out of my greatest self-conquest by talking at the wrong time and being silent at the wrong time, so that in the end I am the victim of her merciless desire for vengeance. My reconciliation with her was perhaps the most fateful step of the whole affair. I realize now that as a result of it Elisabeth thinks she has a right to take her revenge on Miss Salomé.

His misgivings about his sister rose to such a pitch that he shocked Overbeck by expressing fears that his planned reunion with her in Naumburg in September would lead to "horrible scenes" during which his long-smoldering hatred would break out in words and actions. Overbeck begged him not to go, but in vain. Nietzsche spent a month with his relatives, a month filled with mutual recriminations and heated arguments.

The cause, however, was not Lou—Nietzsche had expressly forbidden any mention of her or Rée—the cause was Elisabeth's friendship with Förster. From his mother Nietzsche learned that Elisabeth had spent much time with Förster before he had left for Paraguay, that she was deeply committed to Förster's ideas and even talked of joining him. The good old lady, who considered Förster's Paraguay scheme quite impractical, was appalled by such talk and tried to enlist her son's support in making Elisabeth change her mind. Nietzsche was stunned when he heard this news. That his own sister was considering making common cause with a man whose ideas he abhorred was incredible. Elisabeth knew how much he detested Förster's vulgar anti-Semitism, and as for Förster's Aryan ideals, they were patently absurd. All this talk about a pure German race was nonsense, utter nonsense. Elisabeth was betraying him and his philosophy by embracing it.

During the ensuing arguments Elisabeth defended her friend passionately. If she had to choose between him and her brother, she would choose her friend. She wrote Förster:

> My brother's goal is not my goal, his entire philosophy goes against my grain. I was excited when I read the first part of *Zarathustra* and thought that my brother's ideals could become mine. His striving for the superman

Bernhard Förster before his marriage to Elisabeth Nietzsche, ca. 1884.

seemed something admirable and I thought that you with your colonizing venture had taken the first step toward it. In the meantime the second part of *Zarathustra* has appeared and my excitement is gone. I see now that the superman is not my ideal.

She compared Förster's article on "National Education" with *Zarathustra* and found the former far more to her liking. Angered and humiliated by such talk, Nietzsche noted that "people like my sister must be irreconcilable enemies of my thoughts and my philosophy. That lies in the nature of things." And once again he left Naumburg vowing never to return. It was impossible for him to live in Germany. The climate was intolerable and the people unbearable. He detested their Teutonic self-righteousness, their noisy patriotism, their beer-hall politics. As for his relatives, the thought of living with them made him shudder. They had no idea that the dynamite he was carrying in his head would blow up their cozy Christian world. His dear foolish little mother would be horrified if she knew what he was writing. And his beloved Llama had shown by her friendship with Förster that she lacked any understanding of the revolutionary nature of his philosophy. He had nothing in common with them and would continue his solitary existence to the end.

Elisabeth too resolved to leave Germany. Her sense of adventure had been aroused by Förster's descriptions of his travels in Paraguay. She felt frustrated in the small-town atmosphere of Naumburg and irritated by her mother's carping criticism of her friendship with Förster. For years her mother had urged her to find a husband, but when she had finally met a man who appealed to her, her mother objected to him. Thank God she did not have to listen to her. She was thirty-seven years old and quite capable of making up her own mind. In any case her mother would not object to Förster, if he proposed marriage. Elisabeth's real regret was that Förster had not proposed, although she had given him sufficient encouragement during the long hours they had spent together before his departure. When the question of love and marriage had come up, Förster had always evaded a direct answer by saying that his heart was dead and that all he could offer her was his sincere friendship. Her brother's objections to Förster were more painful to Elisabeth than her mother's. She would have liked the two men to be friends. But there had been such a change in Fritz after his break with Wagner that she did not believe in him anymore. She felt free, at last, to express her own thoughts and follow her own star. She would show both him and her mother that she was no longer dependent on them. Her life was her own and she knew what she wanted. She wanted to join Förster in Paraguay—not as his friend but as his wife.

8·To Catch a Husband

ONCE ELISABETH had decided that she wanted to marry Förster, she pursued her goal with her customary energy. Since an ocean separated her from her husband-to-be, she was forced to capture him by correspondence. This she did with conspicuous success. Letter writing had been a passion of hers from childhood. She wrote quickly and easily in the chatty style of a schoolgirl bubbling over with the latest gossip. She did not weigh her words, and when she was angry, she wrote letters so offensive that the recipients of her verbal insults threatened to sue her and they frequently did. The strategy she used in her letters to Förster was simple: She inflated Förster's ego by telling him how much she admired his pioneering spirit and how grateful she was that he had introduced her to a whole new world of ideas and actions. Knowing that Förster dearly loved his mother, who lived in Naumburg, Elisabeth told him in the first letter she addressed to Paraguay in January 1883 that she often visited the old lady and talked with her about him. "As I reflected on my way home, how many people will want to follow your example and serve under your leadership, it seemed to me as though you were about to become a fairy tale figure like 'Goldner,' who traveled into the blue yonder and found, without suspecting or expecting it, a people and a kingdom."

Förster would have been amused by such sophomoric flattery if he had had a sense of humor. But he was deadly serious and felt indeed like a modern Siegfried, who was single-handedly fighting the dragon of Jewish corruption and in search of a new home for his Aryan brothers. It was a hard and demanding task. He had gone to Paraguay with plenty of verbal encouragement from his flag-waving countrymen who dreamed of founding German colonies abroad while they sat comfortably at home. But they were reluctant to support with hard cash pioneering idealists like Förster, who set out to make their dreams come true. In the hope of gaining support from his countrymen for his colony Nueva Germania, Förster wrote articles for provincial newspapers in which he described his travels in Paraguay. According to his accounts, the country, its climate, soil, and resources were ideally suited for cultivation, and there was enough land for every industrious German who wanted to escape the corruption at home and help build a new Germany in the Southern Hemisphere. All that was needed was a little capital and a great deal of hard work. By way of giving his readers a picture of life in his new home, Förster described the cabin in which he lived, a humble dwelling within a grove of orange trees. Elisabeth was disillusioned by this account and suggested that he improve the looks of his cabin by adding spacious, vine-covered verandas

> so that your home becomes worthy of you. An acquaintance of mine, who does not wish you well, favored me with a newspaper article that presented a rather pitiful and no doubt untrue picture of your life-style and living conditions. It made me sad. I wish you could shame these liars by building a stately mansion which you would call Försterhof. Just think how grand it would sound: Förster of Försterhof.

Förster had quite other worries than building himself a stately mansion— his meager resources were totally insufficient for such a grandiose project, and, besides, he was spending much of his time on horseback in search of a tract of land suitable for his projected colony—but he was moved by Elisabeth's obvious concern for him and his undertaking. He took time to answer her letters carefully, told her of his disappointments and successes, and sent her presents as tokens of his friendship: a book, a piece of native cloth, a Goethean sonnet. It was the sonnet, which Elisabeth received in January 1884, that raised her hopes and caused her to write a letter that amounted to a declaration of love. In Goethe's poem, a woman in love tells her lover that she is writing him, although there is really no reason for a letter; nothing has happened that needs to be told, she is writing simply because of her longing for him. Förster told Elisabeth in an accompanying note that this "beautiful sonnet"—he changed it to fit his own circumstances: a lover is addressing a woman he loves—came to his mind as he was about to write her: "May it convey the mood I am in as I pick up my pen."

Elisabeth seized the opportunity Förster offered her to lay bare her own heart. Although it was January and in the middle of winter, her heart was filled with the turmoil of spring. "You have robbed me of my sleep, for these Goethean verses are dangerous for one's peace of mind." She was excited to hear that he longed for her, but could she believe him? She feared he had a wrong impression of her. She was not at all as clever as he thought.

> All my knowledge is but a weak reflection of your own tremendous

mind. . . . My talents are practical. That is why all your plans and magnificent ideas excite me: they can be translated into actions. And that is why I am at a loss what to do with my brother's philosophy. I do not see at all what can be done with it.

She tells Förster that Naumburg had not been the right place for him to get to know her. Her mother's and her brother's jealousy had prevented her from being herself. Moreover, she had always been afraid to show her true feelings toward him because "I feared the power of your personality. I feared the loss of my golden freedom." Her real self, she confessed, was a mixture of a passionate heart and a cheerful head. Many men had admired her without moving her in the slightest, while in his presence she had always secretly trembled. In a long postscript she added:

Perhaps I have read something into your letter which you did not mean at all. I am terribly ashamed, but do not be too greatly surprised. Others have raised doubts in my heart. I have always been proud of our friendship. I was happy and it suited my enthusiastic nature that I was not involved emotionally. Besides, your confession that your heart was dead, made me feel safe. I was therefore bitterly hurt when people doubted our friendship and tormented me with their cheap jokes. It made no difference how much I protested, insisting that my dignified age would protect me from follies . . . and now I am so foolish myself. I am mortified. I should really not mail this letter, but I shall so that you see what turmoil you have caused with your spring letter. I have completely lost my cheerful head and my heart remains filled with follies and doubts. Please burn this letter—please!

Förster did not burn it. He kept it and reread it often in the light of a camp fire or before falling asleep on the coarse mattress of his cabin. He had grown very fond of Elisabeth, but knowing her deep attachment to her brother, he wondered whether she could enter into a happy union with another man. He himself had experienced a bitter disappointment with a woman he had loved for seven years only to discover that she had been deceiving him all that time. This discovery had been such a terrible blow to him that he felt his heart had died and that he could not love anyone again. He had told Elisabeth the story of his disappointed love, intimating that while he wanted to be her friend he could not be her lover. However, as he reread her letter in the solitude of his cabin, his dead heart began to beat again. The prospect of having a loving woman at his side, who would help and comfort him in his arduous task of carving a colony out of the wilderness, began to look more and more attractive. But was Elisabeth willing to share his simple life? He had no means to support a wife in the style and comfort a European woman was used to. He could not even afford a native servant to help him with his daily chores, although there were plenty of Indian peons eager to keep house for a white señor.

While Förster was still pondering how to answer Elisabeth's letter, he received another one from her. She said she had to write him again quickly to make him forget her "last foolish letter." But foolish or not, her letter expressed a genuine feeling that, she reminded him, had been aroused by the poem he had sent her. Until she had received it, she had believed the story of his dead heart, but why would a man whose heart is dead send her such provocative verses? Still, if she had misunderstood him and had read a too personal meaning into his last letter, she hoped he would forgive her. What really mattered to her was their friendship, which was based on the community of their convictions and the similarity of their goals.

Having said this, she continued in a very practical vein. She told Förster how grieved she was to hear that he had to do all his own housework.

> It saddens me that hands that belong to such an intelligent head have to do such demeaning and ordinary work as cooking, cleaning, and sweeping. I admire the fortitude with which you bear your life, but I would like to make it easier for you, especially since ugly newspaper stories that have been sent to me anonymously paint such a pitiful picture of your existence.

She then told him that she was going to send him eight hundred marks so that he could hire a servant.

"In the Middle Ages people gave the tenth of their possessions to the Church as a mark of their respect for the highest ideals. Why should you refuse to accept my offering? And it isn't even the twentieth part of my fortune." She continued that he could not refuse her gift because she was going to send it before he had time to answer. She would have enclosed it in this letter if she had been able to exchange eight hundred marks into pound sterling. But that was impossible in Naumburg without everybody knowing it. She would have to go to Leipzig for the transaction. Not that it mattered to her what people thought of her sending him money. She could do what she liked with her small fortune, which amounted to twenty-eight thousand marks. But why make an issue of it now?

She concluded her long epistle with a final piece of advice. Instead of trying to recruit pioneers for his colony, he should present the colony in such a favorable light that prospective pioneers would flock to him. "People should volunteer to join you and be glad if you accept them." She clinched her arguments with the suggestion that Förster return to Germany, summon his friends to Bayreuth, and start his campaign for the building of a new Germany in the auspicious environment where Wagner had started the rebirth of the old.

Förster answered Elisabeth's letter in a very guarded manner. He began by admonishing her that she had a greatly exaggerated opinion of him and his talents. "Please let me tell you that I am not the man you take me for." Then he reminded her of the most serious obstacle to their union:

> If your brother or your mother hate me or have a hearty dislike of me, if they suspect me or my ideas, you would be led inevitably into a serious conflict, should you persist in loving me. It is desirable to face this rather

unhappy possibility clearly and in time. Should you be forced one day to decide between either your friend and lover or your mother and brother, you could perhaps make a choice in accordance with your instincts. But let me warn you that I do not believe you could renounce for good all contact with your family. Everybody values his family—you are linked to your blood relatives with particularly close ties and could not cut these ties without seriously endangering your health. Please, my beloved friend, consider this very carefully. I want you to be happy above everything else and shall never do anything to harm your happiness. . . . Finally, I ask you to consider something else. You know parts of my past. You know that I have sacrificed some of the best years of my manhood passionately and devotedly to a woman who seemed to embody my ideal. And now? What does she mean to me? What I to her? What value has the friendship, the love of a man who could make such a grievous mistake? Reflect carefully.

Elisabeth reflected and rejoiced: "Beloved friend," she answered by return, "whatever your heart is or has been—to me it is dearer than the hearts of all other men on earth." She dismissed the objections raised by her mother and brother against her decision to join him by saying: "My relatives think that the sole purpose of my being in the world is to serve their interests and care for their well-being." Well, they were wrong. Her decision to follow the dictates of her heart was irrevocable. She would fight for her freedom.

Moved by such language and no doubt also by the reflection that Elisabeth's fortune would be a very useful asset to his enterprise, Förster confessed that his friendship for her had ripened into love. He would return to Germany at the earliest possible moment and claim her as his own.

Elisabeth's answer was ecstatic: "My beloved friend," she wrote him on the second of August 1884, "I have read your dear, dear letter with tears of joy and cannot stop crying. . . . I feel it in the depth of my being that I love you with my entire soul. I love you passionately and shall always love you." She told him that she had gone to his mother, because she had to confide in someone.

I have told her our strange love story. I have poured out my heart to her—your mother was so dear and so kind and made me feel very happy. Oh, my beloved friend, how did it all happen so miraculously? Or is it merely a blessed dream? All my doubts have disappeared and my soul, firm as a rock, tells me that we belong together and that nothing, nothing can keep us apart.

Förster's replies to such passionate declarations of love became equally passionate. He assured Elisabeth that he was determined to belong to her at any cost, addressed her as his "painfully beloved," and swore that he would be "eternally faithful" to her. Elisabeth accepted these vows with tears of joy and told her mother and her Naumburg friends that she was now engaged to Förster.

This being settled, Elisabeth turned to more practical matters. In long rambling letters she told her fiancé of her plans for their future. She wanted him to return to Germany as soon as possible: "I would be enchanted if you could be here by Christmas." A Christmas wedding would be a very special one, a real "high tide" in her life. But then she asked herself if she had the right to ask him to come home before his work in Paraguay was finished. She reminded him that most people in Germany looked toward Africa when they thought of founding colonies. However,

> that does not matter, for there are different types of pioneers. And Paraguay seems to me particularly suitable for those who have a small amount of capital not sufficient to live on in Germany. Those people long for a simple life, a healthy climate, cheap food, and pleasant surroundings, all of which they will find there.

She told Förster she knew many families who lived in genteel poverty in Germany and would be eager to emigrate to a country where they would get more for their money. In his descriptions of the possibilities for German settlements in Paraguay, she told him, he should give precise information about how much capital was needed, what professions were in demand, and what chances of success there were. She also suggested that he try to negotiate a "most favored nation agreement" between Paraguay and Germany to stimulate trade. Such an agreement would be a great inducement to emigrants; whether it was feasible she did not know, since she did not have the slightest idea how such things were managed. But it was important that they find an answer to the question her mother constantly asked her: "What will you live on?"

> I think first of all of my twenty thousand marks, for, my beloved friend, there must be no difference between what is mine and what is yours. Whatever the future brings, my fortune belongs to you—but I am not going to say anything more, instead I am going to tell you my plan how we might use part of my money.

She went on to explain that her favorite idea was the establishment of a boarding school for boys. "I have read how much wealthy German businessmen in Montevideo and Buenos Aires are spending to give their children a good German education; surely, they could not find anything better than a school directed by you." She reminded Förster that his article on "National Education" contained many excellent ideas for such an enterprise. All that was necessary to establish a boys' boarding school in Paraguay was that they work out a detailed curriculum, get the signatures of some prominent people to attract students from good families, and replace his present cabin with a spacious house.

"What do you say to this plan, beloved friend? Your dear mama thinks that it is excellent, both for your sake and mine, since everybody has told her that I have a great pedagogical talent with both young and old. . . . But please, dear friend, don't be surprised that I praise myself and do not take it for vanity." She admits that she is worried about the future. "I am asking myself constantly, am I suitable for him? Am I not much too old? Does he *really* love me? Why should he love me?'' To be sure, all her friends tried to reassure her by reminding her of her many good qualities and talents, but the surest way to dissipate her doubts would be marriage.

"Dearest friend, please come home as soon as possible and put an end to my worries, sighs, and tears as quickly as possible by a *fait accompli:* our marriage.'' She told him that she did not want a big wedding; only their closest relatives were to be present. After the wedding, they would spend a few weeks in Berlin and then return to Naumburg and live there for a time in her mother's house before setting out for their pioneering life in Paraguay. "You are smiling at these bold plans?'' But they were the result of her courage of desperation. Everybody—her mother, her brother, her other relatives, and her friends—deplored her decision to leave her fatherland. She was surrounded by so much wailing and moaning, as if she were about to die rather than start a new life. She did not know how much longer she could bear the uncertainty. Hence a quick marriage was imperative. "After a *fait accompli* everybody calms down very quickly.''

Her suggestion that they remain in Germany for at least six months after the wedding was a concession to her mother, who had some plans of her own.

As you know, my papa was a tutor at the Court of Altenburg; his pupils were the three princesses: Therese, who has remained unmarried; Elisabeth, who is now the grand duchess of Oldenburg; and Alexandra, now the Grand Duchess Constantin of Russia. I am named after all these three princesses, and they look upon me as their godchild—the oldest and the youngest of the three, whom we know personally, have all been much interested in our welfare. Princess Therese, in particular, is a good friend of ours. My dear mama thinks that if she were to pour out her heart to her, she would try to help us. The daughter of the Grand Duchess Constantin is the queen of Greece, who has seven sons. And my dear mama dreams that you might become the tutor of some of them. I realize all this is a bit foolish because of the language differences, not to mention the growing power of the Jews. Besides, court life is probably not your ideal, although Athens and the Acropolis would be very tempting. But this thought consoles mama, and surely if friends and well-wishers want to do something for us, they will do so only after a *fait accompli.*

Elisabeth's letters reached Förster in Asunción, where he had returned after prolonged and often dangerous travels through the interior of Paraguay. Since he was preoccupied with many practical problems that had to be solved before he could think of founding a colony, he did not pay much attention to Elisabeth's plans. All he wanted was that she share his pioneering life. He hoped she would join him quietly and quickly and was upset when he read her long descriptions of what people thought of their love story. He was particularly irked when she referred to her "dear beloved brother Fritz.'' "Sometimes a voice within me rises and asks: 'Is it right that I leave my brother? Is it not my duty to remain here and take care of him?'—Alas, I feel now how deeply I love you, and that I can do nothing but love you.''

Elisabeth's coupling of her love for him with her love for her brother grated on Förster and made him wonder about their joint future. "Do you really love me enough to leave all those you have loved for my sake?" he asked her. "Yes, yes," she replied. She had said good-bye to her brother and "on the last day of our reunion we felt, without talking about it, that our beautiful past was finally over and God only knew when we would meet again—perhaps never. It was a very painful farewell."

Her only wish now was for Förster's early return. She hoped he would be back in Germany by Christmas, and she proposed to meet him secretly in Berlin because she wanted to spend some time alone with him before he came to Naumburg. When Förster wrote her that he could not return before March at the earliest because he was in the midst of an important land transaction that required considerably more capital than he possessed, and explained that for an investment of five thousand marks one could purchase a very handsome piece of property in Paraguay, she wrote back and told him she was sorry she had not known that land investment in Paraguay was profitable, or she would have sent him five thousand marks herself. Since it was now too late to send it to Paraguay, she would send it to Hamburg so that he would have it on his arrival. In addition, he could count on the rest of her capital, some eighteen thousand marks, "which are meant for my dowry, the journey, and the setting up of our household."

Förster could not very well reject such a generous offer. It was the first substantial sum promised him for his colony. He accepted it, returned to Germany in March, and married Elisabeth on the twenty-second of May, Wagner's birthday. He picked that day, although—or perhaps because—he knew that his brother-in-law's feelings would be hurt by such an ostentatious demonstration of his devotion to the man who had publicly scorned Nietzsche.

The wedding took place in Naumburg amid a small circle of relatives and friends. The only member of the Nietzsche family who was conspicuously absent was Elisabeth's beloved brother, Fritz.

9·Knight, Death, and Devil

NIETZSCHE WATCHED the unfolding of events in Naumburg from his temporary homes in Nice, Venice, and Sils Maria with a multitude of contradictory emotions. He wrote Overbeck that "Dr. Förster's return from Paraguay has caused great jubilation in Naumburg. My sister's marriage will perhaps benefit me, too: she will now be fully occupied and possess someone whom she can trust completely and to whom she can really be useful; neither has always been possible so far as I am concerned." To his mother, who shared his misgivings about Elisabeth's choice of a husband, he confided that the spring of 1885 was one of the most melancholic springs of his life.

That his faithful Llama had become the wife of another man was bad enough, but that she had married an agitator for ideals he had overcome hurt him deeply: "The instinct of your love should have warned you from doing that." He was reluctant to meet his brother-in-law and was relieved when he heard that Förster was equally hesitant to risk a personal meeting. Förster wrote him that he dared to doubt that "a personal meeting before our departure would give us any lasting pleasure."

Since her brother refused to come to her wedding, Elisabeth asked him to send her, as his wedding present, Albrecht Dürer's engraving *Knight, Death, and Devil*, which had been hanging in their Basel home. It depicts a knight in armor who is riding through a rocky ravine toward his distant castle. Looking straight ahead, his mouth tightly clenched, he is oblivious of two grim companions close at his side: Death holding up an hourglass, and a swine-snouted devil sneaking behind him with a pickaxe. The drawing symbolizes Christian fortitude in the face of danger, temptation, and death. Nietzsche loved the picture and had given it to the Overbecks for safekeeping when he left Basel.

I have been approached with the wish (upon my enquiry what sort of a "wedding present" I might give) that Dürer's engraving *Knight, Death, and Devil*, which you have, should travel with the two emigrants to their new and distant home as a valuable and brave token of truth. I am really rather unhappy to take it away from you, for you, a voyager and solitary in your own way, may need such a consoling piece as much as any emigrant.

But perhaps it is too gloomy for your taste, so if you like, send it to my sister.

Overbeck complied promptly with his friend's request. The engraving arrived in Naumburg in time for the wedding and was greatly admired. "My relatives have thanked me so profusely that I must assume that I have surpassed the notion of a wedding present. However, I trust the future of the young couple will be more cheerful than is depicted in this sinister picture."

Nietzsche was not the only one who wondered about his sister's future. His mother was even more worried, and Elisabeth herself succeeded in overcoming her doubts only by plunging headlong into a hectic round of activities. She assisted her husband in writing a book on Paraguay, which was intended both as a guide to prospective colonists and as an advertisement for "New Germany." She wrote numerous letters to her friends and acquaintances informing them that it was a profitable investment to buy land in Paraguay, she addressed envelopes, and she prepared press releases. From the time of Förster's arrival in Naumburg at the end of March 1885 to the middle of February 1886, when she left for Paraguay as Förster's wife, her mother's house on Weingarten was the center of propaganda for Paraguay and anti-Semitism.

In the preface to his book, Förster explained why many Germans like himself felt compelled to leave their fatherland—"not because they wanted to, but because moral and material misery made life in Germany impossible for them, their fatherland having become a step-fatherland." He blamed alien ideas for the decline of German virtues and charged that the modern liberal trend in education endangered the moral fiber of her youth. Many parents decided to leave Germany in order to raise their children in a morally healthier climate than that which prevailed at home. It was a great pity that the majority emigrated to the United States of America, for "whenever a German becomes a Yankee mankind suffers a loss." To prevent this calamity, Förster set out to find a land where the endangered German virtues could be preserved and passed on to posterity. His Eldorado was sparsely populated Paraguay. There he proposed to found an ideal community.

He proposed to recruit some twenty families as a nucleus, preferably farmers, artisans, and workers with sufficient savings to pay into the communal treasury no less than one thousand and no more than ten thousand marks each. When a capital sum of one hundred thousand marks had been secured, the heads of households would elect a commission of two or three men who, under Förster's leadership, would search out a suitable tract of land. He mentioned some fifty thousand acres, a territory the size of a German dukedom, consisting of pasture lands and virgin forest. Title to this land could be either acquired by purchase from private landowners or secured from the government of Paraguay by depositing some securities as "earnest money" and signing a contract which stipulated that the land would be settled with a specified number of colonists at an agreed-upon time. However acquired, title to this land would remain the property of the colony in perpetuity. Spokesmen

for the colony would ensure the colony's right of self-government by entering into a formal agreement with the government of Paraguay.

According to Förster's proposal, each pioneer-family would receive a plot
of the communal land as their personal property, which they could cultivate
as they wished and which they could pass on to their heirs. But they could not
trade it or sell it. It would return to the colony if they left. The capital of the
colony—one hundred thousand marks contributed by individual colonists—
would be used to purchase land, cattle, and horses. Förster estimated that by
breeding and selling cattle the communal capital would earn about nine percent interest. He was less specific about the cost of such necessary public
works as roads, wells, dikes, or the construction and maintenance of a school
and a church. But he was sure that the collective industry of German peasants
and workers would overcome all obstacles.

His main appeal was to the national pride of his countrymen. To arouse
their enthusiasm for the building of a new home in the virgin forests of
Paraguay, he traveled across Germany from border to border. Spurred on by
his wife, he spoke before Wagnerian societies, colonial clubs, civic groups,
and farmers' and workers' associations. His theme was always the same. He
warned his countrymen of the impending loss of their national heritage, for
which he blamed international Jewry; the apathy of German officialdom, including Bismarck; the materialistic tenor of the times; and "not least, the
regrettable German habit of eating meat." Förster was a fanatic vegetarian.
His backers were the Naumburg banker E. Kürbitz, a long-time adviser of
the Nietzsche family in financial matters, and Max Schubert, an industrialist
from Chemnitz who shared Förster's political views. The editor of the
Bayreuther Blätter, Freiherr Hans Paul von Wolzogen, was an enthusiastic
supporter of Förster's colonial project and promoted it in his journal with
patriotic fervor, as did the editors of many provincial newspapers. By contrast, the liberal press of Berlin was openly hostile; it ridiculed Förster's ideas
and cast aspersions on his character. Förster fought back by suing a number
of editors for slander and continued his propaganda campaign with undiminished vigor: part Don Quixote, part Pied Piper of Hamelin.

Nietzsche's reaction to the public furor aroused by the activities of his
sister and her husband was astonished disbelief and a mixture of admiration
and envy. He wished people would pay half as much attention to his ideas as
they did to the dubious project of his brother-in-law. To be sure, Förster was
not the only agitator for colonies. In the 1880s, colonial clubs sprang up like
mushrooms after a summer rain in every German town and hamlet. Books,
pamphlets, and newspaper articles were published, read, and hotly debated.
And resolutions were passed demanding the establishment of German colonies. Passionate patriots exhorted Bismarck to extend the protection of the
Reich to those colonies that had been acquired by German merchants on the
east and west coasts of Africa and New Guinea. Their motto was: Trade follows the flag. University professors pointed out that it was in Germany's
national interest not to be left behind France and England in the race for col-

onies, and they hinted darkly at a need for *Lebensraum*: Living space must be secured for Germany's rapidly expanding population.

The philistine character of much of this agitation offended Nietzsche. He told his sister that it went against his aristocratic grain that she intended to make common cause with a bunch of peasants. And as for Förster's much-vaunted "German virtues," Nietzsche was extremely scornful; nor was he interested in "keeping this splendid race pure—on the contrary."

When Elisabeth told him that her husband insisted on calling her Eli, instead of Lisbeth or Lieschen, he reminded her that *Eli* was a Hebraic word and meant "my God or perhaps my Goddess." He added sarcastically that he was surprised a convinced anti-Semite such as Förster would use an expression sacred to the Jews as a term of endearment for his wife. He himself would continue to call her Llama, although that word too had a Hebraic meaning.

But in spite of the condescending tone in which Nietzsche talked about his brother-in-law, he could not help but feel envious of the attention that Förster's ideas received, while his own went completely unheeded. He complained that a conspiracy of silence kept his name from the public. Everything and everybody seemed to conspire against him: his wretched health—he feared that he was going blind; the indifference to his work and his mission by the public, by his friends, and by his family; and as a final blow, the criminal behavior of his publisher Ernst Schmeitzner, who refused payment for the books he had sold and demanded an exorbitant price for the unsold copies.

All spring Nietzsche was in a melancholic mood. He became more and more depressed as he reflected on his failure to find readers. He was forty-one years old, had published thirteen books—books that would change the face of the earth, if they were read. And now that he had finished the fourth and final part of *Zarathustra*, the crowning glory of his philosophy, no publisher was willing to publish it. It was a humiliating experience for which Nietzsche put the blame squarely on Schmeitzner. People did not read his books because his publisher failed to promote them. And why didn't Schmeitzner promote them? Because—and this was the ultimate insult—he had gone bankrupt promoting hymnbooks and anti-Semitic pamphlets.

By the end of the summer Nietzsche's relations with his publisher had become so bad that he decided to make a personal effort to find a solution. Much as he dreaded the thought of a journey to Germany, he left his Swiss mountain retreat, Sils Maria, in the middle of September in search of another publisher. He divided his time between Leipzig, the center of the German publishing world, and his family home in nearby Naumburg.

He wrote Overbeck in October:

> You will be surprised to find me in Leipzig, but I felt an irresistible urge this autumn to go to Germany once more (where neither my body nor my dear soul has anything to seek in future) in order to be together once again with my mother and my sister—who knows, perhaps for the last time. . . .

I have not yet seen Dr. Förster, for he is in Westphalia making speeches and alternately riding his two horses—Paraguay and anti-Semitism. He will do the same in Saxony in November.

Förster's absence was fortuitous. And although Elisabeth complained about it in her letters to her husband, she enjoyed her brother's company, particularly on days when her mother, too, was absent visiting relatives. Once again they shared the intimacy of the home of their childhood; once again they talked nostalgically about the past and made plans for the future. Elisabeth tried to persuade her brother to come to Paraguay with them. She told him that her husband loved and respected him and would welcome him with open arms. To her husband Elisabeth wrote: "Fritz loves you very much and is very much interested in our project. I really think he will join us. Yesterday we counted up his fortune. It amounts to four thousand five hundred thalers; a very nice capital for investment."

While his sister was writing her husband in this vein, Nietzsche wrote Overbeck that after careful study of the Paraguay project he had definitely decided against it, mainly because he feared the climate would not suit him:

> Otherwise the idea seems quite sensible. It is a great country for German agriculturalists, and a man from Westphalia or Pomerania can set sail to it cheerfully if he does not have too grandiose expectations. Whether it is the right place for my sister and my brother-in-law is quite another question. I confess my mother and I are often terribly worried.

Förster had asked Elisabeth to supervise the publication of his Paraguay book before he left on his lecture tour. He had not found a publisher and was getting it printed at his own expense. It irritated him when she wrote and told him that her brother had read the manuscript and had made suggestions concerning its style and format. More than pride of authorship was involved. Förster felt that by asking her brother to correct his style, Elisabeth had betrayed his trust and was siding with her brother against him. He had always feared that this might happen. He knew that Elisabeth was much closer to her brother than sisters normally are and sensed in Nietzsche a rival for his wife's affections.

Nietzsche directed his major criticism against the book's frontispiece. It showed Förster's face, featuring a high forehead, dark eyes fearlessly facing the world under bushy eyebrows, a straight nose, and a mouth overshadowed by a large mustache that blended into a neatly clipped beard. The face of a man of intelligence, courage, and perseverance. This impression was further emphasized by a broad, bemedaled chest; the signature "Dr. Bernhard Förster" in upright Gothic letters; and the Goethean motto: "In defiance of all obstacles, stand your ground!" Förster was proud of this picture. It represented the same type of German manliness that he advocated and that he felt was reflected in Dürer's engraving. He was therefore annoyed when Elisabeth wrote him: "Fritz thinks that since you are your own publisher, people might consider your picture an act of vanity. In any case, he does not think it is necessary for a book of this kind." Förster considered it a gratuitous insult to be reminded by his brother-in-law that he had not found a publisher for his book—after all, Nietzsche had not found one either. Besides, his book was meant as a practical guide to colonists, who would buy it by subscription. And his picture was an important part of the book because it showed prospective colonists the kind of man their leader was.

When Förster heard that Elisabeth, with her brother's help, had rewritten the introduction entirely—"I am sending you the introduction once more, so that you do not get a shock when you see it in print, because it is altered somewhat"—he lost his patience and ordered his printer not to pay any attention to Elisabeth's corrections but to print the book as he had written it. The printer, who had been dealing exclusively with Elisabeth, sent her the postcard with the new instructions that he had received from Förster. Elisabeth was dumbfounded. "You could hardly have expressed your lack of confidence in a more unfriendly manner," she reprimanded her husband. "I have carefully followed your instructions, and now you order the exact opposite. It is therefore impossible for me to help you anymore. Since you have no confidence in me, I do not want to have anything further to do with the whole book affair. Why did you intentionally hurt me so much?"

Förster was far too busy making speeches and trying to gain followers and financial support for his New Germany to pay much attention to his wife's complaints. His book was one more headache. He was making considerable propaganda for it, but there were very few subscribers. Elisabeth warned him that his violent anti-Semitic speeches—she called them *Judenreden*—scared off buyers. Förster suspected that his wife's sudden caution concerning his speeches was another sign that she was succumbing to her brother's influence. He knew that Nietzsche was scornful of his anti-Semitic crusade because he was unaware of the pernicious influence of the Jews. Förster had often reminded Elisabeth that her brother lived in an ivory tower, which was why he failed to understand how subtly the Jews undermined German culture. Wagner was a far more astute observer and he did understand. Why was it, Förster wondered, that Elisabeth seemed to share his views when she talked with him, and her brother's when he was gone? Was she honest with him or with her brother?

Elisabeth, too, was having second thoughts about her husband. She found it hard to write to him because his mistrust had saddened and depressed her:

> I have tried to hide my grief here. I am anyhow so miserable these days that a little more pain does not matter now. I feel very sorry for my poor, dear Fritz, he is so lonely in the world and I have so much reason to worry. And if you are so unkind to me, all my distress and my worries culminate in the one question: Do Bernhard and I really love each other enough to face this difficult life together? . . . Your brothers and sisters are also wondering and have doubts about your love for me. They ask themselves if I can be satisfied with it.

She concluded her tearful epistle by asking him not to send her any money. She did not need it, for she had sold sixteen copies of his book for forty-eight marks. "Perhaps it would have been better if I had not written this letter. You will not enjoy reading it in the midst of all your work." She signed herself as "your very depressed Elisabeth."

Förster was equally depressed. Not only because of his growing doubts concerning his marriage of four months, but because of the very poor response he received from his countrymen. Evening after evening he spoke to them in small, smoke-filled taverns or large lecture halls appealing to their patriotism and exhorting them to save the fatherland by supporting his cause. But when the collection came at the end of the evening, and he asked for contributions or pledges, the response was disappointing. He shared his disappointment with Elisabeth, who began to feel sorry for him and urged him to come home "so that we can console each other. . . . But please do not tell my mother anything about the poor financial result of your lectures. It is not necessary. She would only see it as a foreboding of our future, and make life even more difficult for me." She wondered whether it would not be wiser if they did not spend much more time in their beloved but expensive fatherland. But then, what does it matter: "If we are to perish, a thousand marks more or less will not save us." Assuring her "dearest heart" that, in spite of everything, she loved him and longed for him, she ended her consoling letter with the expression of "tenderest love."

Thus reassured, Förster continued his efforts and succeeded in recruiting a small band of pioneers who were willing to follow him across the sea and make a new home in Paraguay. But Elisabeth insisted that before they left Germany, her brother and her husband must meet. Reluctantly, the two men bowed to Elisabeth's wishes and agreed that the most suitable occasion for such a meeting was Nietzsche's forty-first birthday, the fifteenth of October. The meeting took place in Naumburg as Elisabeth had planned, and it went off without incident. Both men were on their best behavior, avoided political arguments, and drank to each other's health and good luck. Nietzsche wrote Overbeck:

> I did not find Förster unsympathetic, there is something sincere and noble in his character, and he seems a man of action. I was surprised how many things he accomplished and with what ease. In this respect, you and I are different. Admittedly, his values are not mine. Everything he does is done too quickly—we, you and I, consider these kinds of people overhasty.

As for Förster, he thought that his brother-in-law was a typical German professor with his head in a cloud of theories, and completely out of touch with reality. Nietzsche was obviously in poor health, half blind and unfit for work—no likely candidate for pioneering in Paraguay. The contrast between the fierce tenor of Nietzsche's writings and his gentle, almost feminine manner surprised Förster. He was glad that he had met his brother-in-law. There was no need to worry anymore. If Nietzsche was indeed his rival for Elisabeth's affections, he had nothing to fear, for Nietzsche was an invalid and much more to be pitied than feared.

After this one meeting the two men never met again. When Elisabeth asked her brother to invest some of his money in her husband's colony, he agreed reluctantly but stipulated that his piece of Paraguayan real estate be named *Llama land* and not *Friedrichshain*, as Elisabeth proposed.

Before her departure for her new home in the middle of February 1886, Elisabeth sent her brother a gold ring as a token of her affection, with the engraved inscription: "Remember B. & E. with love." Nietzsche accepted the ring but told his mother: "I confess that this combination Bern and Eli still offends me. Quite apart from Förster's views, there is no affinity between him and me. It is fortunate that he is gone."

In a printed farewell message sent from Hamburg, Dr. Bernhard Förster and his wife Elisabeth informed their friends that their address henceforth would be Asunción. Just before embarking on the steamer *Uraguay*, which was to take them to their new home, Elisabeth noticed that both her engagement ring and her wedding ring had disappeared. She was disconsolate, but it was too late to make inquiries at the railroad station. The die had been cast; even without a wedding band Elisabeth's fate was linked to Förster's for better or for worse.

PART III
1886-1893

10·The Queen of Nueva Germania

*A*FTER A STRENUOUS ocean journey that lasted almost a month, the Försters and their small band of pioneers arrived in Montevideo where they boarded a paddle steamer that took them up the river Paraguay in five days to Asunción. They disembarked on a hot and sultry day late in March. Although Elisabeth had been warned by her husband not to expect a European city, she was shocked by the pitiful appearance of the capital of her new homeland. There were no public buildings of any distinction. The massive imperial palace was an overgrown ruin and bore mute witness, as did many other buildings, to a succession of wars and revolutions. A few one-story stone buildings formed the commercial core of the city, which was laid out in a monotonous series of straight, unpaved streets. The residential sector consisted of clusters of ranchos, straw-covered mud huts, that were surrounded by swarms of half-naked native children.

In her letters to her mother and brother, Elisabeth made light of the depressing appearance of Asunción by calling it picturesque. She praised the city's healthy climate and its good-natured inhabitants, who lived in a state of natural innocence. That they were slothful and slovenly and given to drink, she failed to mention; nor did she mention the frequent cloudbursts that transformed the city streets into rivers of mud within minutes; or that special breed of militant mosquitoes that made life miserable for humans and animals. Like her husband, she described Paraguay as a paradise, a heaven of refuge for Europe-weary Germans.

Her diary presented a more realistic picture of life in her new home. Her husband had installed her in a rented country house several miles outside

95

Asunción. It was furnished in part with furniture they had brought from Germany and was large enough for modest entertaining. But most of the time Elisabeth was not the gracious hostess she depicted herself to be in her letters home; most of the time she was a hard-working peasant woman. Assisted by an unreliable native woman and few equally unreliable peons, she milked cows, made butter, baked bread, and gathered eggs, while her husband spent most of his time in the city conferring with government officials about a suitable tract of land for his colony. It was a slow and wearisome process, although the president of Paraguay, General Caballero, took a personal interest in it. "Bern rides to Asunción to talk with President Caballero about San Salvador," Elisabeth noted in her diary on July 5, 1886. "The president is friendly and obliging. He suggests that Bern submit a specific request." A few days later she noted: "The Argentine ambassador invites us to dinner, but only Bern goes because it is too strenuous for me to get to town." And on the fifteenth of July: "Wash day. Bern visits the president. San Salvador is out. An Italian has got there before us." Two days later: "Bern rides to Lambane with Mr. Matenas and Mr. Torris to look at real estate. We start milking in the evenings. In a bush we find a nest with nine eggs from our brown hens."

Frequently mentioned in Elisabeth's diary is a family Erck. Oscar Erck, a German farmer of a somewhat dubious past, had been one of Förster's first recruits. Like the others, he was anxiously waiting in Asunción for the day when he could settle his family on the promised land. He was Förster's most trusted lieutenant and destined to become the colony's administrator. But like the others, he was kept in the dark about the financial arrangements that led to the acquisition of Nueva Germania.

The main reason why it took Förster a long time to secure the land he needed for his colony was lack of capital. He had not succeeded in collecting one hundred thousand marks before he left Germany. And the response to his appeals from Asunción for increased financial support from his countrymen remained disappointing. But Förster was not willing to admit defeat. If worst came to worst, he was determined to perish rather than to return home a failure. He reminded his wife that Germanic warriors of old returned from battle victorious with their shields, or they were carried off the battlefield on their shields as fallen heroes. Elisabeth shared his feelings. Undaunted by the hardships of her pioneer existence, she spurred him on to ever bolder financial transactions.

During his protracted negotiations in Asunción, Förster made the acquaintance of the wealthy Paraguayan landowner and financier Cirilio Solalinde, who agreed to become Förster's partner in a very tricky land deal. The land in question, called *campo cassaccia*, comprised some one hundred forty thousand acres, mostly virgin forest, near the small town of San Pedro, which lies approximately seventy-five miles north of Asunción. Reputedly the purchase price for this enormous territory was one hundred seventy-five thousand marks. It is not known how much Förster contributed, for when it became evident that it was impossible to cultivate such a huge terrain, Solalinde offered to assume Förster's share on condition that the latter enter into an agreement with the government of Paraguay, which had recently passed a land settlement act in order to attract settlers. Under the terms of that act, the government would buy some forty thousand acres from Solalinde's *campo cassaccia* property for eighty thousand marks and transfer it to Förster, who would merely be required to deposit two thousand marks as security. The catch was that he would obtain legal title to this land only if he succeeded in settling one hundred forty families on it within two years. If he failed, he risked not only losing his deposit but also incurring legal battles with settlers who had paid him money for land he did not own. Since Förster ruled out the possibility of failure, he signed the agreement and by the stroke of his pen assumed possession of a territory the size of a German dukedom.

How little Elisabeth understood the terms of the transaction is shown by the jubilant tone of her diary entry of November 23, 1886: "Solalinde buys camp cassaccia for Bern." That the wily Paraguayan, whose Spanish grandezza Elisabeth admired, had actually sold part of his property to the government for a good profit, and that the government held the legal title to it, does not seem to have worried Elisabeth, who prided herself on being a shrewd businesswoman. What she did understand was that buying undeveloped land and selling it to German settlers could be a profitable business. Hence, she considered it her filial duty to inform her relatives that by investing in land in Paraguay they could become rich overnight. She succeeded in obtaining minor amounts from her mother, her brother, her mother-in-law, and two of her Naumburg girl friends. Even Alwine, her mother's faithful servant, invested part of her savings in Förster's colony and went about Naumburg bragging that she was now a landowner in Paraguay.

As the project grew and more money was needed, Elisabeth remembered her brother's small capital, which was deposited with the banker Kürbitz in Naumburg. She wrote and told him that he could double his fortune if he invested it in their colony, and she urged him to do so. Her request came at a time when her brother's financial future was quite uncertain. He was not sure how much longer he could count on his Basel pension. It had been granted originally for a period of ten years, and there was no certainty that it would be extended, although his friend Overbeck continued to intercede with the authorities of the university on Nietzsche's behalf. But Nietzsche feared that his attack on Christianity and the vehement anti-establishment tenor of his recent writings had offended the conservative Swiss so much that they might consider terminating his pension, which they were not legally obligated to pay. This prospect was particularly serious now that he needed more money than ever because he had to pay for the publication of his books. He estimated that printing costs would run to several thousand marks. Finally, he had serious misgivings about Förster's financial operations, despite his sister's enthusiastic reports. And yet, if his beloved Llama needed his money, ought he not give it to her?

Torn by such contradictory emotions, Nietzsche turned to Overbeck for advice:

My relatives have sent me an excellent plan for their colonial enterprise and want my Naumburg money for it. What do you think of my Basel prospects? I feel I should keep what little money I have for any emergency ... on the other hand, I find it very difficult to say NO in such a stupid money matter.

Nietzsche felt relieved when Overbeck advised him not to risk his money in an uncertain enterprise. He wrote his sister: "Concerning my money, my reason and that of friend Overbeck definitely counsel against tying it up anywhere ... who knows what may happen to me in the next four years. Whether I shall continue to receive my Basel pension now depends on many unforeseeable accidents." [To Overbeck he confided he resented most that by asking him for his money, his sister had forced him to say no.]

Elisabeth became angry when she heard that her brother refused to lend her the money they needed so badly. "It hurt me very much that you could think I would suggest anything uncertain to you and that you insist in remaining a poor man when it would be so easy to double your fortune here."

What rankled her most was that her brother's refusal had been influenced by Overbeck. She had always resented Overbeck's friendship with her brother, and her feelings for Overbeck's wife, Ida, had turned to hatred during the Lou episode. While she was brooding in Asunción over the reasons for her brother's refusal to help her, she convinced herself that Overbeck, although a Protestant theologian, was in reality a Jew. Like her husband, she began to suspect Jewish intrigue whenever anything went wrong with their Aryan project.

But she kept her misgivings to herself and told her brother that she would not hold it against him that he refused to help her in a time of need; on the contrary, she would share her wealth with him, for she was certain their colony would flourish. She admitted that she was getting tired of waiting in Asunción while their house in Nueva Germania was being built, but she echoed her husband's confident reports about the progress their small band of pioneers was making. The edge of the forest had already been cleared and the ground prepared for the first German town to rise in the wilderness. It was fittingly named Försterrode.

Elisabeth's two-year wait ended at long last in March 1888 when the moment of truth came—her first look at Nueva Germania. In a long and jubilant letter she told her beloved *Herzensmutter*

that on March 5 we arrived in our glorious new homeland and took possession of it like kings. ... We did not travel to the colony on the little steamer but on a wagon drawn by six oxen. Bernchen rode at our side. As we were about an hour and a half from Nueva Germania, two Paraguayans appeared and told the wagonmaster wonderful tales, whereupon the latter and his two peons broke into shouts of joy. The most eloquent told me in Spanish that the colony was festively decorated with German flags and everybody was waiting to welcome us. ... It was all very moving. In front of every farm house we passed, people stood festively dressed, presented me with flowers and cigars, and handed me their babies for my benediction.

Suddenly eight splendid horsemen appeared. They were our new Germans who had come to greet us; among them was Herr Erck and other leading colonists. They brought Bern's favorite horse, beautifully decorated with black, white, and red rosettes, which he mounted at once. That was only the first reception, but we were still not in our own country. You ought to have seen the procession: first the wagon, then the riders, and then the long train of people. Now we reached the Aguaraymi, which borders on our property. We were not received with a cannon salute, but cheerful gunshots rang out as we approached and a charming small wagon appeared, decorated with palm leaves like a green arbor and carrying a small red throne. All very pretty. Here I embraced my dear Mrs. Erck. Mr. Erck made a solemn speech of welcome since I had never been here before. Then the procession moved to the port of Aguaraya Guazo, the commercial center of the colony with the store and the immigrant house.

Here the first triumphal arch had been erected and the official reception took place. We sat in the center of a marvelously shady square, and three very beautiful girls appeared, the oldest, about fifteen, was almost a lady; she was pretty as a picture and the beauty of the colony. She recited a charming poem of welcome that her father had written and gave us flowers. Then we ate breakfast, while the populace feasted on wine and cumin. The wives of the colonists, who had been called together, brewed coffee, and our new Germans sat at a long table underneath a beautifully shady tree.

Dear mother, I can only say may God grant that all coming colonists look as decent as the ones who were sitting with us at the head table. They all had such open and honest German faces. Then Mr. Enzweiler, a very industrious and capable colonist, made a speech of welcome, raised his glass and shouted "Long live the mother of the colony," which pleased my heart. You see, the people of New Germany are very gallant: the ladies come first. Then they toasted our dear Bernchen, who replied and thanked the colonists for both of us. There followed another series of toasts. It was all very cheerful, but we had to move on. Accompanied by the sounds of "Deutschland, Deutschland über Alles" we drove and rode to our house, which lies about half an hour from the port.

As we approached the forest we found a second triumphal arch that had been erected by the colonists who live on either side of the forest path. We stopped and inspected their half-finished houses where people live so comfortably. That would not be possible in any other climate. Again we received flowers and solemn good wishes. At last we approached our own house, where a third triumphal arch had been built. The house itself was decorated with foliage. Here a charming little girl presented us with bread, salt, and the keys to our spacious home. From outside it looks surprisingly ugly, but inside it is grand, with high ceilings, large and cool. You have no idea how hot it is here. We call this style of house the "icebox style," because the roof reaches very far down, which keeps it pleasantly cool at all times of day. The three rooms in the center are very large and almost eighteen feet high.

Gradually everybody left and we remained at home—to work. The festivities were over, and now there was work, hard work. Life is not easy

förſterhof.

Elisabeth's home in Nueva Germania.

because we have too many possessions. In addition, the floors in three small rooms had still to be laid, the provisions arrived and there was so much confusion that at times I did not know where to begin.

But as regards the colony, I never imagined it to be half so magnificent. Everything is marvelous. Everything looks so professional and grandiose. Our administrator and our other officials are gentlemen and very well suited for their positions.

I confess that often before falling asleep I lie in bed wondering how we got the money for such a grand enterprise. God must have blessed it. He turned every mark a loving heart gave or loaned us into five. There is no other explanation. We own a magnificent property, a large house, five small ranchos and three medium-sized ones. We have hundreds of heads of cattle, eight horses; we own a store with six thousand marks' worth of goods; we pay an official administrator, an agricultural administrator, a storekeeper, a land surveyor, and an agent who escorts colonists from San Pedro. Besides, we employ twenty peons, servants, cooks, etc. We can afford to pay good salaries and wages, and although we are often worried, there has never been any lack of money. Good heavens! People think that Bern married a very rich woman because they do not know how we did it. They all assume that I am rich. But you know better. You know the real reason: It is God's blessing on honest work.

The dear, excellent Mr. Kaiser from Dortmund, who has just arrived with six people, has been very much impressed with the grandeur of the whole enterprise and is quite upset because he thinks that Bern has been far too modest in his reports about this magnificent colony. He is delighted to be here and told me in confidence: "Well, my dear Frau Doktor, it is quite apparent that you must have invested a quarter of a million here." Bern and I laughed when we heard this. It is true that we have debts, but they are ridiculously small in comparison with our property.

Farewell, dear *Herzensmutter*, I must finish this letter. We are only half furnished and are expecting four houseguests. It is a time of hard work but also a very happy one.

Franziska wept with joy, and she read and reread her daughter's letter. She felt like begging Lieschen for forgiveness for her opposition to her marriage to Förster. Thank God her worries had been unnecessary. Lisbeth was right: The Lord had richly blessed her, blessed be the Lord. She sat down at once and told her son the glad tidings. To make sure that he understood them fully, she enclosed her daughter's letter.

Nietzsche was impressed. Although he continued his refusal to invest his money in Förster's "anti-Semitic enterprise," he proudly told his friends:

My sister has written a long and frankly enchanting report about her arrival and royal reception in Nueva Germania. The undertaking really assumes a grandiose aspect. . . . "It is possible that one of the world's greatest railroads, which runs from the mouth of the La Plata to the Panama Canal will either pass through the colony or close by—the line through Bolivia and Peru. The building of this railroad can bring a fortune, for the colony has magnificent alpine forests and two tributaries of the main river. General Osborne, formerly the ambassador of the United States to Argentina, is currently negotiating with the government about this railroad, which is his dream and his life's goal." (He told my sister, as he bid her good-bye, that it was his fondest wish that he would arrive one day by train and renew his acquaintance with the little queen of Nueva Germania.)

Nietzsche wrote the last phrase of this letter in English, hence Elisabeth probably inspired it. She was determined to show her brother that he had been mistaken in his opinion of Förster and wrong to doubt the success of their enterprise. And she succeeded.

Nietzsche envied his sister's rapid rise to fame and fortune, which contrasted so markedly with his own solitary boardinghouse existence.

A few days ago I made the following inventory of my possessions: four shirts, four nightshirts, three woolen shirts, eight pairs of socks, one good coat, one heavy overcoat. The winter coat from Naumburg, still quite good although I rarely wear it, two black pants, one very heavy pair of pants, two black vest coats, the last two Naumburg vests, which would be good if they were not too short, and one pair of slippers.

These were his possessions, he told his mother, while his sister and her husband had become the largest landowners in Paraguay and played an important role in the social and political life of their adopted country. "I have just heard indirectly and accidentally that Dr. Förster's influence has grown so greatly that it is by no means outside the realm of possibility that he will be the next candidate for the presidency of the Republic," Nietzsche wrote Overbeck in February 1888.

His brother-in-law's spectacular success made his own failure to receive any recognition even more humiliating, and it strengthened his resolve to force the world to take notice of him. In a spurt of furious energy he wrote a number of provocative pamphlets in which he vented his scorn on every successful man and every popular idea. He declared war on Wagner and Bayreuth, on Bismarck and the German Reich, on nationalism and democracy, and pronounced a solemn curse on Christianity. A host of brilliant aphorisms burst out of his feverish brain, climaxing in the *Ecce Homo*, an autobiographical essay that he wrote to celebrate his forty-fourth birthday and in which he proclaimed his immortality. Imperceptibly during the late fall and winter of 1888 Nietzsche approached his Rubicon, the line that separates sanity from insanity. At the same time, his sister and her husband fought desperately to secure the future of Nueva Germania, which had looked so promising a few months ago but was suddenly threatened by the specter of financial collapse.

Under the terms of the agreement between Förster and the government of Paraguay, one hundred and forty families had to be settled in his colony by August 1889. To meet this deadline, Elisabeth and her husband kept up a steady barrage of letters, reports, and appeals, which were published in the *Chemnitzer Kolonialnachrichten*, the official organ of the Chemnitz Colonial Society, which Schubert had founded to support Nueva Germania, and in the *Bayreuther Blätter*. German readers gained the impression from reading these accounts that life in Förster's colony was truly idyllic.

What a chance we offer German workers who are wasting away in poverty, sickness, and despair in many parts of our old fatherland. We give them bread, while liberal social democracy only gives them stones. . . . We are dreaming of a rebirth of our race, which is getting weary and old. . . . When the ax resounds in the primordial forest, when we clear the underbrush with the sweat of our brow to prepare the fertile soil for cultivation, when we dig trenches to drain stagnant water—how far all these activities seem from the sacred hill of Bayreuth. But we feel in our hearts that it is precisely this kind of work that makes us the spiritual heirs of Richard Wagner.

By means of such lyrical language, Förster hoped to attract colonists and investors.

His wife pursued the same goal, but her descriptions of life in Nueva Germania, although equally enthusiastic, were interlaced with practical hints for would-be colonists, polemics against the colony's detractors, and laments about the lagging support from their old fatherland. A long article, entitled "A Sunday in Nueva Germania," which she wrote for the *Bayreuther Blätter* in December 1888, begins with this idyllic picture:

It is Sunday, the middle of summer, and half past four in the morning. A gentle darkness still lies over New Germany. . . . The spacious yard, filled with shady trees, which extends beyond the manor house and is bordered on both sides by farm buildings, offers a very picturesque sight at this early morning hour. Brightly colored hammocks hang everywhere among the trees, the farm wagons, and the entrance hall. They are covered with mosquito nets (which are more necessary against the heavy night dew than against the few mosquitos). Those are the sleeping quarters of our Paraguayan servants; fourteen at the moment. In the middle of the yard blazes a bright, open fire with a kettle of boiling water on it. Around it crouch peons (Paraguayan workers), who drink the favorite drink of all Paraguayans, *yerba maté,* out of small hollowed-out pumpkins through thin reeds called *bombilla.* Even in this early morning hour they chatter cheerfully and laugh happily. The Paraguayans are a very good-natured, harmless race with certain childlike traits that one must never forget in dealing with them. . . . The best method of keeping Paraguayan servants is to treat them firmly but kindly, like children, to let them keep their own ways in eating, drinking, and working, and to give them little presents from time to time as a sign of appreciation. It is enough to give them cigars or freshly baked bread, which they consider a delicacy. . . . But let us return to our Sunday morning. The master of the house now appears. The peons rush up to him to fulfill any wish he may have. The Paraguayans are very obliging and respectful toward their masters. The horses are brought, groomed and fed. . . . Our German gardener brings cucumbers and melons from our garden. Then comes breakfast. The Germans drink coffee and milk and eat bread with butter and cane syrup, or cornmeal and syrup. The peons usually eat boiled or cooked mandioka roots, but since those are scarce just now, their Sunday breakfast today will be bread and syrup.

This description of a Sunday morning in New Germany is followed by an account of the monthly meeting of the colonists in the afternoon. They are all honest Germans, who indignantly protest the horrible lies that "a certain Julius Klingbeil, an Antwerp tailor, is spreading in Berlin about the colony and its people." Elisabeth insists that it was most unfortunate that this unsavory character ever set foot in Nueva Germania, for his slanderous accounts are damaging the reputation of the colony, particularly his charges that Förster lacked legal title to the land he was selling. Elisabeth took great pains to refute this charge:

It seems to us that a false importance is given in Germany to the fact that one hundred and forty families must be settled within two years. It is true, my husband accepted this condition and deposited securities valued at two thousand pesos. However, since the government has not the slightest interest in having unsuitable people brought into the colony merely to reach this figure, it is ready at any time to rescind the two-year clause at my husband's wish and extend the date stated in the contract for three or four more years. This extension would not affect the question of title, which is so much talked about and exploited by our enemies. My husband, who has the assurance of the government, will go to Asunción in May and request the right to issue legal titles. His request will no doubt be granted.

In December 1888, when Elisabeth expressed confidence in her husband's ability to extricate himself from the two-year clause of his contract, she did so without knowing—or caring to know—the fine print of the document Förster had signed. As far as she was concerned, it was a minor point and could be corrected easily. Förster knew better. He knew that if by August 1889 there were not one hundred and forty people settled in Nueva Germania, all the land he had sold would revert to the government of Paraguay. Since he was in no position to return the moneys he had received from the settlers, he feared there would be violence and he would be the object of universal condemnation. The closer the date of reckoning came, the more morose did he become. Elisabeth's willful ignorance of what was at stake added to his depression. She refused to face the reality of ruin and insisted that all he had to do was to go to Asunción and request an extension of the two-year clause. He would try that, of course, but he was not very hopeful that he would succeed.

Elisabeth wrote her mother that she had spent a very cheerless Christmas because Bernchen had been so moody. She had to remind him constantly that his life's motto was "to prevail in spite of all obstacles." She hoped he would take it to heart in the new year.

11·1889: Drama and Tragedy

URING 1888 all signs pointed to the approaching final phase of Nietzsche's illness. The poison that had been in his body all these years was slowly but inexorably destroying his brain, a process that increased the irritability of his nervous system and affected his physical and mental state. He spent the first quarter of the year in Nice, alternating between moods of deep depression—"there were days and nights when I did not know how to go on living, and when a black despair overwhelmed me, worse than I have ever known before"—and jubilant affirmation—"I say to myself at every healthy moment 'much has been accomplished in spite of everything—very much.' "

At the beginning of April he left Nice for Turin, but fell sick before he reached it and spent two "horrible days" in the little town of Sampierdarena near Genoa. The moment he entered Turin—"that princely residence of the seventeenth century"—his health improved, and when the news reached him that the Danish literary critic Georg Brandes had given a series of lectures on his philosophy, his depression vanished and gave way to a mood of euphoric elation. At last the conspiracy of silence that had dogged him at every step and prevented his ideas from becoming known was broken. Proudly he informed his friends that Brandes's lectures were a brilliant success. "The lecture hall is packed every time. More than three hundred listeners. All leading newspapers bring reports." And while congratulating his sister on her "royal reception" in Nueva Germania, he told her, "I, too, have reason to be a little proud. Brandes is giving lectures at the University of Copenhagen 'om den tyske filosof Friedrich Nietzsche.' What do you think of that?"

His feverish brain was bursting with ever bolder ideas, which he scribbled down hastily and almost illegibly because his fingers could not keep up with the *tempo fortissimo* of his mind. He felt he was finally reaching his goal; he was erecting the triumphal arch of his philosophy. "To my own surprise," he told Overbeck, "the final draft of the first book of my *Transvaluation of All Values* is already half finished . . . this work cuts through millennia. The first book is called *The Antichrist.* I swear that everything that has ever been said critically about Christianity is mere childishness compared with it." During a ten-day respite from his philosophic labors, he wrote *The Case of Wagner*, a merciless declaration of war on his former friend. He hoped it would cause a sensation, and he was right: "My publisher tells me that he has received so many orders (after the first announcement in the trade journal) that the edition of a thousand copies can be considered exhausted." And jubilantly he added that he now had readers everywhere: "In Vienna, St. Petersburg, Paris, Stockholm, New York. My future works will appear simultaneously in many languages . . . the Swedish genius Strindberg is writing letters to all the world: *Carthago est delenda, lisez Nietzsche.*" As the year progressed, his mind, taut to the breaking point, worked on ever more provocative projects. Philosophizing with a hammer, he declared war on every god and on every idol sacred to mankind. Socrates, Christ, Luther, Rousseau, Kant, Schiller, Schopenhauer, fell victim to the sharp, rapierlike thrusts of his mind. He called Christianity "the one great innermost corruption, the one great instinct of revenge, the one immortal blemish of mankind," and declared as decadent all such modern ideas as nationalism, socialism, and democracy. He was writing, he insisted, for a race of men that did not yet exist—"the lords of the earth," a master race with a terrible will to power, the barbarians of the twentieth century. Carried away by the vehemence of the ideas that flashed through his brain, he asked:

> Do you know what this world is to me? Shall I show it to you in my mirror? This world, a monster of energy, without beginning, without end, an eternally fixed quantity of force which neither increases nor decreases, which is not used up but only transformed . . . this world is the will to power—and nothing besides. And you yourselves are the will to power and nothing besides.

Upon reaching his forty-fourth birthday on October 15, 1888, he took stock of his life and wrote *Ecce Homo*, an autobiographical essay scintillating with magnificent madness: "I know my fate. Someday the remembrance of something monstrous will be linked with my name—I am not a man, I am dynamite." He felt like a king traveling incognito as he walked through the streets of Turin, and he told his mother that everybody treated him like a prince, "including my peddler woman who will not rest until she has found the sweetest of all her grapes for me." Overbeck was startled when Nietzsche wrote him that he was working on a memorandum for the courts of Europe, in which he proposed the formation of an anti-German league: "I mean to constrict the Reich into an iron shirt and provoke it to a war of desperation."

He demanded that the German emperor and all anti-Semites be shot. On the thirty-first of December he confided to Peter Gast in a tone of awful finality that he had crossed the Rubicon. Henceforth, he lived in a land not inhabited by rational beings. And he now signed his letters with Nietzsche Caesar, Dionysos, or the Crucified.

It took two months before the news of her brother's collapse reached Elisabeth. She was far too occupied with her own problems to pay much attention to the increasingly more strident tone of her brother's letters. Six months had passed since her spectacular arrival in New Germany. What had begun so auspiciously was followed by a series of reverses that threatened the very existence of their colony. The hoped for support from their financial backers in Germany failed to arrive, the number of colonists did not increase as rapidly as they had expected, and, worst of all, some of the colonists who had come were so disillusioned by what they experienced that they began to leave. In the midst of these disturbing developments Elisabeth discovered that her husband was quite incapable of coping with practical problems and left her almost solely in charge of running the affairs of the colony. In her letters to her mother she complained occasionally about her heavy responsibilities, but continued to enjoy her role as the reigning queen of Nueva Germania and still found time to carry on her correspondence with her brother.

On the occasion of his forty-fourth birthday she wrote a long letter to her dear *Herzens-Fritz* and congratulated him on his rising fame:

> For fame is a sweet drink. Personally, I would have wished you another apostle than Mr. Brandes; he has peeked into too many pots and eaten from too many plates. However, one cannot choose one's admirers and one thing is certain: He will make you fashionable, for that is what he understands. But I cannot suppress a well-meant piece of advice. Avoid a personal meeting, exchange pleasantries with him by correspondence, but do not look at him too closely. Two of our friends know him and agree that he has a flair for the most interesting personalities, and that he makes himself interesting through them. It pleases my heart that there can be no longer any talk about a "conspiracy of silence" and that through Brandes many genuine admirers who suit you will hear about you. . . . My dear *Herzens-Fritz*, once again your dear birthday is here. It makes me think of the many years we have wandered through life together and now, unfortunately, are so far away from each other. How much joy and grief we have experienced. Is life worth living?

If Nietzsche had received this letter at any other time, he would have smiled and dismissed it as merely another example of his sister's sophomoric style. But since it reached him at the height of his euphoria, when he felt like an uncrowned king, its condescending tone offended him, the more so since he had just heard rumors that Förster's enterprise was in deep trouble. He felt that his sister had deceived him with her grandiose account of her "royal reception," which he had accepted at face value and passed on to his friends. Hence, he lost no time to inform Overbeck that "in Paraguay things are as

bad as they can be. The Germans, who were lured over there, are in rebellion
and demand their money back—but there is none. Acts of violence have
already occurred. I fear the worst. This does not prevent my sister from writing to me for October 15 with the utmost scorn: Was I perhaps trying to become famous, too—that would indeed be a sweet affair. And what scum I was
associating with—Jews, who had been licking all plates, like Georg Brandes.''

Nietzsche's angry reaction to his sister's letter and the distorted version of
it he gave Overbeck shows how deeply Elisabeth had wounded him. Her marriage had been a cruel betrayal. It had opened his eyes to the true character of
his faithful Llama. She had never understood him, she had not the faintest
notion of his philosophy, she had remained what she had always been: a petty, spiteful creature imbued with a self-righteous sense of middle-class
morality. It was ironic that she was his sister. He would tell her that.

While Nietzsche brooded over the unfortunate role his sister had played in
his life and penned ever-more-savage attacks against her, Elisabeth was fighting for the survival of their colony. More and more colonists, who had left
Germany in the hope of finding an easier life in Paraguay, discovered that
this was not the case. Clearing the forest and cultivating the heavy, claylike
soil, so highly praised in Förster's book and articles, proved a backbreaking
and often hopeless task. Despite hard work, most colonists were worse off in
New Germany than they had been at home. They lived in primitive huts, had
to buy most of their food in Förster's store, found no market for the produce
they grew, and were exposed to the daily irritations of a number of subtropi-
cal pests. Disillusioned, they accused Förster of having misled them and demanded their money back.

In his propaganda brochures, Förster promised that he would refund the
purchase price for the land and any improvements made on it, if a colonist
wished to leave Nueva Germania. But it became evident very soon that in order to make good his promise, Förster would need much more capital than he
possessed. He was forced to take out loans at exorbitant rates of interest and
finally had to invent subterfuges for his inability to return monies he owed.
This gave rise to the charge that Förster was a swindler and his entire colonial
enterprise a fraudulent land speculation. This charge was at first privately
uttered by disgruntled colonists but brought into the open by the angry Antwerp tailor, ominously named Klingbeil—"resounding ax"—who in 1889
published a one-hundred-and-sixty-page book entitled *Revelations Concerning Dr. Bernhard Förster's Colony New Germany in Paraguay*. It caused a sensation.

About the time when Klingbeil's book appeared, Elisabeth heard that her
brother had become deranged and committed to an insane asylum. Her first
impulse had been to rush home and take care of her beloved Fritz:

> If I could only get away from here and had the money for the journey, I
> would leave at once. I am tormented by the thought that the worst would
> have been avoided if I had stayed in Germany . . . Bernhard does not show
> the slightest sympathy for my grief. On the contrary, he does everything

he can to make life as hard as possible for me. His behavior is taking all the joy out of my life, for I remember how loving Fritz has always been (the ugly letters he wrote me were nothing but a sign of his first attack of chloride poisoning). Fritz never once said an unfriendly word to me and I thanked him by leaving the poor dear heart to his fate . . . I am of course an "excellent wife" when I take upon myself joyfully every burden without ever asking anything for myself. My only concern is the success of our work. I only think of Bern and the colony (I spend literally nothing on myself except for buying two pairs of shoes a year). I have not received any presents for Christmas or my birthday. I have been forced to think more of myself during the last six months because of a serious eye infection and my great grief. And I feel very strongly now that Bern is a terrible egotist. It hurts me very much . . . I know quite well that without me this entire colonial enterprise would have been a very uncertain affair. I am saying this without pride and merely to explain why I have left my poor Fritz in the lurch.

Since Elisabeth got no sympathy from her husband, she fell to solitary brooding about the cause of her brother's collapse and convinced herself that he had poisoned his brain by taking overdoses of chloride as a sleeping medicine. She had frequently warned him of this drug: "If only I had remained near him, I could have prevented his sickness or at least started the right treatment at once. The cause of his sickness is chloride, nothing else; he is suffering from chloride poisoning." Overbeck should have taken him to a hospital, not a lunatic asylum. Her misgivings about Overbeck had been right. He was not a true friend of her brother's. He had probably been jealous of him all these years. By committing him to an insane asylum he had seriously damaged Fritz's reputation. Indignantly, she wrote her mother: "I hear that Overbeck is a Jew; that speaks volumes and I believe it." But Elisabeth's grief for her brother and her indignation with Overbeck were overshadowed by events much closer to home—events that were precipitated, though not caused, by Klingbeil's book.

Klingbeil was an enterprising German tailor who had settled in Antwerp and carried on a small but profitable business there. By dint of hard work and modest living he had accumulated a small capital, which he wanted to invest in a German colony since the Antwerp climate did not agree with him. He was of peasant stock and longed to return to the land. In search of a suitable place, he had come across Förster's Paraguay book. Förster's descriptions of the favorable living conditions in New Germany and the book's tone of honesty and patriotism—convincingly reflected in the manly features of Förster's face—made a profound impression on Klingbeil. He corresponded with Förster—who assured him that New Germany was a haven of refuge for German patriots. On the strength of these assurances, Klingbeil had paid down a deposit of five thousand marks for a piece of property. He arrived in the colony in March 1888, accompanied by eight eager young compatriots.

Already during the journey, however, Klingbeil began to have doubts about Förster's financial transactions, for he heard that under the terms of

Förster's agreement with the government of Paraguay, no legal title to the land he sold could be issued until certain conditions had been met. Klingbeil was told that Förster could not possibly meet these conditions and was therefore in a critical mood when he reached his destination.

What he saw in New Germany quickly confirmed his fears. He noted that most of the colonists lived in miserable huts, while Förster's home was spacious and comfortable:

> Nothing was lacking to make life pleasant; comfortable armchairs, couches, a piano, large curtained doors, and handsome stone floors. Many a colonist must have felt sad when he compared Förster's elegant home with his own miserable hut, which lacked even those amenities of life that the poorest day laborer enjoys in Germany—not to mention the pitiful food. I have often heard bitter complaints that Dr. Förster leads a life of ease at the expense of the colonists' savings.

Klingbeil's originally favorable impression of Förster was quickly shattered when he met Förster in person, for

> the man possessed none of the qualities we had expected. He could not look you straight in the eye. Restlessly, like the bad conscience personified, the haggard man with his unsteady, ugly eyes walked back and forth across the room; during the conversation he jumped absentmindedly from one topic to the next. If it were not for the fact that his actions show cunning and calculation, as I shall have occasion to prove, you might think that the man was crazy. It is revolting to witness how he endures the tyranny of his domineering wife, who insists that she and her husband are the rulers of the small principality, as she calls the colony.

During Klingbeil's first meeting with Förster, Elisabeth, "who represented the practical point of view," brought the conversation back again and again to the question of money.

> Finally, she came straight out and asked her husband: "Dear Bernchen, would you not offer Mr. Klingbeil the customary one percent monthly interest, if he would pay today the twenty-five hundred marks he owes us in October?" Angrily, the Doktor replied: "Why should I do this? I do not need the money that badly." Unfortunately, we did not know then that Frau Förster's sly suggestion and her husband's cursory rejection was a comedy merely enacted to deceive the victim, for even then the Doktor was paying sixty percent interest in Asunción for a loan of two thousand pesos.

Klingbeil's book contains even more serious charges: "With much elegance Frau Doktor displayed a large map of the colony showing that all available lots had been sold." This was not true. The names of all the so-called buyers had been used without their knowledge. "Not one had actually bought a lot." Even so, Klingbeil himself fell victim to Elisabeth's salesmanship and paid the twenty-five hundred marks for a lot that, she insisted, would otherwise be sold to someone else. While Förster seemed to him a pathetic mixture of cowardice and ambition, his wife "possessed an incredibly high degree of courage." He added that it was too bad that "Elisabeth makes use of her heroic trait for very ignoble ends." To watch "the little woman, always elegantly dressed, skittering around the table clutching a map, her mouth, her hands, and her feet in constant motion," amused the Antwerp tailor. There was no doubt in his mind that Elisabeth wielded the real power in the colony and that her husband was merely her mouthpiece: "What a sad life he must lead with a domineering wife like her."

Klingbeil's accusations coincided with the deepening crisis in Förster's personal life. He had had misgivings about his marriage from the start, for he knew that Elisabeth was a very headstrong woman. But he had hoped that by taking her away from her family and her native surroundings to a country she did not know, he could assert his role as husband and provider. This hope, he soon realized, was an illusion. Elisabeth took over the reins of his colony right away and relegated him to a subordinate position, very subtly, to be sure, for outwardly she deferred to him on every occasion. But there was no doubt in anyone's mind who was the master of Försterhof. Hurt at the core of his male pride, Förster became moody and despondent. His despondency intensified when he noticed how deeply Elisabeth was affected by her brother's illness. He felt that she all but blamed him for it because she reminded him constantly that Fritz would not have broken down if she had been with him. What Förster had feared all along had happened: If his wife had to choose between him and her brother, she would choose her brother. This knowledge saddened him because both he and Elisabeth had been shocked by Nietzsche's scurrilous attack on their patron Richard Wagner. He began to wonder whether Elisabeth secretly shared her brother's views on Wagner, while she professed the contrary to him. Was she honest with him? And what future was there for a marriage built on dishonesty?

The burden of this question lay heavily on Förster's mind, when Klingbeil's accusations appeared in print. He tried to defend himself by calling upon those colonists who were content with their lot to bear witness on his behalf and refute "Klingbeil's lies." But his German backers became suspicious and refused further support until the whole matter had been cleared up. This refusal made Förster's financial situation untenable. When his efforts to take up additional loans in Asunción failed, he was at the end of his rope. Facing the specter of bankruptcy he left Asunción toward the end of May, a defeated and despondent man. He did not return home to seek comfort in the arms of a loving wife. Instead, he went to San Bernardino, a Swiss colony, where he had lived as a bachelor when he first came to Paraguay and dreamed the dream of founding a German colony. There on June 2, 1889, he wrote the following letter to the director of the Chemnitz Colonial Society:

> Dear Mr. Schubert—The strange conduct of the Chemnitz Colonial Society deprives me of the last possibility to maintain myself here economically. My physical and mental state is such that I must assume I shall soon be relieved of my hard task. This is my last request: Please continue to put your considerable talents, your strength and your youthful en-

thusiasm in the service of the worthy enterprise that I have started. Perhaps it will prosper better without me than with me. Believe me, New Germany deserves to be supported rather than many other colonial enterprises. It can become an honorable monument for all who participated in the establishment of this colony.

Cordially yours,
Bernhard Förster

One day after he had written this letter, on June 3, 1889, Förster was found dead in his room in San Bernardino. When the news of his death reached Elisabeth, she displayed all the signs of grief of a loving wife who has suddenly lost her husband, although her love for Förster, never very strong, had declined considerably during her marriage, especially in the months after she heard of her brother's illness.

But she realized at once that the mysterious circumstances surrounding her husband's death would have serious repercussions in New Germany and made sure that a death certificate was issued, declaring that Förster had died of a sudden faint caused by an "ataque nervioso," a nervous disorder. Signed by a Paraguayan doctor, this death certificate was of dubious value both medically and legally and did not prevent the press in Argentina and Germany from reporting that Förster had killed himself by taking poison, exactly as Klingbeil had predicted he would. However, it was a useful document, for it permitted Elisabeth to refute these "malicious allegations" and to assert that her husband's untimely death at forty-six was due to overwork in the service of his new fatherland. By assuming the role of the widow of a patriotic martyr, who was carrying on her husband's work alone and unafraid, Elisabeth could count on a considerable amount of public sympathy. Her new role helped her greatly during the difficult negotiations with her husband's creditors and the government of Paraguay. She fought bravely for over a year to keep control of her colony, but neither her tears nor her business acumen proved equal to the financial straits in which she found herself. On August 1, 1890, the queen of Nueva Germania was forced to abdicate.

Ownership of the colony passed into the hands of an international corporation—the Sociedad Colonizadora Nueva Germania en el Paraguay. The majority of the stockholders in the new corporation were non-Germans. Elisabeth succeeded, however, in persuading the chief stockholder to retain her late husband's administrator, Oscar Erck, in that position. Since Erck was used to following her orders, her behind-the-scenes influence on the affairs of New Germany remained considerable. But she was not content to stay behind the scenes. She wanted to regain German control of New Germany. To achieve this objective, she traveled to Germany at the end of 1890 in a fund-raising effort that was to provide her with the means to continue her colonizing work and ensure immortality for her late husband.

12·Homecoming

As Elisabeth's train approached Naumburg, a few days before Christmas 1890, her mind wandered back to the scene of her departure almost five years ago. She remembered her mother's worried face—poor Mamachen had never been reconciled to the idea that her Lieschen would leave home and fatherland for the wilds of Paraguay. She remembered her husband comforting the two old ladies—his mother and hers—who had come to see them off, by assuring them they would all meet again in a few years either in Naumburg or in Försterrode, the town he was going to build. And she remembered her last meeting with her brother, who had been in such good health and high spirits. That had been five years ago, only five years, but they seemed like an eternity. Bernhard was dead, his work unfinished, leaving her with a legacy of disappointed hopes. And her poor beloved brother? She dreaded the thought of meeting him, although she knew that he was no longer confined to an asylum and that her mother was taking care of him at home.

When the train pulled into the station, Elisabeth recognized them at once: her little mother leading her brother gently by the arm, as though he were a child. He walked stiffly upright, like a Prussian soldier on parade, clutching a bunch of roses in his right hand. Elisabeth's eyes filled with tears as she walked up to them and heard her mother reminding Fritz to give her the flowers. He did so gravely, called her Llama, and babbled happily about his life in the army. Elisabeth exchanged a quick glance with her mother, embraced her brother, and wept.

Later that evening, after Alwine had taken Fritz to his bedroom upstairs, she and her mother sat in the living room and talked for hours about the two tragedies that had befallen them. Elisabeth explained that Bernhard had been on his way home when he was stricken in San Bernardino. She denied vehemently the rumors of his suicide, which had appeared in German newspapers, by asserting that only Jewish papers spread such vile lies because the Jews hated her husband. But she would not let his memory be besmirched; she would sue the editors for slander. That was why she had come home: to fight for her husband's good name, his work, and his ideals. New Germany was a monument to German industry, German courage, and German faith. She was determined to regain full control of it. With the help of such staunch supporters as Count von Volzogen, the editor of the *Bayreuther Blätter*, who had just published a long poem eulogizing Bernhard as a fallen hero, "a Germanic warrior welcome to Valhalla," she would arouse the German public and remind them of their duty to support their pioneering countrymen. She would go to Berlin and plead the case for German colonies with the officials of the foreign office. Since Bismarck had declared that he "was not a colonial man," she would address her appeal directly to the Emperor. She would seek an audience with the All-Highest and enlist his support for New Germany. She would also approach the ecclesiastical counselor of the Lutheran Church, Provost von der Goltz, and ask him to help her build a Christian church in Nueva Germania. And she would write a book about her colony. Germany must be told what had been accomplished in Paraguay and what still needed to be done.

Franziska listened to her daughter's vehement eloquence in subdued silence. She had hoped that Lieschen had come home to help her take care of her brother. But nothing seemed farther from Elisabeth's mind. She was completely wrapped up in colonial affairs and lived in a world totally foreign to her mother's. But Franziska knew that it was useless to remonstrate with her daughter. Elisabeth was obviously not staying home, and her son's care would remain her responsibility. While she was pondering the meaning of this news, the quiet of the night was suddenly shattered by a fierce, animal-like howling from Fritz's room. Elisabeth stopped talking and stared at her mother. Franziska nodded sadly and told her that, although her brother was mostly quiet now, there were moments when he burst into terrifying rages. It was dangerous to be near him then. He had once grabbed her by the throat and almost throttled her. At the beginning of his illness these rages had been frequent, and if Professor Overbeck had not rushed to Turin immediately after having seen the letter Fritz had written to Jakob Burckhardt, the Italians would have confined him to one of their notorious institutions for the insane. God knows what would have happened to him there. They owed a great debt of gratitude to Overbeck, who had behaved like a Good Samaritan and a true friend. Not only had he brought Fritz, his books, and his manuscripts back home, but he had seen to it that Fritz would continue to receive his Basel pension. It had been her greatest worry that he would lose the pension, and even now she worried day and night about his future. What would he live on if she died, and who would take care of him?

Elisabeth brushed aside her mother's worries. If worst came to worst, she would take care of her brother in Försterhof in Paraguay. But he had to get well first, and to get well he had to be treated right. He was not a mental case at all; he suffered from chloride poisoning. That had been her diagnosis the moment she had heard of his breakdown. And if she had been in Overbeck's place, she would have taken Fritz at once to a hospital. By committing him to an insane asylum, Overbeck had made a very serious mistake. Even a sane man loses his sanity in such places. She also told her mother not to worry about her brother's finances. She would look into them in due course.

During the following months Elisabeth devoted most of her time to her colonial work. From her mother's home in Naumburg she carried on an extensive publicity campaign on stationery with the printed letterhead: "Dr. Eli Förster of Försterhof, Nueva Germania." She addressed petitions for support to government officials and colonial societies, prepared memoranda about the agricultural and industrial potential of New Germany in which she pointed out that German tea and tobacco importers would reap rich profits by investing capital in her late husband's colony. She appealed to the Protestant clergy for contributions to a Christian church and worked on her Paraguay book.

She compiled the book—a hodgepodge of previously published newspaper articles, testimonial letters by colonists in praise of Förster, and sharp polemical pieces directed against Klingbeil—for two reasons: to vindicate her husband and to arouse support for Nueva Germania. In the preface she explained that after her husband's untimely death the fate of the colony and a mountain of debts had weighed on her—"a weak, brokenhearted woman." For more than a year she had borne this heavy burden, hoping that her German countrymen would come to her rescue. When they did not, she was forced to surrender control of her colony to an international corporation, which could not be expected to maintain the German character of New Germany. She had returned to Germany to make a personal appeal to the patriotic conscience of her countrymen to assist her in regaining German control of the colony by setting up a German corporation that would buy back the shares presently held by foreigners. In addition, she was inviting contributions for a German Lutheran church and parsonage. Both were very badly needed to provide guidance for colonists to live truly Christian lives.

Franziska, who was fully occupied with taking care of her son, was amazed by her daughter's wide-ranging activities. Lieschen was like a dynamo going at full speed all the time. One day in Naumburg, she was in Berlin the next day, in Magdeburg the following, then in Leipzig and Chemnitz. When she was at home, she carried on a vast correspondence and still found time for her Paraguay book. It appeared in late spring 1891, barely five months after Elisabeth's arrival in Germany, and was well received by reviewers interested in the cause of German colonies. The cosmopolitan press ignored it, and it failed to generate significant financial contributions. But it added to Elisabeth's reputation as a courageous and energetic woman who was carrying on her husband's work, undaunted by the difficulties left in the wake of his death. She cultivated the image of a widow in mourning by always dressing in black. She wore long silk or taffeta gowns, fashionably cut, and modish black hats bordered by small veils that set off her pale and still youthful face to good advantage. By her own account, she had become "an influential woman."

During these months of hectic activity Elisabeth did not have much time for her brother, who was sitting in an armchair or lying on a couch upstairs, totally unaware of what went on below. Only on an occasional evening would Elisabeth go up and read to him from *Zarathustra*, which he seemed to enjoy, although he did not understand it. But as time went on, Elisabeth began to notice that while her own reputation as a woman pioneer was limited to a small coterie of people interested in colonial affairs, her sick brother's fame was rapidly spreading among the intellectual elite. In Berlin she met ardent young admirers of her brother who were completely indifferent to her colonial concerns, but looked upon her with awe when they discovered that Frau Doktor Förster was Nietzsche's sister. They venerated Nietzsche as the fountainhead of the fraternity of truly free spirits, a solitary voice extolling individual merit in a society that was increasingly becoming mass-oriented. Their number was small but their devotion intense, particularly when they learned that their idol had been plunged into mental darkness. So far from detracting from Nietzsche's influence, his illness surrounded him with an aura of mystery and added to the impact of his ideas by giving them the weight of the utterances of an ancient prophet. Elisabeth had not foreseen this turn of events. She had feared that if it became known that her brother had been in an insane asylum, his writings would be discredited as the outpourings of a sick mind. The ardor of her brother's youthful disciples surprised and moved her.

One of them, a handsome young man of artistic temperament, made a lasting impression on her. His name was Koegel—Dr. Fritz Koegel, she noted from the card he gave her: "First lieutenant of the reserve of the Tenth Infantry Regiment number 134." Koegel, in turn, was attracted to Elisabeth, because she was the sister of the philosopher he admired and—although she was twenty-five years older than he—because of her feminine charms. After meeting her by chance at a social occasion in Berlin, he sent her a note the following day thanking her for "the delightful hours" he had been privileged to spend in her company. He drew her attention to a number of articles on her brother that had appeared in the *Vossische Zeitung* and the *Freie Bühne*, written by Lou Andreas-Salomé. Elisabeth was first taken aback and then furious. Here was that terrible creature again, who had caused so much mischief between her and her brother. Now Lou was exploiting her brief acquaintance with Nietzsche by selling his ideas to Jewish papers. It was preposterous. She asked Koegel to keep track of any further articles by Salomé and to send them to her. Then she decided to look into her brother's contracts with his publishers. If others could make money through him, it was time that Fritz made some money himself.

Fritz Koegel in 1893 when he was Elisabeth's trusted friend and Nietzsche's editor-in-chief.

Strictly speaking, it was her mother's responsibility, as her brother's legal guardian, to find out what financial arrangements he had made with his publishers. But Elisabeth knew that her mother had never taken much interest in her brother's writings and was completely in the dark about his dealings with printing firms and publishers. Hence, she undertook to clarify the matter herself by requesting through a Naumburg lawyer that each of the three firms that had published Nietzsche's books—Fritzsch, Schmeitzner, and Naumann—submit detailed accounts of the number of copies they had printed and sold. The answers she received were not encouraging. Schmeitzner replied rather irritably on September 1, 1891, that he had sold to Fritzsch for a few thousand marks all his remaining copies of Nietzsche's books, because they had laid in his warehouse "heavy like lead and unsalable." He added that the literary world started to take notice of Nietzsche only after it became known that he was insane. Now his books were in such demand that new editions would probably become necessary. Schmeitzner estimated that he had personally lost some twenty thousand marks by publishing Nietzsche and closed with the pointed remark: "No other publisher would have published these volumes of aphorisms because nobody bought them."

Elisabeth received a similarly discouraging answer from C. G. Naumann, the publisher of her brother's last works. Naumann was a Leipzig printer who published books only at the author's risk. According to the accounts the firm presented to Elisabeth, her brother still owed them nearly sixteen hundred marks for four of his books that had been published since 1886: *Beyond Good and Evil, On the Genealogy of Morals, The Case of Wagner, Twilight of the Idols.* Naumann declared that of 6,200 copies printed, 2,801 had been sold, leaving 3,399 on hand. Elisabeth was not satisfied with this answer and examined Naumann's statement closely, particularly the items concerning printing and advertising costs. Considering the figures too high, she submitted them to other printers for examination. They agreed that Nietzsche had been overcharged. Elisabeth was furious and threatened to sue Naumann. She was particularly indignant that Naumann had issued second editions of some of her brother's works without authorization. To this charge, the owner of the firm, Constantin Naumann, replied that he had consulted both Professor Overbeck and Heinrich Köselitz, better known as Peter Gast, who had assured him that Nietzsche's guardian, Frau Pastor Nietzsche, had given her consent. When her mother confirmed Naumann's statement, Elisabeth angrily warned her that by having given Overbeck a blanket permission to authorize the publication of her brother's writings, she had made herself liable to criminal charges, because one of the books Naumann had printed and was about to release was the fourth part of *Zarathustra*, which contained a blasphemous attack on Christianity. Did Franziska not realize that the antidefamation laws were strictly enforced? Besides, her brother had always insisted that *Zarathustra* IV must not be made public in its present form.

The good pastor's widow was horrified. She begged Overbeck to tell Gast that although she had given her consent for the publication of *Zarathustra* IV, she had done so without knowing its content. Now that her daughter had told her what the book contained, she had to withdraw her consent, the more so since she was certain that her brother, Pastor Edmund Oehler, who was her son's second guardian, would never allow such a book to be published. Upon Elisabeth's suggestion she sent a telegram to Naumann, ordering the sequestration of *Zarathustra* IV. Naumann was understandably annoyed and, on his part, threatened to sue. Gast, who had prepared *Zarathustra* IV for publication, was furious and informed Frau Pastor Nietzsche that since a thousand copies had already been printed, it would cost her some three to four thousand marks to reduce the book to pulp now. Privately, Gast told Overbeck: "One could laugh oneself sick at the thought that two pious women and a country parson sit in judgment on what can and cannot be published of the writings of one of the fiercest anti-Christians and atheists.''

Gast resented Elisabeth's interference because he considered it completely unwarranted. He had been in close touch with Nietzsche all the years when Elisabeth was in Paraguay, and he knew what his friend wanted to have published. When Nietzsche's growing blindness had made it hard for him to read proof-sheets, Gast had undertaken this chore at the expense of his own work. He had made stylistic suggestions and proposed book titles. Indeed, during the most productive period of Nietzsche's life, "maestro Pietro," as Nietzsche affectionately called Gast, had been closer to him than anyone else, with the exception of Overbeck. It was absurd for Elisabeth to come back from Paraguay and assert her authority over her brother's work, which she did not even know. If she thought that *Zarathustra* IV was blasphemous, her Christian conscience would be horrified by the ferocious curse her brother had pronounced on Christianity in *The Antichrist*, or by the contemptuous remarks he made about her in *Ecce Homo*. Gast considered the proposed suppression of *Zarathustra* IV a crime.

Peter Gast, ca. 1890.

Much to Gast's surprise, Elisabeth, who had instigated the suppression of *Zarathustra* IV by frightening her mother with the possible consequences of its publication, suddenly changed her mind and wrote him: "Do we have the right to withhold from the world forever these magnificent ideas?" She hinted that while she was still against the work being published in its present form, a somewhat less offensive version might be prepared—a hint that so shocked Gast that he informed Overbeck that Elisabeth was about to "mutilate *Zarathustra* IV."

Actually, what Elisabeth wanted was to find a publisher for all of her brother's works, including *Zarathustra* IV, a few selections from unpublished manuscripts, and the rights of translation into foreign languages, in return for a life annuity for her brother and the guarantee that the publisher would accept liability for any legal action taken against the author. When Elisabeth told him of her plan, Gast was highly amused, for which publisher would grant an annuity for life to an author whose books sold about three hundred copies a year and who, despite his present state of health, could become quite old. He also resented Elisabeth's continuing denunciations of Naumann, whom she called a penny pincher and a crook, who had overcharged her poor brother. Gast had never encountered any difficulties in his dealings with the firm and was on particularly cordial terms with the firm's youngest member, Gustav Naumann. If Naumann had indeed overcharged Nietzsche, he stood to lose a considerable sum by Elisabeth's decision to suppress *Zarathustra* IV.

Elisabeth had planned to return to Paraguay at the end of November 1891, but decided to remain in Germany until a solution had been found to the question of her brother's publisher. She sensed that this question was more important to her in the long run than her own work in New Germany. For unlike her mother, her uncle, or even Gast and Overbeck, Elisabeth was convinced that her brother's rapidly rising fame would lead to a corresponding rise in the sale of his books, and she was determined to obtain as favorable a publishing contract as possible. She insisted that all that was needed now was an alert publisher who would seize the moment—when so many articles began to appear about her sick brother in newspapers and literary journals— to promote the sale of his books. She brushed aside her mother's objections that it was in poor taste to publicize Fritz's illness, by saying that since the public seemed more inclined to buy the books of a sick philosopher than a sane one, it would be foolish to prevent a publisher from advertising her brother's fate. It could not be kept secret in any case and was widely known already.

Elisabeth's intensive search for a publisher climaxed in a brief note she sent to Gast on January 17, 1892, informing him that "a solemn decision concerning the publisher of the works of our beloved patient" was about to be taken. At the same time she assured Gast that she had told all interested parties that no decision would be made without his consent. Elisabeth's deference to Gast in this matter was the result of a very practical consideration. She knew that Gast was the only one who could decipher her brother's almost illegible handwriting and that without his help the publication of the manuscripts of Nietzsche's final phase was all but impossible.

As far as Gast was concerned, the most suitable publisher for Nietzsche's works was and remained Naumann. He was therefore relieved when he heard that Gustav Naumann and Elisabeth had settled their differences and reached an agreement. The firm withdrew its claim for sixteen hundred marks, acquired the remaining copies of Nietzsche's books, and paid the author thirty-five hundred marks for them. On February 9 a formal contract was drawn up, with Naumann agreeing to pay Nietzsche's guardians fifty marks per proof-sheet and accepting liability for any legal actions against the author. Jubilantly, Elisabeth wrote Gast:

> The contract with Naumann was signed last Tuesday. Fritzsch wired indignantly. He had obviously wanted to offer more favorable conditions. But it was useless. Nietzsche and Wagner do not belong in the same publishing house. What do you think about the publication of *Nietzsche contra Wagner?* The moment is very favorable for France. *Zarathustra* IV will now also appear very soon.

A few weeks later she told Gast that she was urging Naumann to bring out a cheap, popular edition of her brother's works, suitable for hundreds of his youthful admirers who could not afford the standard edition. Naumann was willing to do so but balked when she insisted upon the same royalties that had been agreed upon for the standard edition. When Gast reminded her that Naumann was justified in offering lower royalties for a popular edition, she told him "in plain language" that as long as her mother and her brother were alive she would insist on the highest royalties from any publisher. She was getting tired of Naumann's haggling over every penny, for, if properly promoted, royalties for her brother's works could easily amount to twenty-five thousand marks. Gast laughed incredulously and did not believe his eyes when he saw this figure. Obviously Frau Förster was indulging herself in a financial daydream. Authors of popular fiction might earn royalties of such magnitude; to expect that an eccentric philosopher like Nietzsche would ever attract a mass market was absurd.

However, Gast had learned to keep his doubts to himself. He knew it was useless to argue with Elisabeth. Once she had made up her mind she was inaccessible to arguments. And she had made up her mind that her brother's writings had the potential of a mass appeal, provided they were efficiently promoted. If she did not have to return to New Germany, she would take charge of the publicity herself. Unfortunately, she could not delay her return journey any longer; she was six months late as it was, and her presence at Försterhof was urgently needed. She asked Gast to continue his editorial labors, exhorted him to present a truly heroic picture of her beloved brother in the introductory essays he was writing for each volume, and on July 9, 1892, she embarked with a heavy heart for Paraguay. To her grieving mother she confided before she left that if she could find a buyer for Försterhof, she would sell it and return to Germany.

13·Flight

*E*LISABETH ARRIVED in Nueva Germania on the first Sunday in August 1892 and was warmly welcomed back by the colony's administrator, her friend Oscar Erck, who thanked her in the name of the colonists for promoting their cause so effectively in Germany, in particular for her success in persuading the Royal Ecclesiastical Council of Prussia to provide a Protestant clergyman for New Germany and pay his salary for two years. Her reception on Försterhof by her numerous native servants was equally cordial. She was pleased to find that, although she had been away much longer than she had planned, her authority in the colony seemed unimpaired. Reassured, she took over the reins with undiminished zest and sent glowing reports of the rapid material progress Nueva Germania was making to her German backer, Max Schubert, the director of the Chemnitz Colonial Society.

Schubert was puzzled by these reports, which contrasted sharply with letters, highly critical of the way the colony was run, that he received from individual colonists. One told him bluntly that it was doubtful that Frau Förster's return would benefit the colony, for: "I do not believe that she has been cured in Germany of her disease which borders on megalomania; on the contrary, her alleged successes concerning the clergyman, etc., have probably made her even more conceited and domineering."

Other colonists became indignant when they discovered that her Paraguay book repeated the same misleading accounts about the fertile soil of Nueva Germania's forest lands that her husband had made in his book. In open letters to the editor of the *South American Colonial News*, a paper devoted to the dissemination of information about prospects for German settlements in Latin America, they declared that while it had been rashness on Förster's part to make such statements, it was unpardonable that Elisabeth repeated them, when she knew that they were untrue, since all attempts to settle in the forest had failed.

Elisabeth replied to these charges not by trying to refute them but by directing sharp personal attacks against those who made them. She called them "slanderers and miserable good-for-nothings" who befouled their own nest. And by publishing laudatory letters, written upon her request by colonists who were beholden to her, she made her accusers appear as ungrateful liars. These insinuations caused a furor and led to demands that Frau Doktor Förster leave the colony. But since Elisabeth still wielded considerable power, these demands were at first voiced only by a few brave spirits. The majority of the colonists kept quiet for fear of reprisals.

In the midst of this controversy, which became increasingly more acrimonious, and in spite of the exhausting daily chores that her pioneer life and her administrative duties demanded, Elisabeth still found time for her correspondence with her mother and Peter Gast. In a long letter written at the end of November she congratulated Gast for "the magnificent introduction" he had written for *Zarathustra* IV. She was ecstatic because "it is impossible to give a better picture of our dear, world-conquering hero. I am reading your introduction again and again and am transported into a state of rapture. What marvelous things you say! Nobody has ever portrayed his personality and philosophy so accurately and completely." She added mournfully that she herself was living in an intellectual desert: "An indescribable homesickness overcomes me at times and I must call upon all my inner resources to continue unflinchingly my hard task. It is extremely difficult for a woman alone to pursue such a goal, undismayed by the praise or blame of her associates, who are often motivated by petty and personal concerns."

She mentioned that she was encountering heavy financial losses and was longing for the past, when it had been her great good fortune to live closely to the noblest spirits of the age: "Oh, how happy I would be to be near my beloved brother, even in his present state, and how I envy my dear Mama for being able to take care of the loved one." She closed her letter by saying that she wished Gast could live in Berlin for a time because, there, a devoted "Nietzsche Circle" existed that would pay him homage and welcome him with open arms. She mentioned in particular a young man, Dr. Koegel, who cared deeply for her brother.

The most prominent themes of Elisabeth's letters to her mother were likewise her homesickness and her concern for the fate of her brother's books and manuscripts. She admonished her mother to take good care of all of Fritz's writings, letters, and notebooks, and was chagrined when she learned that Franziska had given Gast, who had visited Naumburg on her brother's birthdays, some unpublished manuscripts. Franziska realized herself that she ought not to have done that, for, after telling her daughter about it, she remarked: "You are perhaps not pleased with it, because I gather from your last letter that you intend to make money out of these manuscripts." This was indeed Elisabeth's intention. She needed money more than ever now that her own investments were in jeopardy. As long as she was the mistress of Försterhof, her capital was safe, but what would become of it if she were forced to leave New Germany, as her accusers demanded, before she had found a buyer? And even if she succeeded in selling it and left the colony abruptly, would it not look as though she had deserted her husband's work? A strategy had to be worked out that permitted her to leave New Germany without loss of face or money.

She told her mother that she would try to sell Försterhof quietly. When she had succeeded, her mother was to send her a telegram requesting that she return home at once because her presence in Germany was urgently needed since her brother's illness had taken a turn for the worse. A similar announcement was to be given to the press. Franziska assured her daughter that she would of course "play the role of a concerned mother." She would not only send such a telegram, she would send, in addition, a bank draft for seven hundred marks so that Elisabeth could undertake the journey home at once. And she would be careful not to mention Elisabeth's homesickness to anyone in order not to provide hostile colonial reporters with ammunition against her daughter. Franziska was quite aware that the appearance of her daughter's flight from New Germany must be avoided at all costs.

The plan worked. In April Elisabeth told her mother that she had sold Försterhof, including her furniture, to a Baron von Frankenberg-Lüttwitz. However, it would still take some time before she could return home because she was too deeply embroiled in colonial affairs. She hoped to be home by Christmas. What she failed to tell her mother was that by directing a sharp, personal attack against one of the most popular colonists, Elisabeth had aroused such widespread anger that more and more people demanded her removal from New Germany. These demands were openly voiced in a letter to the *Colonial News*, which for years had published Förster's picture on the front page. The paper's editor stated that he had reluctantly come to the conclusion that he must publish this letter, which contained such bitter accusations against the widow of a venerated pioneer; but "German colonial policy has made so many serious mistakes that necessity and not delicacy must now govern our actions." The gist of the long letter was that by her words and actions Elisabeth had lost the confidence of the colonists and that it would be in the best interest of all concerned if she left New Germany. The editor of the *Colonial News* agreed with the sentiments expressed by the colonists and added in a postscript: "The first requirement for any effective improvement in the affairs of Nueva Germania is the removal of Frau Doktor Förster."

When this letter appeared, Elisabeth had already left the colony and was on her way home. She did not dignify it with a reply but bided her time and published her official farewell to Nueva Germania in the *Bayreuther Blätter* almost a year later. Once more she told the story of her beloved husband's heroic efforts to regenerate his fatherland by founding a colony of noble spirits in the virgin forests of Paraguay. She repeated that after his untimely death, caused by overwork and worry, she had felt duty-bound to continue his work: "But alas, how little can a weak woman do!" She had spared no efforts to spread the truth about Nueva Germania and was happy to learn upon her second and final return to Germany that the German Colonial Society Herman in Berlin had decided to buy back Nueva Germania from the foreign corporation that now owned it. She appealed to her countrymen to buy Herman shares to provide the necessary capital for this purchase.

Should people question her right to make such an appeal, since she was no longer officially connected with the colony, she replied that she was motivated by her love for her husband, whose ideals she shared, and wanted to make sure that he had not died in vain. Her feelings toward New Germany were those of a mother who cannot take care of a beloved child anymore and wants to see it in good hands. She concluded her stirring patriotic appeal with the words: "I must say farewell to all colonial affairs because another great task now awaits me—the care of my dear and only brother, the philosopher Friedrich Nietzsche."

PART IV
1894-1900

14·My Brother's Keeper

*E*LISABETH WAS shocked when she saw her brother again on her arrival in Naumburg in September 1893. She had only been away a year, but during that time his condition had deteriorated rapidly. He hardly walked anymore, sat apathetically in a wheelchair, or lay on his couch staring ahead of himself without uttering a sound for hours. Her mother and Alwine took care of him, and there was nothing for Elisabeth to do. But she had not come home to become a nurse for her sick brother; she had come home to preside over the execution of his literary estate, which was rapidly increasing in value, and to establish herself as his representative. As such, her name Eli Förster was obviously unsuitable because it referred to her colonial past. Her credentials as the representative of Friedrich Nietzsche would be far more convincing if her name was Nietzsche. Hence she must assume her maiden name again.

Soon after her return, she started to sign her letters as Elisabeth Förster-Nietzsche, and to make sure that her hyphenated name was legally valid, she requested and obtained a court order for this change. By the stroke of her pen she joined the two men in her life who had scrupulously avoided meeting and whose world views were poles apart. Some of Nietzsche's closest friends, such as the Overbecks, who knew Nietzsche's contempt for Förster's ideas, resented her action and continued to address her as Frau Förster, which Elisabeth found insulting. It was one more reason for her smoldering anger toward the Overbecks. They treated her as if she were still the little girl who had taken care of her brother's household in Basel, and they did not acknowledge that, since then, she had become an author and a widely ac-

*Elisabeth in 1894, after
the death of her husband.*

claimed woman pioneer. Unfortunately, she had to avoid an open break with them because of her mother's insistence that but for Overbeck her brother would have lost his Basel pension. But she hoped that Nietzsche's rising fame would increase his royalty earnings sufficiently so that they were no longer dependent on the goodwill of Basel and Overbeck. In any case, she would not be deterred by Overbeck's criticism from playing her dual role of widow in mourning and loving sister. It was right that her name reflected that role.

During the long ocean crossing Elisabeth had drawn up a plan of action she intended to follow when she reached home. Her major project was to write her brother's life. Nietzsche's growing fame made more and more people wonder who he was, this revolutionary iconoclast, where he came from, and why he had gone mad. Elisabeth had read a number of newspaper stories on her brother by people who had never met him and articles by others, like Lou, who pretended to a knowledge they did not have. Since nobody knew him as well as she did, it was her duty to present his picture to the world in a manner that would appeal to his admirers and enhance his reputation.

In addition to writing her brother's life, she would supervise the publication of his books. She would request a statement from Naumann about the number of copies that had been sold during her absence. She was irked that she had not received such a statement before her departure from Paraguay. In view of her own uncertain financial future, she had to know what royalty income to expect. Then she would ask Gast what he had been able to prepare for publication during the past year. She would encourage him to write an introductory essay to each of her brother's works. She herself would gather together all of Fritz's manuscripts, notebooks, and letters. She knew that there was a trunkful in her mother's house, and she thought there must be other papers scattered about. It was important to preserve every line her brother had written, because every line was potentially worth its weight in gold.

Naumann's answer to Elisabeth's request about the sale of her brother's books contained two startling surprises: There had been such a demand for Nietzsche's writings in the last twelve months that the firm had decided to bring out a collected edition of his works under the general editorship of Peter Gast; and, to satisfy the curiosity of Nietzsche's readers, Naumann announced that they proposed to publish a biography of Nietzsche written by Gast. When she heard this, Elisabeth became furious. Nobody had the right to publish her brother's collected works without her permission and nobody was entitled to write his life. She told Gast "in plain language" that if he wanted to write a scholarly biography of Nietzsche, that was his affair, "but his life, my dear Herr Köselitz, his life I am going to write myself. Nobody can do that as well as I." By way of mollifying Gast for her blunt warning not to encroach on her territory, she called him "the high priest at the Nietzsche altar, the true apostle of his teachings, the keeper of the sacred flame."

But her gentle tone evaporated quickly. A few days later she was again very angry and lectured Gast in a long letter about the inequities of Naumann's treatment of her. He had no right at all to bring out a collected edition of her brother's works. It was beyond her why Gast defended the actions of this insolent fellow. "You must understand one simple fact, dear Herr Köselitz, you can only be editor with my consent, my wholehearted, unreserved consent. We must cooperate as good comrades or not at all." In conclusion she added that it had occurred to her that Gast wanted perhaps to be relieved of his editorship and devote himself to his own work. She begged him to tell her honestly if this was the case. She would respect his wishes, although she realized that she would never find anyone else "who could publish her brother's works with so much love and understanding."

The truth of the matter is that while Gast wanted to continue his work as Nietzsche's editor, Elisabeth was not at all sure that he was the right person for it. She had renewed her acquaintance with Fritz Koegel soon after her arrival in Naumburg by inviting him to visit her. In long and intimate talks she had given Koegel an insight into the many problems she faced with the publication of her brother's writings. She could not possibly undertake this difficult task alone; she needed help, and in many respects Gast was the ideal editor. He was intimately familiar with her brother's works and had editorial experience. The trouble was, he was very obstinate. He refused to take her advice by claiming that he had been authorized by her brother to edit his works, and, worst of all, he always sided with Naumann against her. It was true, he had written some excellent introductions, but in his description of her brother's friendship and later feud with Wagner he had used unnecessarily offensive language. Since Elisabeth valued her own friendship with Cosima, she felt it was not necessary to dwell on her brother's break with Wagner. Gast failed to understand that and was obviously not the right person to edit Nietzsche's correspondence with Wagner, which she hoped to publish. Koegel agreed and told her that if she considered him suitable and wanted to entrust him with it, he would "joyfully undertake this honorable task."

In thanking Elisabeth for the cordial reception she had given him in Naumburg, Koegel wrote her a note, telling her that he felt "enveloped in an aura of friendship which moves me as though it were a familiar and trusted one." Elisabeth was flattered by the young man's courtesies, and the more she saw of him, the better she liked him. Koegel was a man of the world, a real gentleman, a good musician, and an excellent *causeur*. He moved in a circle that included some of the most distinguished men and women of the German capital. It was a far cry from the petty bourgeois world of the bohemian Peter Gast, who had retired to his native village of Annaberg with her brother's manuscripts. But since her mother had given Gast permission to edit her brother's works, it would be difficult to get rid of him, unless he withdrew voluntarily.

Koegel agreed that Gast's dismissal was a delicate matter. It was, in fact, impossible as long as Gast enjoyed the support of Nietzsche's guardians. He advised Elisabeth to obtain authorization from her mother and Nietzsche's second legal guardian, her cousin, Dr. Adalbert Oehler, to assume control over the editorship of her brother's published and unpublished works. As a first step in this direction, Elisabeth informed Gast in October that he would soon receive an official request from her attorney to return all of Nietzsche's manuscripts and notebooks in his possession: "The guardianship has requested that I prepare a complete inventory of all existing manuscripts and establish a register and archives. I myself have many pieces. And I do not need those you have before the end of October, because the archives room and furnishings will not be ready before then."

Elisabeth's reference to an "archives room and furnishings" concerned a structural change in her mother's house in Naumburg that she had undertaken with her mother's tacit, if not enthusiastic, approval. She insisted that it was unworthy for an author who was rapidly becoming internationally famous to have his books and manuscripts stored in dingy rooms. By breaking out a wall between two small rooms on the ground floor, a larger, more dignified setting for Nietzsche Archives could be created. It would serve as a central collecting point for all her brother's memorabilia, which would be stored in specially built cabinets decorated with a carved insignia of Zarathustra's animals—eagle, serpent, and lion. In this dignified environment she would receive all visitors who wanted to pay homage to the author of *Zarathustra*. There would also be easy chairs, a sofa, and a piano for use on special occasions, when she wanted to entertain her brother's admirers. Although Frau Pastor Nietzsche had misgivings about her daughter's social ambitions and doubted that her home, which harbored her invalid son, was the proper place for it, she reluctantly gave her permission for the remodeling project. At the end of the year Elisabeth opened the first Nietzsche Archives on the ground floor of her mother's house on Weingarten 18 in Naumburg. From then on she conducted her voluminous correspondence on stationery bearing this name in large Gothic letters. In less than three months the transformation of Dr. Eli Förster of Försterhof, Nueva Germania, into

Elisabeth Förster-Nietzsche of the Nietzsche Archives, Naumburg an der Saale, was completed.

Gast was dismayed by Elisabeth's request that he return her brother's manuscripts, because he felt that "by this return one of the most significant events in the history of the human spirit would be destroyed. I must have all the notebooks in my possession, if I am to complete the great work which nobody but me can complete—I am convinced of that." He explained that Nietzsche's most brilliant thoughts—he called them "volcanic eruptions of soul and spirit"—that were written in the autumn of 1888, were hieroglyphic symbols and completely illegible except for him who had been intimately familiar for years with Nietzsche's handwriting, vocabulary, style, and train of thought. Instead of returning the notebooks to Naumburg, Gast suggested that Elisabeth come to Annaberg for a visit to see for herself how carefully he guarded these "most precious treasures."

But Elisabeth would not hear of that. She ordered Gast by telegram to meet her in Leipzig on October 23 and hand over her brother's manuscripts. Reluctantly, Gast obeyed. In the course of their conversation, Elisabeth asked him angrily who had appointed him editor. At the same time she informed him that she planned to publish a number of her brother's Basel lectures in literary journals. She had discussed the matter personally with the editor of the *Magazin für Literatur.* What she did not tell Gast was that she had corresponded with Koegel about selling some of her brother's unpublished manuscripts to the highest bidder among editors of literary magazines. Koegel had told her that the *Deutsche Rundschau* paid the highest royalties, but that both the *Magazin für Literatur* and *Zukunft* paid very well. Koegel had volunteered to talk with each of the editors about Nietzsche's articles, and since they were the work of an author who was deranged, "I shall, of course, demand special honoraria *(Affektionspreise).* I am sure they will pay them." This was the kind of language Elisabeth liked to hear. She was irritated when Gast reproached her for wanting to publish her brother's writings in popular journals. The author, Gast insisted, would deeply resent it. Stung by this reproach, Elisabeth replied: "Don't get the idea that I have the publication mania. My mission in the next ten years is to plant the personality of Nietzsche, as the noblest figure of light, firmly into the hearts of people. That is the sole reason for all my private publications."

In the same letter she mentioned that, as a result of a recent article in the *Zukunft,* there was now a popular clamor for the publication of *Antichrist.* This was a delicate matter, since they were both agreed that *Antichrist* could not be published at this time and in its present form because its violent treatment of Christianity made the author liable for prosecution under the Prussian antiblasphemy law. "We must tell nobody, but nobody, that we cannot publish it because of its content," Elisabeth exhorted Gast.

Hence the following lie has occurred to me: A closer examination of the manuscript has shown that part of it is missing and before all existing manuscripts are reviewed, copied, and registered—a time-consuming process in view of the author's very difficult handwriting—any publication now is out of the question. You must make Overbeck and Naumann believe this lie. I will tell it to Mama, the Magdeburg guardian, and everybody else. It is not pleasant, but it cannot be helped. The four above mentioned are the only ones that may have suspicions, but Overbeck has no proof.

It is unlikely that Gast enjoyed the role Elisabeth asked him to play. He knew that Overbeck, for one, would not be deceived by Elisabeth's disingenuous explanation for the suppression of *Antichrist*, because he had read the manuscript, indeed, he had copied it. But Gast had a conciliatory disposition, and although he complained to Overbeck about Elisabeth's frantic efforts to make money out of her brother's unpublished manuscripts—he called it Frau Förster's money-madness—he agreed to continue working under her supervision. She urged him to publish his introductory essays to her brother's works in book form, because "seven prologs to Nietzsche's works would make a very popular book."

At the same time that Elisabeth was encouraging Gast to help her with the publication of her brother's works, she urged Koegel to come to Naumburg and take Gast's place as Nietzsche's general editor. It was a flattering offer for a young man of artistic temperament who was about to enter a career in the consular service. And the main reason for Koegel's hesitancy to accept it was his distaste of becoming the instrument for Gast's dismissal. He recognized Gast's shortcomings as an editor, deplored Gast's cavalier treatment of Nietzsche's texts, and agreed with Elisabeth that it was unreasonable of Gast to claim that he, and he alone, was authorized by Nietzsche to edit his works. But it was one thing to agree with Elisabeth's objective criticism and quite another to share her personal contempt for Gast, whom she called a clumsy proletarian, a boor, and an ignoramus. "Please do not talk to me anymore of Köselitz," Elisabeth implored Koegel. "I simply cannot stand him. You know more about Nietzsche and understand him better even now than this clumsy clod will ever be able to in all his life."

But Koegel demurred. "I cannot help myself," he told Elisabeth, "but an open breach between me and Köselitz must be avoided, as far as I am concerned. Incidentally, your mother shares my view. I am as little inclined toward unconditional hatred of people as toward unconditional love. My passion is spent on causes."

Elisabeth dismissed such protestations as youthful rhetoric. She knew that the position she was offering Koegel was far too tempting to be declined. And she was right. After months of reflection Koegel agreed to write Gast and tell him that he could not continue to edit Nietzsche. The letter, a thirty-eight-page document, is a detailed critique of Gast's shortcomings as an editor. It begins with the statement that Gast did not have the right to edit Nietzsche's collected works, because nobody had authorized him to do so, and ends with the remark that he, Koegel, was unfortunately not in a position to assume the editorship, because he had other plans for his life. This remark may have been true at the time Koegel wrote his critique, but it is also possible he made it to spare Gast's feelings. At any event, barely three months after Koegel had dismissed Gast on Elisabeth's orders, he told her that after having talked the matter over with his father, he was now ready to assume the position of editor-in-chief of Nietzsche's collected works. Elisabeth was jubilant, although she had already hired a young man from the Goethe-Schiller Archiv in Weimar to help her with the edition.

Gast accepted his forced separation from a task that for years had been a labor of love rather than a profitable occupation, with surprising equanimity. He told Overbeck that he was glad to be relieved of the work and expressed confidence in Koegel, calling him a very sensitive young man who was devoted to Nietzsche's ideas: "Dr. Koegel and his assistant Dr. Zerbst will bring out a very good edition of Nietzsche's collected works." But Overbeck remained skeptical. He winced when Elisabeth wrote him that:

> Dr. Koegel has a truly eminent mind; the gentlemen of the Goethe-Schiller Archiv, with whom we are on the most cordial terms, continue to make most flattering remarks to me about his extraordinary artistic and scholarly talents. His temporary assistant, Dr. Zerbst, was also a nice person but quite unfamiliar with editorial or philological work, while Dr. Koegel knows everything.

The casual manner in which Elisabeth referred to Dr. Zerbst's brief tenure at the Nietzsche Archives offended Overbeck's sense of fairness. He suspected that other than scholarly deficiencies had caused both Gast's and Zerbst's fall from Elisabeth's grace, and he followed the fortunes of the Nietzsche Archives with increasing misgivings.

Koegel's presence in her Naumburg home was a source of constant enjoyment for Elisabeth. He was a very talented young man, played the piano with considerable skill, and entertained her for hours with songs he had composed. She was moved when he dedicated to her a series of Keller poems he had put to music, although she chided him gently by suggesting that he should dedicate these beautiful songs to some charming young girl. Koegel rejected her suggestion by declaring flatly: "I shall never again dedicate songs or books to charming young girls but rather to those who once were young and charming." And in answer to another suggestion by Elisabeth that he use his knowledge of economics to write a book about it, he replied: "I shall hardly ever write a book about import or export statistics, but perhaps one about the psychology of colonization."

Elisabeth proudly introduced her handsome young protégé to her Naumburg friends and was duly envied. Everybody wanted to know where she had met him and by what means she had enticed him to exchange Berlin for sleepy old Naumburg. Even her mother came to like him, although she was sorry that he had replaced her son's long-time friend Peter Gast. What the old lady did not like were those long social evenings, when music and laughter filled the festively lit archives room, while she was sitting upstairs in the dark, anxiously watching her sick son's restless sleep.

15·Poor Koegel

*I*N HER DEALINGS with Koegel, which led to the outcome Elisabeth had desired from the beginning, she took pains to point out to the young man that in addition to the honor he stood to gain by becoming the editor of her brother's works, she would see to it that he would receive adequate compensation. She realized that he was just about to enter a career in the consular service, but promised that if he committed himself to staying with her until the editorial work was completed, she would pay him an annual salary equivalent to that of a university professor. Since Elisabeth was in no position to make such an offer, she turned to Naumann and proposed a three-year publishing contract for her brother's collected works. Under the terms of that contract the firm would pay a total of twelve thousand marks in advance royalties or four thousand marks each in 1894, 1895, and 1896. Koegel, as editor-in-chief, should receive an annual salary of twenty-eight hundred marks, the remaining twelve hundred marks were to be paid into her brother's estate, which was administered after Pastor Oehler's death, by his two guardians, her mother and her cousin Dr. Adalbert Oehler.

Concerning her own compensation as director of the Nietzsche Archives Elisabeth made special arrangements with the guardians. She counted on two additional sources of income: monies that were still owed her in Paraguay and royalties from the book she was writing on her brother's life. It was projected to be in two volumes. Since she was a quick worker, she planned to have the first volume finished within a year. It would portray her brother as a healthy young man, a brilliant student, and a budding genius, and hence present a striking contrast to the somber picture of his present state. Elisabeth expected that her book would be widely read and attract readers to her brother's works, because the relationship between genius and madness was being widely discussed at the time, often in connection with Nietzsche. If Naumann, who was to publish her book as well, mounted a coordinated publicity campaign, Elisabeth was certain the firm would quickly recoup the advance royalties she demanded.

Gustav Naumann, the firm's junior partner, agreed with her and persuaded his uncle to accept the contract as proposed by Elisabeth, although it entailed the risk that, if for some reason the editorial work was delayed, the firm would lose money, as it had during Elisabeth's controversy with Gast. However, Nietzsche was rapidly becoming what the trade calls "a hot property," and provided his works were published according to an agreed-upon timetable, a handsome profit would accrue to both publisher and author. Accordingly, since Naumann was concerned about the person of the editor-in-chief, an appendix was added to the contract concluded between Nietzsche's guardians and Naumann on April 24, 1894, stating that "basic changes in the editorial plan for the collected works, including a change in the person of the editor, require the consent of the firm C. G. Naumann." The contract named Dr. Koegel and Dr. Zerbst as editors, with the understanding that Koegel was editor-in-chief and Zerbst his assistant.

The ink was hardly dry on this contract when Elisabeth regretted that it included Dr. Zerbst, whose presence disturbed the harmonious relationship between her and Koegel. She was daily growing fonder of the young man, enjoyed his company, his conversation, his piano playing, and the attention he paid her. Being older and more experienced than Koegel, she tried to put him at ease by encouraging him to flirt with her, although he warned her that "if I once indulge in such follies I do not start with some lighthearted fireworks but go very much further." This was a tantalizing confession for a widow young at heart, and all the more reason why Dr. Zerbst's presence was unwanted. Hence Elisabeth soon began to complain to Naumann and to her cousin about Dr. Zerbst. He was a very slow worker, a poor proofreader, and totally unfamiliar with her brother's works.

> This is the situation: Dr. Koegel does ninety-nine percent of the work, Dr. Zerbst one percent. Nobody can say that this is a fair distribution of the work load. Our good little doctor has become merely an ornament here and is almost useless. To his excuse I must say that it is extremely difficult for anyone to compete with Dr. Koegel's enormous capacity for work. Dr. Koegel is the genius of the edition.

Made to feel that he was an unwelcome intruder by both Elisabeth and Koegel, Dr. Zerbst reacted accordingly. He protested to Naumann about the treatment he was receiving and threatened to sue if Elisabeth made any further disparaging remarks about his work. But in the end he realized that, regardless of his contractual rights, his position had become untenable and he resigned after his demand had been met that part of his salary be paid. No sooner had Zerbst left than Elisabeth volunteered to take his place as proofreader, although she was fully occupied with her brother's biography. She would now be able to work in the closest proximity to her admired protégé. Much to her annoyance, her mother raised objections to that plan, ostensibly because proofreading was bad for her daughter's eyes, but actually because Franziska considered it unseemly for Elisabeth and Koegel to spend hours together in the privacy of the Nietzsche Archives. Neither she nor Alwine could be present because they had to look after the invalid upstairs, and although her daughter was forty-eight years old, Franziska did not think it looked right for Elisabeth and the young man to work together unchaperoned.

Elisabeth protested violently. She reminded her mother that she had lived and traveled abroad for years unchaperoned and was old enough to protect her reputation. When, after two months of heated arguments, no accommodation had been reached, Elisabeth decided to set up a household of her own. She rented a large apartment not far from her mother's house and on September 1, 1894, established the Nietzsche Archives there. For more than a month she and Koegel worked uninterruptedly, editing volume after volume of her brother's collected works.

But to squash any possible gossip about her relationship with Koegel, and since the contract with Naumann included an assistant editor, Elisabeth invited Dr. von der Hellen, a married scholar whom she had met at the Goethe-Schiller Archiv in Weimar, to join Dr. Koegel. She hoped that von der Hellen's presence would expedite the editorial work, which was entering into a more difficult phase now that unpublished manuscripts had to be edited, and was very pleased that von der Hellen got on well with her young protégé. The Koegel-Hellen team worked harmoniously for a few weeks, while Elisabeth concentrated on her own writing. In the evening she would often invite the two gentlemen and Dr. von der Hellen's wife to dinner. She was an excellent cook and an efficient supervisor of her domestic help. The table setting and decor of her intimate dinner parties became the talk of the town. Lieschen Nietzsche had class—even her enemies had to admit that. Sometimes after dinner Elisabeth would ask Koegel to entertain them with his songs. She was deeply moved one evening when he sang one of her brother's poems that he had set to music.

Unfortunately, and much to Elisabeth's dismay, the pleasant working and living relationship between Koegel and von der Hellen did not last long. Koegel became increasingly irritated by von der Hellen's critical attitude toward him and his work. He complained to Elisabeth that von der Hellen was interfering with his function as editor-in-chief. When Elisabeth tried to mediate, Koegel felt offended and reproached her for siding with his critic against him. Being an artist by temperament, Koegel objected to von der Hellen's scholarly approach and was jealous of any sign of respect Elisabeth paid him. He began to hint darkly that she would have to choose between him and von der Hellen; if she did not, he would be forced to challenge von der Hellen to a duel. Confronted with this ultimatum, Elisabeth decided to separate the two antagonists. She suggested that Koegel take a leave of absence from his work at the archives with full pay, get some much-needed rest at his family home in Stassfurt, and prepare a register for the eight Nietzsche volumes he had edited. At the same time she informed von der Hellen that his work at the Nietzsche Archives would have to be terminated.

Koegel accepted his "temporary banishment" with sorrow and resentment. He wrote Elisabeth that the worst that could happen to him now was for him to be forced to leave unfinished the work he had started: "I would be tormented by the thought that it was not an honest difference of opinion about the quality of my work that stopped me from finishing a task I am proud to perform." He implied that he was afraid of Elisabeth's fickleness, for while she encouraged his advances, she seemed to enjoy hurting him. To regain his peace of mind, he traveled to Italy.

Elisabeth finished the first volume of her brother's biography during Koegel's absence and sent it to the printer early in 1895. Because the second volume was to deal with her brother's life during the period when she had often not been with him, she planned a pilgrimage to all the places where he had lived during his solitary wanderings. But before she could set out on this journey, she had to put the affairs of the Nietzsche Archives in order. With von der Hellen gone and Koegel on an extended leave, during which he kept Elisabeth in the dark about what he was doing and where he was, she had to find somebody else to help with the edition. Once again she turned to the Goethe-Schiller Archiv in Weimar, and from the group of young scholars working there, she invited Rudolf Steiner to come to her assistance. Steiner, who was later to become the leader of the anthroposophic movement, had just published a book on Nietzsche. He agreed to join the Nietzsche Archives in Naumburg on a "temporary assignment."

When Steiner discovered that Nietzsche's sister did not have any real understanding of her brother's philosophy, he volunteered to give her private lessons. Elisabeth accepted the offer and enjoyed Steiner's stimulating discourses on her brother's thoughts concerning the transvaluation of all values, a topic with which she was unfamiliar and one which went against her grain. She became quickly fond of the sensitive young man, who was so erudite and had such a profound grasp of the ideas her brother had scribbled down during the last hectic months of his life. The idea occurred to her that Steiner was perhaps more competent than Koegel to edit these thoughts, and she decided to ask him to do that. When Koegel heard of Steiner's presence at the Nietzsche Archives he hurried back to Naumburg from Florence, where he had been sightseeing and composing. He met Steiner and liked him. He liked him even better when Steiner assured him that he had no intention of joining the Nietzsche Archives on a permanent basis.

Between April, when Koegel returned to Naumburg, and August, when Elisabeth left for her travels in search of her brother's past, the air in the Nietzsche Archives reverberated with optimistic discussions about the future. Elisabeth was in very high spirits. Her book was receiving excellent reviews; even Gast, who had every reason to be critical, commented very favorably on it, and it was eagerly bought. Moreover, the royalty income for the eight volumes of her brother's works, which had appeared during 1894, was considerable. Naumann paid fourteen thousand marks into her brother's account. From this sum, the guardianship gave her six thousand marks for her work as director of the Nietzsche Archives and her brother's official representative. Finally, Naumann estimated that royalties from the French and English editions, which Koegel was also preparing, would amount to another fourteen thousand marks; six thousand marks from the English and four thousand each from the French and American editions.

Within a year, the bleak financial future that Elisabeth faced when she returned from Paraguay had become a prosperous present. She was well on the way to becoming the recognized spokesman for an author who had risen overnight from obscurity to international fame and who, while still alive, lay entombed in a grave of madness. In the eyes of the world the sister of the mad philosopher became an object of reverence. Most reviewers read her book on her brother's life as a young man, in which she played an important role, in that light. They looked upon Elisabeth Nietzsche as the representative of a genius who had been driven to madness because nobody had paid any attention to him while he was sane. Elisabeth basked in the universal acclaim that she was receiving and departed for Italy in search of her brother's past with a high sense of adventure, leaving Koegel in charge of the affairs of the archives. She was rudely awakened to the realities of a hostile universe by the derailment of her train near Munich, and although she escaped with minor cuts and bruises and a very bad shock, she wondered what would happen to the archives in the case of her death. To protect the archives against such an eventuality, she informed her cousin that he should "follow Dr. Koegel's instructions scrupulously, because he knows my wishes better than anyone else."

Retracing her brother's footsteps, Elisabeth traveled to Sils Maria, Venice, Genoa, and Turin. But while he had stayed in second-rate boardinghouses or dingy rented rooms, Elisabeth resided in first-class hotels that catered to international society. In Sils Maria she had a rendezvous with Meta von Salis, a young Swiss lady from an old aristocratic family, who was a friend of her brother's during the last years of his life. Nietzsche had been attracted to her by her intelligence and her independent spirit. Unlike other casual female acquaintances he made in the years of his migratory existence, Meta aroused his admiration because she did not put on the airs of an emancipated woman, although she was one of the few members of her sex who had earned a Ph.D. degree in philosophy, wore short hair, and disregarded the conventions of her class. Meta looked down with aristocratic disdain on the antics of the militant suffragettes of her time. As a serious student of philosophy, she was fascinated by Nietzsche's writings and moved, after she had met him, by the nobility of his character and the simplicity of his life-style. When she wrote her book of reminiscences, she called it *Nietzsche: Philosopher and Nobleman*.

What impressed Elisabeth was Meta's aristocratic birth. It flattered her vanity that her brother's friend, and now hers as well, was a true blue-blooded baroness, who traced her origin back to one of the oldest patrician families in Switzerland and who owned the ancient castle Marschlins. For years Elisabeth had wished to be included in the select circle of Europe's aristocracy, and now her wish had come true. She was surrounded by titled ladies and flattered by the attention she received from men of distinction, including—she says—a number of marriage proposals: "Last September, just before the *Antichrist* was about to appear," she confided to the wife of her cousin, "I received a marriage proposal from a member of high society. He insisted that I was meant to shine in his circle. I declined only because I could not have continued working for the Nietzsche Archives because his condition for marriage was that the *Antichrist* must not be published."

Upon Koegel's urging and without telling her mother, who was greatly upset when she heard of it, Elisabeth had agreed to the publication of *Antichrist,* to which she had been strongly opposed a few months before. She had done so because Koegel had assured her that he would personally accept any legal consequences, but primarily because "we are very good friends and complement each other in all our ideas."

During Elisabeth's absence Koegel kept himself busy trying to decipher Nietzsche's hieroglyphic notebooks. He came across a number of passages in which Nietzsche made very angry remarks about his sister, expressing disgust that he was related to her at all and forbidding her to read his books because she was totally incapable of understanding them. Koegel made copies of these passages, for there were moments when he shared Nietzsche's misgivings about Elisabeth. She attracted and repelled him at the same time. And yet, when she was gone, he felt lost amid the pile of manuscripts and he missed her volatile presence.

In a letter he sent her to Sils Maria he complained that: "A very lonely life begins for me now. My conversations with you have become solitary moral strolls; and in the evenings I copy manuscripts. Imagine how starved for human warmth I shall be in a few weeks—good people call it love." Being occupied at this time also with the English edition, he signed his letter in English "poor Koegel." Little did he know how prophetic these words were.

16·Mother and Daughter

*F*RANZISKA WATCHED HER daughter's relentless drive with a mixture of pride and sorrow. She was proud of Lieschen's accomplishments and delighted to hear the many laudatory comments made to her about her daughter's biography. Naumburg resounded with praise of Elisabeth's book, and everybody wanted an inscribed copy. Overnight Lieschen Nietzsche had become a famous writer. Only her mother expressed misgivings, but not publicly, for she loved her daughter and wished her well. But she was hurt when she discovered that her own role in her famous son's life was barely mentioned. According to Lieschen, the most influential woman in her brother's and her own life had been their father's mother, Grandmother Erdmuthe. This was, of course, not true, and Franziska resented it as an undeserved slight against herself and the entire Oehler branch of the family.

In letters to other family members, she complained bitterly about the "false picture" her daughter had "conjured up."

Lieschen refuses to admit that I had the least influence on Fritz's development. The only thing she cannot deny is that I bore him. But what would have become of the two children if four highly nervous females had brought them up? Nobody but me cared about their education. Lieschen thinks they became model children, as she portrays them, entirely on their own.

To correct her daughter's picture, Franziska started writing her own account of her children's lives. But she did not have the strength to finish it. She was approaching seventy and was fully occupied with taking care of her sick son. It was a duty of love that she refused to share with anyone, except her faithful Alwine, although it meant that she had to spend all her son's waking hours with him and often watch over him at night.

Her maternal instinct warned her that her son would not want to be seen by strangers in his present unhappy state. And to the best of her ability, she tried to shield him from visitors. But on one occasion, when she was absent from Naumburg, Elisabeth invited the painter Stöving to come and paint her sick brother's portrait, although she knew that her mother vigorously objected to the idea because there were sufficient pictures of her son when he was well. Elisabeth argued that her brother's numerous admirers had a right to know what the author of *Zarathustra* looked like now.

Stöving painted two oil portraits, a large one showing Nietzsche on the veranda of his mother's house, like a sick bird in a cage, and a smaller one in which Nietzsche stares ahead of himself with the expressionless stare of the insane, his face a sickly yellow, his dark hair showing dull streaks of gray. Franziska was horrified when she saw them, and outraged when she heard that her daughter had given permission for these "horrible pictures" to be publicly exhibited in Leipzig, Berlin, and Munich: "Nobody understands why you did this to your brother. Dr. Zeller said that these pictures show Fritz with the face of a criminal, and Adalbert's wife exclaimed she would destroy them if she were the mother."

Elisabeth brushed aside such reproaches, for she knew what she was doing: The more people talked about her brother, the more books were sold. But as long as her mother had the authority to interfere with her way of promoting Fritz's ideas, her hands were tied. Clearly, a way had to be found to wrest from her mother control over her brother's literary estate. This was not easy as long as her mother was in sole control of his physical care. Hence, as a first step, Elisabeth suggested that a professionally trained male nurse be hired to help with the caretaking. But Franziska would not hear of that. She was convinced that her son benefited far more from her motherly care than from the treatment by a professionally trained nurse. To make her mother change her mind, Elisabeth turned to Dr. Gutjahr, their family doctor and a good friend of hers. He was one of the few people in Naumburg with whom she could talk about her brother's philosophy. Much to her surprise and chagrin, Dr. Gutjahr sided with her mother against her by declaring that Franziska was an exemplary nurse and that nobody could do more for her son than she.

In an outburst of anger Elisabeth wrote Dr. Gutjahr a ten-page letter in which she denounced her mother in the most violent terms. She called her "a woman without character, unloved by her children and unloving—a pious fraud." Dr. Gutjahr, who had known Franziska for years and who knew how devoted she was to her children, was appalled and did not know what to do with Elisabeth's letter. It deserved an answer, but not from him. Should he show it to the old lady, who was already burdened with a load of sorrow? For almost a month he carried it in his pocket during his almost daily visits to his

Friedrich Nietzsche, portrait of the sick philosopher by Stöving, 1894.

patient. But Franziska, who had heard that her daughter had written bitter letters to others about her, became suspicious and pleaded with Gutjahr to be honest with her and let her see her daughter's letter. Gutjahr still hesitated for some time, but he finally decided that the old lady had a right to know what her daughter had written.

Franziska burst into tears when she read Elisabeth's letter. She was particularly hurt by a passage in which Elisabeth quoted her brother as saying that if he and his sister had not lived apart from their mother, "she would have driven us both to suicide or madness." The idea that her beloved sick son had said such a terrible thing about her preyed on her mind. Angrily, she confronted her daughter and wanted to see Fritz's letter. Elisabeth, equally angry because of what she called Dr. Gutjahr's violation of confidence, declared that Fritz's letter was among the documents she had lost in Paraguay. This answer did not satisfy Franziska. She refused to believe that her beloved son had written such a letter at all and since there was no proof, called it a "ghost letter," the figment of Elisabeth's imagination. Elisabeth protested fiercely that what she had written was the truth, although it was a bitter truth for a mother to be told that her children did not love her, because they felt that her love for them was not genuine.

The acrimonious controversy between Franziska and her daughter continued for months and involved many members of the family, for both women tried to enlist support for their positions. Elisabeth, who had started the quarrel because she wanted to prove that her mother was unfit to take care of her brother, wrote her uncle, Pastor Schenck:

> Imagine the terrible tragedy, my poor, dear Fritz being cared for by a mother who makes a spectacle of everything she does, now also of her sick son and her taking care of him. Fritz has dreaded this all his life, that is why he always called me when he needed somebody to take care of him. In 1880 he made me give him a solemn pledge never to let his mother take care of him. That is why I returned home three years ago, the moment I learned that he had left the asylum. But now Mother feels that she can boast that she is taking care of her famous son; she says that no power on earth can take him away from her. All last year she tormented me and the poor invalid so much with her jealousy—Fritz showed much more love for me than she liked—that I moved into my own apartment. I did not want to torture the poor invalid unnecessarily. This is the truth.

Elisabeth's unfilial outburst against her mother did not endear her to those who knew and respected Frau Pastor Nietzsche, and she began to feel increasingly isolated in Naumburg. Her brother had been right when he called it a stuffy and gossipy town. She sensed that the good burghers of her native town resented her life-style, her social activities, parties, travels, and, above all, her close association with numerous young men. And she began to think about other possible locations for the Nietzsche Archives.

The trouble was that any move from Naumburg would cost money, and although royalties from her brother's books were increasing rapidly, she could not dispose of them. For under the law, Franziska, as her son's legal guardian, was the only one authorized to administer his finances. She had given Elisabeth six thousand marks from the fourteen thousand marks royalty income Nietzsche's books had earned, insisting that this sum was more than enough to cover her daughter's expenses. Money was a topic Elisabeth could not discuss with her mother, for all her mother knew about money was that it must be saved. A ridiculous notion, Elisabeth thought, and doubly ridiculous in their case, when there were no heirs. It made much more sense to spend and enjoy your money while you can, and let posterity take care of itself.

This being Elisabeth's conviction, it was obviously necessary to eliminate her mother's control over Fritz's finances, for she could represent him properly only if she had untrammeled access to his funds. She discussed this problem on many occasions with her protégé Koegel, who was knowledgeable in financial matters. Koegel suggested that she approach her mother with the proposition that Frau Pastor surrender to Elisabeth the rights to her son's writings in return for a fixed sum of money. By investing this sum she could count on a definite amount of annual income, sufficient to take care of Nietzsche as long as he lived, and would avoid the uncertainties of royalty income varying from year to year. It was a sensible suggestion, except that neither Elisabeth nor Koegel possessed the capital needed to make such an offer. They made calculations about the amount that would provide a reasonable annual income for Nietzsche. The major source of his current income was his Basel pension of sixteen hundred marks annually. Assuming an average five percent rate of interest, a capital of thirty thousand marks would earn fifteen hundred marks interest annually. This was the sum Koegel suggested Elisabeth should offer her mother for the rights to her brother's works. Since Nietzsche's books had earned fourteen thousand marks in one year, it was not a very lucrative offer. But it was much more than either of them possessed. There was, of course, the possibility of a bank loan, but in that case securities are needed and these they did not have either. After lengthy discussions Koegel volunteered to approach some of his wealthy Berlin friends and admirers of Nietzsche and ask them to provide the necessary securities for such a transaction. In return they would become co-owners of Nietzsche's manuscripts and trustees of the Nietzsche Archives.

Koegel's proposal was the egg of Columbus. It opened a new world of activities for Elisabeth. As the sole owner of her brother's literary estate she could manage it according to her own wishes and unhampered by her mother's bourgeois scruples. She urged Koegel to approach his friends and find out if they were willing to participate in this scheme. Koegel did so and before long had recruited four of his Berlin acquaintances, among them the well-known, wealthy cosmopolitan count, Harry Kessler. Elisabeth succeeded in enlisting the support of her friend Meta von Salis. All five guarantors agreed to deposit securities, valued six thousand marks each, in a Berlin bank. In return, the bank agreed to grant Elisabeth a loan of thirty thousand marks at three percent interest.

Even before the intricate transaction, which involved numerous legal documents, was completed, Elisabeth approached her mother and her cousin with mysterious allusions to "anonymous donors" who had given her thirty thousand marks to enable her to acquire the rights to her brother's works. Her cousin, who sympathized with her desire to control the publication of her brother's writings, because he realized that Frau Pastor was neither interested nor competent to do so and might, in fact, try to prevent publication of manuscripts that offended her Christian conscience, listened to Elisabeth's proposal with an open mind. But Franziska was dead set against it. She refused to believe that there were any anonymous donors and suspected that her daughter intended to borrow the money and that she would have to pay interest on it. She knew her daughter's careless handling of money and considered it her duty to prevent a transaction that would place a further burden on Elisabeth. Besides, she resented the whole idea of selling her son's literary estate. As long as he lived, she owed it to him to protect the products of his mind. Elisabeth, who feared that her mother's reluctance to sign the surrender documents might jeopardize the entire transaction, appealed in lengthy letters to all who had any influence on her mother, to help her persuade Franziska to sign.

Franziska tried to resist her daughter's pressure by also seeking help from her friends. She became alarmed when she learned that her daughter had written Overbeck and inquired whether it was true that her brother's Basel pension was about to be terminated, indicating that, as far as she was concerned, this was quite acceptable, because her brother's income from his writings was now more than adequate for his upkeep. Indeed, Elisabeth suggested that Nietzsche might wish to return to Basel some of his pension money. Franziska was horrified when she heard this and hurriedly advised Overbeck not to take her daughter's suggestion seriously. On the contrary, she begged him to reassure her that her son would receive his pension as long as he lived. Thereupon Elisabeth wrote again and asked Overbeck to remind her mother that nobody could guarantee that and urged him to advise Franziska that her son's future would be secure if she accepted the offer of the anonymous donors and signed the surrender document.

Perhaps you are astonished and wonder: "Why does Frau Pastor not want to sign?" Well, the simple but very confidential reason is her passionate and childish jealousy of me. She is annoyed that many good people trust me. That the donors insist they must remain anonymous, hurts my poor mother most of all. The whole bad situation is the result of the biography. My poor mother has put it into the heads of all the Oehlers that because my brother always insisted on his descent from the Nietzsches (he did not want to be an Oehler), they must all feel slighted. ... I must emphasize that the good donors are willing to give me the money only because they want to enlist my energy and my knowledge of my brother for the archives, and because I am the only person to whom the archives can be sold. Mama, being a guardian, can legally buy nothing from her son. Only if somebody has bought the archives can legally valid arrangements be made for the future.

It is unlikely that Overbeck was impressed with these arguments. He knew that as long as Franziska lived, her son's finances were in good hands. And after her death Elisabeth would inherit what she wanted to buy now. Why was she in such a hurry? Knowing Elisabeth, Overbeck suspected that her reason for wanting to obtain sole control over her brother's writings was her imperious nature. She chafed under her mother's tutelage. She wanted to establish herself as the unquestioned authority of her brother's life and work. This went against Overbeck's grain, and he sympathized with Franziska. Nevertheless, upon Elisabeth's urgent request, he agreed to a personal meeting with her in Leipzig. It took place on September 19, 1895. They talked for three hours in the parlor of the Evangelische Vereinshaus. Overbeck records that "she received me, splendidly dressed in a flowing black-silk robe enthroned on a couch, and tried to gloss over the first few painful moments with a torrent of words, her face bearing the expression of a mournful Niobe; she clutched a handkerchief in her hands ready for tears." In the course of the conversation, Elisabeth insisted repeatedly that the cause of her brother's sickness was chloride poisoning. It was most unfortunate that it had not been diagnosed correctly at the time. Her poor brother might have been saved if he had received the correct treatment. Now, of course, it was too late. Overbeck, who had vivid recollections of the macabre scenes of Nietzsche's insanity he had witnessed in Turin, listened silently to Elisabeth's barrage directed against him. She seemed quite unaware how deeply she offended him by her self-righteous assertion that she, and she alone, knew the cause of her brother's collapse. But it was useless to argue with Elisabeth when her mind was made up. Overbeck remembered that during the years of his life before his collapse, Nietzsche had often referred to Elisabeth as the great misfortune of his life. Her tirades now confirmed his suspicions that Elisabeth's main concern was to monopolize her brother's work. He agreed to furnish information about Nietzsche's life during the time she was in Paraguay, but refused to give her copies of Nietzsche's letters to him or advice about the publication of his friend's manuscripts. He made it quite clear to Elisabeth that he did not want to have anything to do with the Nietzsche Archives.

By contrast, Overbeck sympathized with Franziska's anguished outcry that it was "a mental confusion on my daughter's part to want to buy from me with money from strangers the literary treasures of my son, our mutually beloved patient, hence our family treasure." And he shared the old lady's suspicion concerning the anonymous donors: "It is a matter of thirty thousand marks, supposedly given by friends, although there is a complete mystery who these friends are who offer to give money from such idealistic motives, if the guardians surrender the archives to my daughter." What baffled Franziska most of all was why Elisabeth wanted to make this change, because neither she nor her nephew had ever interfered with the running of the archives. The whole scheme seemed to her unnecessary and unworthy and she resisted it.

The year 1895 was drawing to a close and the struggle between mother and daughter remained unresolved. The longer her mother resisted signing, the more frantic Elisabeth became, going so far as to threaten to go to court and have her mother declared incompetent to be her son's guardian. Weary with worry, Franziska fell sick and on December 18 gave in to her daughter's demands by signing a document prepared by Elisabeth's lawyer in which she surrendered all her rights to her son's works to Elisabeth. But no sooner had she signed than she regretted it. She wrote her nephew: "I testify herewith that I have given my signature just now for the surrender of my son's literary treasure for money from strangers only at the request and urgings of my daughter, Frau Doktor Förster, hence—under duress."

Elisabeth was jubilant. She embraced and kissed her "beloved Mamachen" and told her that now everybody could sleep more easily. She had finally reached her goal and now was the sole mistress of the Nietzsche Archives.

17· The Case of Elisabeth

*A*S IT TURNED OUT, Elisabeth's jubilation was premature. According to the surrender document that her mother had signed so reluctantly on December 18, 1895, Elisabeth had to pay thirty thousand marks into her brother's account by February 1, 1896; otherwise the agreement was null and void. Once again, as so often in her life, Elisabeth was under time pressure. To be sure, Koegel had assured her that he had firm commitments from four friends to deposit securities worth six thousand marks each in a Berlin bank, and Meta von Salis had agreed to do likewise, but the necessary legal documents had not yet been drawn up, nor had a bank been approached. To expedite matters, Elisabeth sent Koegel to Berlin after Christmas. He reported to her in a long letter that after exhaustive discussions with his Berlin friend Dr. Hecker, a lawyer and himself a guàrantor, they had decided to ask the guarantors to make their deposits in cash rather than in securities, because only "a Jewish banker" would be willing to lend money on securities of private persons. And they both felt that it would be a serious mistake to accept Jewish money, because "the Jews would then boast that they had financed Nietzsche and the press and literary journals would soon echo with the proud refrain: 'Our people are the only champions of freedom of thought.' "

Elisabeth was dismayed by this unexpected turn of events. Her main concern was to get money before February 1; it made no difference to her where the money came from. She was equally disturbed when she learned that Dr. Hecker's mother was among the guarantors. This would give Hecker two votes in the five-member board of trustees she envisaged for the archives.

She told Koegel that she was not in favor of this arrangement and wrote Meta von Salis that she had again taken personal charge of the transaction.

I am terribly afraid that because of the obstinacy of some individuals the whole arrangement will fail. A difference concerning the banker has arisen between Dr. Koegel and Dr. Hecker on the one hand, and Count Kessler and Dr. Richter on the other. The former insist on von der Heydt, who does not show much interest, the latter on von Mendelssohn, who is willing to loan thirty thousand marks on securities. But the other two object to him because he is Jewish.

Koegel's attitude irritated Elisabeth. As far as she was concerned, Jewish capital was just as good as Aryan. She reminded Koegel that her brother who, she insisted, did not like the Jews any more than she did, had said that he needed Jewish capital for the propagation of his ideas. Besides, Robert von Mendelssohn was a descendant of the famous philosopher and his family had been Christians for three generations. She complained to Meta that Koegel had been too much influenced by his friend Hecker, who seemed to hold a personal grudge against Mendelssohn. It was therefore very unwise to have both Hecker and his mother on the archives' board of trustees. She suggested that if Meta would increase her six thousand mark share to ten thousand, she, Elisabeth, would add another two thousand and they could dispense with Mrs. Hecker. Since, in that case, Meta would have two votes on the board, Elisabeth proposed that she transfer her second vote to Rudolf Steiner: "He is an excellent serious scholar, in his late thirties, and really unusually interesting and attractive, a genuine admirer of Nietzsche. He has been here only a short time to work in the archives; he lives in Weimar, where he edits the scientific writings in the Goethe-Schiller Archiv."

Elisabeth concluded her long letter with a sigh about the dilatoriness and squabbling of men: "It makes me sick. And in a week from today the whole matter must be settled. Men are much more jealous of each other than women. I wish they had your highmindedness." Signing herself as "deeply depressed," she waited anxiously for Meta's reply. It arrived just in time. Meta agreed to deposit securities for ten thousand marks, and Robert von Mendelssohn made the loan that officially established the Nietzsche Archives. On February 2, Elisabeth joyfully told her friend: "Everything is now in good order, and I embrace you in warm, heartfelt gratitude."

Having passed this hurdle, Elisabeth threw herself with renewed energy into her work. She was determined to finish the second volume of her brother's biography, for which she had received advance royalties, while Koegel prepared for additional volumes by sorting the material contained in Nietzsche's notebooks. It proved a frustrating experience because the sheer mass of these almost illegible aphorisms that Nietzsche had scribbled down during the final phase of his illness defied any attempt at arranging them in a meaningful order. To make things worse, the notebooks contained contradictory entries about a major work Nietzsche planned to write, or said he had written. He called it *The Transvaluation of All Values* and claimed that it represented the triumphal arch of his philosophy, based on the twin pillars of "Eternal Recurrence" and "Will to Power." Athough no such manuscript existed, Elisabeth expected Koegel to produce one out of the chaos of the notebooks. But Koegel, whose editorial skill was generally admired (Elisabeth told her cousin "the gentlemen of Weimar are absolutely amazed how quickly Koegel works"), was noticeably slowing down. He had edited eight volumes in 1894, but only two in 1895. In 1896 he began work on Volumes 11 and 12, but far too leisurely for Elisabeth's taste. Since her income depended on the royalties she received from each volume—she had already received two thousand marks in advance for Volume 11—these delays worried her.

She blamed the stifling atmosphere of Naumburg for the difficulties that Koegel and she herself experienced, and decided to move the Nietzsche Archives to Weimar. She had long felt ill at ease in her hometown, and now that she was the mistress of the archives she was no longer dependent on her mother's approval. Weimar was far enough from Naumburg to permit her freedom of action, and close enough to permit visits to her mother and brother should it become necessary. In addition to being the historic center of German culture, Weimar was the residence of the Grand Duke Alexander, whose court contained some of the most brilliant men and women in Germany. It was a city that held the arts in high regard, and it was the seat of the newly founded Goethe-Schiller Archiv. Elisabeth had established cordial relations with many young scholars working there, most recently with Rudolf Steiner, whom she had begun to admire greatly. She secretly hoped that he would join the Nietzsche Archives before long.

Franziska was very unhappy about her daughter's intended departure from Naumburg: "That my daughter intends to exchange Naumburg for Weimar because she believes she will find there greater understanding for Fritz's philosophy, has caused me much grief. However, she is a very restless spirit and has her will in whatever she wants to do." Elisabeth tried to console her mother by pointing out that Weimar was not very far and that she could be in Naumburg in a couple of hours. In the company of Meta von Salis, who visited her and whom she now addressed as "dearest heart," she traveled to Weimar, found a spacious apartment not far from the center of town, and at the end of August moved all her own belongings and her brother's notebooks and manuscripts to her new home. Her address was Wörthstrasse 5. It was the third move for the Nietzsche Archives in two years.

Koegel was too much occupied with his personal affairs to pay much attention to Elisabeth's move to Weimar, although it presented a potential threat to his position as editor-in-chief. He had fallen in love with Emily Gelzer, daughter of Elisabeth's Jena friends, and had been incautious enough to extol Emily's beautiful voice and charming personality to Elisabeth in long letters he wrote her while he was on a holiday hiking in the Alps. Elisabeth's answers were apparently chilly, for Koegel complains of her "grumpy letter": "It is unfair of you," he wrote back, "to expect much *esprit* from me now—

do I not have the right to rest awhile, even though it may be the official duty of the Nietzsche editor to have and to show wit at all times."

When Koegel returned from vacation, Elisabeth forgave him his transgressions. She even wished him luck when he confided to her that he intended to propose to Emily, but she suggested that, since he now needed more time for his personal affairs, it would be in his interest if Dr. Steiner could be prevailed upon to become assistant editor. Koegel objected violently. Such a suggestion, he said, reflected on his editorial competence. He promised, however, to have Volume 11 ready for publication early in January 1897. Thus reassured, Elisabeth wrote her publisher Naumann that "although Dr. Koegel is occasionally a difficult person, and there are times when he does little or no work, he is still the best editor we could wish for."

In November, when Koegel announced his engagement, Elisabeth told him half in jest, half seriously, that she would refuse him her blessings unless he promised to edit Volumes 11 and 12 before the end of January. After Koegel had done so, Elisabeth wrote Naumann on November 26, "in a state of deep emotion," that she was very happy about this turn of events and planned to give an engagement party for the young couple in the Nietzsche Archives. A few days later she received a printed engagement announcement sent her by the bride's parents and was furious to notice that no mention was made of Koegel's position as Nietzsche editor. She took this as a personal insult and started a series of actions that embroiled her, Koegel, Steiner, and Naumann in a bitter quarrel, including threats of dueling and lawsuits.

It began with a letter. Early in December, barely a week after Elisabeth had written to Naumann "in a state of deep emotion," she again addressed him:

> You have probably wondered why no mention whatever is made of the Nietzsche Archives in the announcement of the engagement. I consider this very offensive. I was mistaken when I thought that Koegel would marry into a good Nietzsche tradition. Gelzer and her Basel relatives respect Koegel but consider his position at the Nietzsche Archives as though he were a high executioner. I believe everything can change very much. But let us not get upset too early. Console yourself with the thought that I have found a far better editor for the *Transvaluation*. Everything changes, everything—except you and I.

What Elisabeth meant, although Naumann did not know it, was that in a fit of spite Elisabeth had offered Steiner Koegel's position as editor-in-chief. In a confidential talk with Steiner on the eve of the engagement party she was giving for Koegel and his bride, Elisabeth had complained that Emily Gelzer was not a suitable wife for the Nietzsche editor, nor was it likely that Emily would want her husband to continue in this position. It was, therefore, necessary to make other arrangements. Would Steiner accept this honorable and remunerative task?

Taken by surprise, and knowing that Koegel would resent being replaced behind his back and feel that he was the victim of an intrigue, Steiner not only declined the offer but begged Elisabeth not to make any mention to anyone that they had even discussed such a possibility. Elisabeth promised but repeated that she hoped Steiner would reconsider should Koegel resign from his editorship, as she suspected he would.

Since Elisabeth knew that any change in the person of the editor needed the approval of the publisher, she bombarded the youngest member of the firm, Gustav Naumann, whom she trusted and liked, with letters containing mysterious hints about "threatening events to come." For example, in the letter in which she invited Naumann to join the engagement festivities she had planned for Koegel and his bride on Sunday, December 6, she writes:

> I would very much like to talk with you confidentially. This seems to be a time of great conflicts. I cannot describe what I have suffered in the last few weeks. It is almost like three years ago when I discovered that the excellent Peter Gast was not the suitable editor. Next week everything will be decided, but on Sunday we will forget the seriousness of life and be cheerful.

Elisabeth did not know that Gustav Naumann was on very friendly terms with Koegel, whom he respected both as a friend and an editor. Her hints that she planned to dismiss Koegel disturbed Naumann. But friendship apart, he was convinced that it was in the best interest of the firm that the present editor be kept. Naumann was therefore in a wary mood when he reached Weimar, and he participated with misgivings in the engagement party.

Elisabeth, who played her role as hostess with disarming charm, had invited a number of Nietzsche admirers from Weimar, as well as Koegel's bride and sister, Steiner, and Naumann. She was in a very animated mood. Music and laughter filled the air of the festively decorated rooms of the archives. At the appropriate moment, Elisabeth proposed a champagne toast to the young couple, wishing them many years of happiness. The company cheered and emptied their glasses in honor of bride and bridegroom. As an expression of his appreciation for the friendly wishes, Koegel proposed that Emily sing a few of his songs while he accompanied her at the piano. Elisabeth used this occasion to draw Naumann aside and whisper to him: "Koegel is not really a philosopher; he is an artist, a musician. He cannot possibly edit the *Transvaluation* volumes. Dr. Steiner, on the other hand, is a philosopher who can and will edit them." When Naumann tried to remonstrate with her, she cut him short, stating: "In these matters I am always right."

During the course of the evening Elisabeth became increasingly irritated by the attention Emily was receiving from her guests. Everybody was captivated by her vivacity, her charm, and her beautiful voice. Later, when the conversation turned to Nietzsche's philosophy, Emily made some disparaging remarks. She disagreed with the treatment of women in Nietzsche's writings; in particular, she objected to Zarathustra's statement: "If you go to women, don't forget the whip." When she was told that Zarathustra did not make the statement, but that it was the advice an old woman gave him, Emily said that this made it even worse. Elisabeth thought that such talk was both stupid and tactless. Did Emily not realize that she was a guest in the

Nietzsche Archives? But what infuriated Elisabeth was Koegel's attitude. He agreed, or at least pretended to agree, with everything his bride said. To see "the Nietzsche editor capitulate to a silly sophomore" was more than she could bear. She decided then and there that "Emily was simply impossible for the Nietzsche Archives," but she kept this decision to herself. As the party ended she kissed Emily and once again wished her happiness and good luck.

That same night Naumann told Koegel at the Weimar railroad station that Elisabeth planned to dismiss him, and that Steiner had agreed to edit the final volumes. Koegel, who had noticed a change in Elisabeth from the moment he announced his engagement, reminded Naumann that under the terms of the publishing contract she could not dismiss him without the consent of the publisher. Naumann agreed and reassured Koegel that he would urge his uncle not to give his consent. What upset Koegel most was Steiner's part in this affair. He considered it a betrayal of trust, for Steiner had always assured him that he did not want to become Nietzsche's editor; they had a gentleman's agreement on that. In Koegel's eyes Steiner was a hypocrite who had been plotting behind his back with Elisabeth to usurp his position. Although Naumann put the blame for the intrigue squarely on Elisabeth, Koegel, pale with rage, insisted that to protect his honor he would challenge Steiner to a duel. To calm him, Naumann advised his friend not to draw too hasty conclusions from what he had told him, and he suggested that Koegel request a personal meeting with Steiner and Elisabeth to clear up the matter.

In the presence of his friend, Dr. Hecker, Koegel confronted Elisabeth and Steiner in the Nietzsche Archives on December 9, three days after the engagement party. A tumultuous scene took place. Threatened by three angry young men — one challenging the other to a duel — Elisabeth, fearful of bloodshed, raised up her hands in a gesture of injured innocence and denied everything. She had never offered Koegel's position to Steiner; Steiner would testify to that. Naumann had been mistaken. It was he who was responsible for the deplorable misunderstanding. But Steiner did not oblige Elisabeth by agreeing with her. He was very angry, and not because of Koegel's threatening gestures. He was angry with Elisabeth for blatantly betraying his trust. On Saturday she had given him her word not to mention to anyone the offer she had made him, and which he had turned down, and on Sunday she had broken it. To clear the air, Steiner explained everything exactly as it had happened. "The scene in the archives ended with a complete unmasking of Frau Förster," Koegel reported to Naumann. "After turning and twisting for a long time she had to admit that she had compromised Steiner."

But according to Elisabeth, what happened that afternoon in the Nietzsche Archives was that "both men fell on me like wild beasts in order to prove that I was a liar through and through, although they knew very well that I sacrificed myself only to prevent bloodshed." She was so firmly convinced of her version of the incident, her own letters to the contrary notwithstanding, that she swore it was the truth, the whole truth. The real culprit of the terrifying scene to which she, a defenseless woman, had been subjected, was Gustav Naumann, who had "invented the stupid fairy tale" that she was plotting to get rid of Koegel. When Naumann heard that Elisabeth had made such charges in letters to his uncle, he asked his lawyer to demand a retraction, else he would sue Elisabeth for libel.

Elisabeth's answer was a masterpiece of double-talk:

> If there is anything dishonorable in the expression "stupid" in connection with "fairy tale," I gladly retract it. It was meant in the sense of "unreasonable," and I merely wanted to express how much it would have gone against all my interests to force Dr. Koegel to give up his position as editor. An intrigue would have been both unnecessary and undignified, because there is a clear understanding between Dr. Koegel and me that each of us can give the other notice any day. Not even the shadow of a binding contract exists between us. I am perfectly justified in reproaching Gustav Naumann that he talked about a matter, of which he knew nothing and which he completely misunderstood, without any authorization on my part, causing a dreadful confusion which can lead to great financial loss for me and the firm C. G. Naumann.

When Gustav Naumann realized that it was impossible to make Elisabeth admit that she had repeatedly urged Koegel's dismissal, he prepared a document, based on quotations from Elisabeth's letters, in which he gave chapter and verse of Elisabeth's untrustworthiness and convicted her by her own words. It is a forty-six-page exposé entitled *The Case of Elisabeth*. Gustav Naumann's lawyer informed Elisabeth that thirty copies of this document existed and that they would be used whenever his client considered it necessary to prove the truth of his statements. At the same time Constantin Naumann, the senior member of the firm, warned her that "Dr. Koegel intends to publish a book under the title *Friedrich Nietzsche and His Sister*. I do not think that a scandal will benefit the works of your brother or your biography."

Elisabeth reacted to these threatening communications with fear and fury. She was furious that Koegel had the audacity to tell her through his friend Hecker that "she did not understand her brother at all, that she was falsifying him, that everything she did was sham, and that she had organized the archives only to satisfy her personal vanity." And she was afraid that if it could be proven that she wanted to dismiss Koegel without obtaining the consent of the publisher, Naumann could accuse her of breach of contract, and she could become embroiled in expensive legal battles just now when she badly needed money.

Her strategy was to deny that she had ever wanted to dismiss Koegel and to assert that she had merely asked him to accept Steiner as his assistant. According to the contract, she was entitled to engage an assistant editor. Naumann pointed out that in a letter to him dated December 16, she had written: "I am giving Koegel notice on October 1 next year." In another letter, written a week later, she asked angrily: "*Who* has given notice to Dr.

Koegel? Who has proposed another editor in his place? Some creature of your imagination." It was useless to argue with her. She contradicted her own words. Gustav Naumann told his uncle that as long as Elisabeth was in charge of the edition the firm was at the mercy of an irresponsible woman. He advised him to insist on his right as publisher and refuse to discharge Koegel. Constantin Naumann agreed with his nephew, but he was an old man and did not want to become involved in a lawsuit. After all, he was making money on Nietzsche and he said that it would be bad business to interrupt the editorial process now. He reminded his nephew that while Dr. Koegel had worked well in the past, his performance lately had been poor. He had not produced one single volume all year. And Elisabeth had reason to be disappointed. If she thought that Steiner's presence would spur Koegel on, it was worth trying.

His nephew argued that the situation was not that simple. Koegel was not willing to accept a second editor, nor was Steiner willing to become one. Hence, if Elisabeth persisted in her campaign to oust Koegel, there might be no one to complete the edition in the near future. And this would mean a considerable financial loss for the firm.

The thought that she might be left without an editor began to worry Elisabeth, too. She spent a dreary Christmas with her mother and her brother in Naumburg and startled her friends by hinting that she contemplated giving up the archives altogether. She felt that she had been treated outrageously by the one man she had trusted more than anyone else. The real reason for Koegel's cruel behavior toward her was that he wanted to have sole charge of the Nietzsche Archives, because he resented having to take orders from a woman. He would not have dared to act as he did if she had been a man. But "a defenseless woman can be tortured to death by educated men. She cannot say, as a man can, 'one more word and I shall kill you.' "

This was the tenor of her letter to her cousin, Dr. Oehler, when she described the dreadful scene in the Nietzsche Archives. She implied that she was the victim of a plot between Koegel and Gustav Naumann, both of whom wanted to gain control of the archives for themselves. Dr. Oehler, who knew and liked Koegel and who was quite familiar with Elisabeth's mercurial temperament, was at first inclined to dismiss the incident as yet another tempest in a teapot. However, when he received a letter from Gustav Naumann addressed to him as Nietzsche's guardian, charging Elisabeth with an attempted breach of contract and enclosing a copy of *The Case of Elisabeth*, which he threatened to make public, Oehler knew he had to act. Assuming the role of Elisabeth's defense attorney, he wrote a seventeen-page counterstatement in which he asserted that Elisabeth had never wanted to dismiss Koegel and that it was her right to engage an assistant editor. As for Gustav Naumann's threat to publicize his "so-called exposé," Oehler called it blackmail and warned the firm that he would take the necessary legal steps to protect his cousin.

Old Constantin Naumann became outraged when he heard what his nephew had done. At a hastily called conference in Weimar on January 17 at which Dr. Oehler, Elisabeth, and Koegel were present, Naumann agreed to punish his nephew for his unauthorized and unpardonable act by expelling him from the firm. Koegel, who swore that he had had no part in preparing the exposé, was told that he could keep his position for another three months, in which time he was to prepare Volumes 11 and 12 for publication. But he was not allowed to work in the archives and he had to make personal progress reports to Elisabeth on Tuesdays and Saturdays. The ultimate decision as to what should or should not be published was henceforth hers alone.

Once again Elisabeth had triumphed. "Dr. Koegel arrived obediently and punctually on Tuesday," she told her friend Meta, who knew only her version of the affair.

He made such a comic impression, like a naughty little schoolboy who wants to be good again: but it is useless. He has threatened me with a scandalous pamphlet, *Nietzsche and His Sister*, he wants to throw dirt and slander on one of the finest relationships, and there is only one answer to this threat—dismissal.

Peter Gast, who had watched the events in Weimar from his observation post in Annaberg with amused interest, reported to Overbeck:

Dr. Koegel has left the archives. His star with Frau Doktor Förster began to sink from the moment he became engaged to Emily Gelzer. It appears that Frau Doktor Förster only permits bachelors to be near her, young men with whom the slight possibility of a liaison exists. At the moment Dr. Steiner is her favorite.

18·Villa Silberblick

*A*FTER HER TROUBLED WINTER, Elisabeth looked forward confidently to the spring. She told her "dearest heart Meta" in a rejoicing mood that she now "had really become conscious of her power." The plot to wrest the archives from her had failed miserably; she, a defenseless woman, had triumphed over a group of scheming men. It was foolish that she had let herself be intimidated by them. She did not need Koegel at all, nor Steiner. She and Meta could edit her brother's works on their own just as well. As for the laborious task of deciphering and copying manuscripts, they could engage a male secretary.

Meta, who remembered Elisabeth's enthusiastic praise of her erstwhile protégé and who had herself formed a high opinion of Koegel, was puzzled at her friend's abrupt change of tune. Elisabeth's idea that they edit Nietzsche's works struck her as very naïve. It showed how little she knew about the painstaking business of professional editing. But Elisabeth would not take no for an answer. Bubbling over with plans for their future editorial partnership, she informed Meta that she had visited her brother's old friend, Professor Deussen and his family, in Kiel and had asked him what he thought of two women editors. He had strongly encouraged her and had introduced her·to all his colleagues in the academic community. As the sister of the philosopher around whom so much discussion was beginning to center, she had received a royal welcome: "I am being terribly spoiled, but it does me good after last year's ignominious treatment." But Meta was not impressed. She was beginning to see through Elisabeth's practice of putting on airs.

When Elisabeth told her that she had promised her friends that she and

Meta, her aristocratic Swiss friend, would spend six to eight weeks in Kiel in May, attending university lectures and enjoying an active social life, Meta did not even deign to reply. It struck her as ridiculous that Elisabeth expected her to enroll under her tutelage at the University of Kiel, when she had completed seven semesters of serious studies at Zürich with a Ph.D. degree. As it turned out, Meta did not have to reject Elisabeth's invitation because in April an event occurred that was to have far-reaching consequences—the sudden sickness and death of Elisabeth's mother.

Franziska Nietzsche had never been seriously ill in all the seventy years of her life. She had worked hard, lived simply, and prayed to God every night for her children, whose ideas she did not understand. Sometimes, in the depth of the night, during her lonely vigils at the bedside of her sick, and suddenly famous, son, she had wondered if his sickness was not God's punishment for having rejected the Savior. But Franziska was steady in her faith and never seriously doubted that the Lord would have mercy on Fritz.

Elisabeth's behavior hurt her far more. She could not understand why her daughter would publish those terrible anti-Christian notes that Fritz had scribbled down when his mind was weakening. She was sure he would not have published them if he had been well. And Lieschen had done it only because she needed money. That had been her curse all her life. She always needed money. She had enacted the "ridiculous comedy" of the anonymous donors also because she wanted to get her hands on her brother's money. That was something Franziska never forgave her and is echoed in the pitiful lament addressed to Overbeck: "Who knows if my son's best friends must not someday come to the defense of his mother?"

Physically exhausted by the demands her sick son had made on her for eight years and worn out by the continuous quarreling with Elisabeth, Franziska's robust health began to deteriorate. Soon after Christmas she complained of stomach cramps. At the beginning of April her condition worsened. Elisabeth was called home to help take care of her brother, but it was soon evident that her mother's case was hopeless. With her body sick and her mind weary of life, the end came mercifully quickly. On April 20, 1897, Franziska Nietzsche was dead.

Elisabeth was now forced either to face the future with her brother in her mother's house in Naumburg or to find a house in Weimar large enough for both of them and the Nietzsche Archives. The idea of returning to her native town was so repugnant to Elisabeth that she did not seriously consider it. Although her apartment was not suitable for her brother and she did not have enough money to buy a house, she was determined to remain in Weimar. In her predicament she turned to Meta, who had helped her before and whose friendship she had cultivated. And once again Meta came to the rescue. She found a villa recently built on the hilly outskirts of Weimar, overlooking the town, that was for sale and would provide an ideal retreat for the sick philosopher. It was not cheap: the owner wanted forty thousand marks for it. Meta was forced to sell some good investments to acquire the necessary capital. But out of reverence for Nietzsche, Meta did so. She was deeply moved by his present pathetic state and felt he deserved to spend the rest of his life in seclusion and to be spared the degradations of being exposed to the idle glances of the curious. These were the considerations that led Meta to buy Villa Silberblick in June 1897.

Elisabeth had inspected the villa before Meta bought it, was delighted with it, and assured her friend that it was precisely the right place for her and her sick brother. Meta offered it to Elisabeth on the condition that she could live in it at a modest annual rental as long as her brother was alive. After his death she had the option of buying it. Elisabeth accepted Meta's offer with an expression of deep gratitude: "I think of you as an angel who, at a time when my beloved brother and I were miserable and needed help, took us by the hand and led us into this house, where we shall live and die."

Before she moved in, Elisabeth decided that the villa, a spacious three-story building, needed improvements if it was to fulfill its twin functions: as a home for her and her sick brother and as a dignified environment for the social functions of the Nietzsche Archives. She engaged a veritable army of carpenters, painters, plumbers, and blacksmiths, and ordered extensive remodeling. A veranda had to be added to the house for her brother, she needed a bathroom, the kitchen needed a tiled floor, a new sink, and a new coat of paint. She decided the guest room, which Meta had reserved for herself, was far too small, and ordered a wall torn out. The combination of two medium-sized rooms created an imposing and truly representative guest room. Elisabeth was very proud of her innovations and informed Meta that she was happy her room was now so attractive: "I have followed your intentions and transformed the two small rooms into an alcove. The room is bright and cheerful and makes a very friendly impression."

Meta had given no instructions for any remodeling and was aghast when she heard that Elisabeth had ordered the work without consulting her, and outraged when she was billed for it. She wrote Elisabeth:

> Dear Elisabeth, Ask yourself calmly what would you think of a woman who orders structural changes against your will in your house and in the room reserved for you? It is surely a daring circumvention of the facts to say that you had followed my intentions. None of my long-term friends — men or women — would have been capable of such a blatant disregard of my personal wishes, to say nothing of my rights.

Deeply disappointed by what she felt was a basic flaw in Elisabeth's character Meta told her that they could not possibly live together now, for

> *you* love luxury and comfort and what impresses people, and you think that you can thus serve your brother's noble goals. *I* would prefer to provide the invalid with every possible easing of his life and for the rest accumulate his fortune through the income from his books by modest and careful living in order to provide a permanent home for his work.

Elisabeth answered Meta's long and reproachful letter in a tone of injured innocence, which she always adopted when she was obviously in the wrong. She emphasized that she was not asking Meta to pay for the structural changes she had ordered without consulting Meta beforehand. There had been no time for consultations because the changes had to be made before her brother's arrival. "I could not wait because the hammering and knocking would have been impossible with the dear invalid in the house. But it seems unfair to make you pay for them." However, if she had to pay for all these expensive alterations in the house and in the garden—"the latter had to be completely landscaped, it was useless as it was, not offering any shade for my dear brother"—she was forced to conclude that she really ought to buy the house now. She told Meta that she was making plans to purchase Villa Silberblick but wondered whether Meta was not perhaps too fond of the house and did not want to sell it.

By way of reassuring Meta, who had spent time and money on acquiring the villa barely two months before and was obviously in no hurry to sell it, Elisabeth emphasized that she would never forget she owed it to Meta's energy and kindness of heart that she had found such a suitable home for herself and her beloved brother. "Unfortunately," she added, "the house is not suitable for everybody. People with small children or anyone sensitive to drafts could not possibly live here, it is always drafty somewhere." Thank God, she and her brother had been immunized to colds by their mother's insistence on ablutions in cold water.

Continuing in a lighter vein, she invited Meta to visit her and see for herself the great improvements in the appearance of Villa Silberblick. She told her friend that she had already received many important visitors, such as Frau von Petry, the painter Stöving, and Count Harry Kessler, whom she called her "bibliographic adviser." They were planning a new edition of *Zarathustra* because "the present one is printed in the style of 'young ladies' poetry books." She expected a stream of important and interesting visitors in the autumn and hoped that Meta would be in Weimar to meet them.

In conclusion, she again brought up the matter of buying the house. Since she would now have to pay two thousand marks for the alterations, she thought she ought to buy it. She hoped that Meta's heart was not set on keeping it. However, Meta already owned a beautiful castle in Switzerland and probably would not mind selling her Weimar villa.

> Please give me the option of buying the house for forty thousand marks during the first year of your ownership. . . . When I arrived here on July 22 early in the morning and looked on the shimmering town below and the far horizons, I told my heart: "A new life, yes a beautiful new life has begun. Without you I would have been stuck in the small house in Naumburg."

Meta's answer arrived promptly and was not comforting. She told Elisabeth that it was not her intention to sell her villa as long as Nietzsche was alive:

> I can only smile that you now criticize my house and garden, which you

liked so well in the spring; that you consider a bathroom necessary when you did not have one either in Weingarten 18, nor in your later Naumburg home, nor in your Weimar apartment; and that the millionaire Count Kessler, your "bibliographic adviser" tells you to look down with contempt on last year's edition of *Zarathustra*. All these things throw a very different light on you than you suspect—not only in my eyes but in the eyes of many people.

Elisabeth found it hard to reply to such plain speaking. She could not understand why Meta was so upset. She had assumed that Meta had bought Villa Silberblick for her brother and would be in favor of any improvements made for his benefit. But perhaps she was mistaken. Perhaps Meta had bought the house as an investment and a tax shelter. She had heard that many wealthy Swiss were buying property in Germany for that purpose. But in that case she had to make other arrangements because she simply had to have a suitable home for herself and her brother. Her cousin was willing to lend her the money so that she could buy a house of her own in Weimar. If Meta did not want to sell hers, she would buy Villa Oberist, which had just come on the market.

Angered by this turn of events, Meta decided to travel to Weimar in the fall and see for herself the alterations Elisabeth had made on her property. She was met at the station by a liveried servant with a ducal crown embossed on silver buttons, who solemnly welcomed her in the name of Frau Doktor Förster-Nietzsche and led her to a waiting carriage. On her arrival at Villa Silberblick Elisabeth, standing in the doorway, greeted her warmly and showed her through the house. On the ground floor was the archives and reception room, furnished with a red velvet sofa and chairs, a grand piano, and cabinets with Nietzsche's books; on the walls were family portraits, Paraguay pictures, Indian pottery, framed lace veils, and pieces of embroidery. Elisabeth's living room was on the first floor, joining a bathroom and her brother's bedroom and veranda. The guest rooms were on the second floor. Meta noticed that the alcove room which Elisabeth had ordered built without her consent was indeed bright and cheerful. But she resented it all the same because she was confronted by an accomplished fact. Elisabeth had obviously taken over her house and there was nothing much she could do. She might as well sell it to her. After a painful scene during which Elisabeth accused Meta of having misled her by pretending that she had bought the house for her and her brother, whereas in truth she had bought it as a tax shelter, Meta abruptly left Weimar. She told Elisabeth that she would correspond with Dr. Oehler about the sale of her house.

Elisabeth continued to pursue her with lengthy epistles, repeating how disappointed she was about Meta's behavior. Why should their friendship be sacrificed to a piece of property? She reminded Meta that she had urged Naumann to publish Meta's "charming little book" on her brother—a phrase that made Meta wince—and had succeeded in obtaining the same royalties for it that she had received for her brother's biography. Was that not an act of friendship? To add substance to her words, she sent her friend, as a Christmas present, an inscribed copy of her brother's poems, a slender volume that she had hastily compiled for the Christmas market.

Meta thanked her for it but insisted that she could not accept any further presents:

> It is better we do not correspond anymore. There are again passages in your last letter that represent a complete reversal of the facts, and I would have to write many pages to correct them. I have neither the time nor the strength for that. Besides, it is unworthy that I defend myself against people toward whom I had the best intentions. I wish you had told me honestly last spring when I wrote and talked about a possible sale of the house after your poor brother's death that you really wanted it for yourself.

How deeply Meta had been hurt by Elisabeth's action can be seen from the letters she exchanged with Dr. Oehler. "Believe me," she warned him, "Elisabeth's position as the sister of her famous brother has gone to her head. Situations can arise when for his sake it is no longer possible to treat her with indulgence." Or again:

> I do not know, dear Sir, if you have any influence on your cousin. If you do, I must draw your attention to something I have repeatedly observed lately—newspaper articles about Nietzsche that begin to irritate all sensitive readers. There was one among others by a Mr. Böttcher, who describes rather crudely that he was allowed to observe the poor invalid first during his sleep, then awake, watching him crouched on a chair as he was being fed a piece of cake. I cannot repeat what people, who have read this article, say about Frau Doktor, but I cannot deny that it is incomprehensible to me that a man who was so sensitive when he was well, is sacrificed to the public now that he is a helpless invalid.

It is unlikely that Dr. Oehler passed on Meta's criticism. He knew that Elisabeth was immune to it. She insisted that nobody was as close to her brother as she and hence nobody else was in a position to judge what was good for him. "Meta has not the slightest idea of the intimacy of my relationship to my brother," Elisabeth boasted in a letter to Meta's friend Hedwig Kym. "It makes me smile, for I could easily show how deluded she is."

Elisabeth was disappointed that her friendship with Meta had come to such an abrupt end. She was fond of her, enjoyed her company, and liked to boast about her friend's aristocratic birth. But she had found other noble supporters and did not need Meta anymore. In her last letter to Meta, written in July 1898, she expressed both her disappointment and her victory: "I am really sorry that our friendship is over for good, for I have liked you very much, indeed I have loved you and I miss you more than ever now that I have triumphed over all men and manikins."

19·Staging Nietzsche's Funeral

*T*HE MOST IMPORTANT of Elisabeth's new friends was Count Harry Kessler, the son of a wealthy Hamburg banker, who had been ennobled by Emperor Wilhelm I. He had made his home in Paris, where Harry was born on May 23, 1868. His mother, who traced her descent from an old Irish family of landed gentry, was a famous beauty. A cosmopolitan by birth, Count Kessler received his elementary and secondary education partly in France and England and partly in Germany, where he attended the universities of Bonn and Leipzig. He had an inquisitive mind and was a keen observer of the contemporary political and cultural scene, which he depicted with literary skill in his diaries. He started keeping a diary when he was twelve years old, in the summer of 1880; his last entry is dated September 30, 1937, barely a month before his death.

Unsurpassed as a chronicler of his time, Kessler performed many important functions in the course of his rich and varied life. He was a discerning connoisseur of the arts, a patron and friend of painters and poets, a museum's director, an author, diplomat, and politician. Vladimir Nabokov calls him: "One of the few true grandseigneurs of our century, a complete and unique cosmopolitan, a European trained in the best humanistic German tradition."

When Elisabeth met him, Count Kessler was twenty-nine years old, unmarried, a tall, slim man with a well-groomed mustache and dark probing eyes. He was independently wealthy but, in contrast to most members of his class and upbringing, deeply affected by the revolutionary ideas of his time. He recognized that Darwin, Marx, Ibsen, Wagner, and Nietzsche, as well as many contemporary writers, predicted the end of an era, and he was not surprised when the First World War shattered the old order in Europe. But again, unlike most members of his class, he did not resent the drastic political and social changes brought about in the wake of the war; he embraced the new order, supported the Weimar Republic, became president of the German Peace Society, and established such cordial relations with left-wing politicians that his detractors called him the "Red Count."

Kessler came under the influence of Nietzsche, like many young intellectuals at the turn of the century, because he was fascinated by Nietzsche's provocative ideas and spellbound by his style. He was one of the first to respond to Koegel's appeal for a deposit of six thousand marks to establish the Nietzsche Archives. With her unerring instinct for the true believers in her brother's mission, Elisabeth cultivated the friendship of this young nobleman. A few weeks after she had moved into Villa Silberblick, she invited Kessler to spend the weekend with her. He accepted and noted in his diary:

> Weimar, August 7, 1897; 5:30 P.M. Nietzsche's manservant at the station . . . liveried, a five-pointed crown on his buttons. The house lies on a hill at the upper part of the town amid a newly planted but still rather bare garden. But the view over town and country is pretty. A spacious interior. On the ground floor archives and reception rooms, on the first floor the private apartments of Nietzsche and his sister, on the second floor my guest room. . . . Everything is solidly furnished but without regard to more refined tastes. It is the home of a well-to-do university professor or a civil servant.

> For several hours Frau Förster gave me a rather long-winded account of her feud with Koegel, Steiner, Hecker, and associates, without enlightening me very much. When she becomes excited, she speaks with a Saxon accent and sometimes she becomes lachrymose. How she says things is often awkward, but what she says is mostly good. For example, comparing Cosima Wagner with Madame de Staël and George Sand, she said she had always admired Cosima who had remained, emotionally, a woman, a loving submissive woman, while the other two great women of the century had really been men. About Nietzsche's present life she is more hopeful after their move to Weimar. He likes his new home. . . . When Frau Förster talks of her brother, it sounds as though he were a very small child, just beginning to talk. She seems to have become so used to considering her brother a babbling infant that she does not comprehend the terrible tragedy of it all. After dinner we talked about the new edition of *Zarathustra* and the poems. Frau Förster offered me Koegel's position as editor, but I declined.

The day following his intimate dinner with Elisabeth, Kessler took an early morning stroll through Weimar, passed the Goethe house, and noted the contrast between that house, where a genius had recovered his health, and the house on the hill, where a genius lay entombed in madness. Elisabeth insisted that before they have breakfast Kessler must visit her brother because he liked having visitors. But as they entered Nietzsche's room, they found that

> he was asleep on a sofa, his mighty head had sunk half-down to the right onto his chest, as if it were too heavy for his neck. His forehead was truly colossal; his manelike hair is still dark-brown just like his shaggy, protruding mustache. Blurred black-brown edges underneath his eyes are cut deeply into his cheeks. One can still see in the lifeless, flabby face some deep wrinkles dug in by thought and will but softened, as it were, and getting smoothed out. His expression shows an infinite weariness. His hands are waxen, with green and violet veins, and a little swollen as with a corpse. A table and a high-backed chair had been placed at the edge of the sofa to prevent the heavy body from slipping down with a clumsy movement. The sultry air of a thunderstorm had fatigued him, and although his sister stroked him several times and fondly called him "darling, darling," he would not wake up. He did not resemble a sick person or a lunatic, but rather a dead man.

Two months later Kessler again spent a weekend with Elisabeth. He went up to his room about ten o'clock after a pleasant dinner at which two young society ladies had been present. A quarter of an hour after he had turned out his light he was suddenly startled by the loud roar of the sick man on the floor beneath him. "I half got up and heard again once or twice the long coarse and moaning sounds which he uttered with full force into the night." The young nobleman shuddered and lay awake for hours wondering what nightmarish thoughts had caused Nietzsche's heartrending outcry.

Kessler was attracted to Villa Silberblick and its mistress because he venerated Nietzsche as the model of a "good European," the prophet of a Europe to come, a Europe without national borders or petty political and economic rivalries. And like most youthful admirers of Nietzsche, he transferred his admiration for his idol to Elisabeth. As Nietzsche's sister, she deserved respect. Kessler does not seem to have felt that there was something morbid about the proximity between the invalid upstairs and the social life, the receptions, teas, and dinner parties, given downstairs in his honor. If Kessler had any doubt about the propriety of Elisabeth's life-style, his diaries do not reflect it. He admired her courage, her fortitude in the face of adversity, and her untiring energy.

She told him that for her next project—after completing the edition of her brother's collected works, which was now planned in two separate formats, medium and crown octave with some fifteen volumes each—she would publish her brother's letters. They were human documents of great literary value. She had asked all her brother's friends and acquaintances who had corresponded with him to let her have his letters. Some had donated them to the Nietzsche Archives; others had demanded money for them. She had paid Malwida two thousand marks for her brother's letters, and his former publisher Schmeitzner almost three thousand. These expenses were a considerable drain on her resources, but she was determined to make the archives a comprehensive repository of all of her brother's writings. The only person who had refused to cooperate was Overbeck. His negative attitude toward her and the archives hurt her deeply.

Count Kessler promised to help her to the best of his ability in achieving her objective. He introduced her to a number of influential people, such as the Belgium architect Henry van de Velde, who was beginning to make a name for himself as the creator of a new art style, and the mistress of one of the most elegant literary salons in Berlin, Caroline Richter, the daughter of the composer Meyerbeer. Elisabeth was received in these circles with curiosity and awe. She was well known as the author of Nietzsche's biography and as a frequent contributor to literary journals. Always modishly dressed in long black silk or taffeta gowns, chic little black hats with veils, or large brimmed ones with feathers and plumes, she moved with ease among the literary and political elite of Berlin who attended the splendid dinner parties given by Caroline in her palatial home. Villa Silberblick was modest compared with palace Meyerbeer, but it could be made more impressive by suitable remodeling. Elisabeth decided she would talk to van de Velde about that.

At present, her most urgent need was to find an editor who could be relied on to finish what Koegel had started. There was no lack of applicants for the position. Many young scholars who wanted to make a name for themselves as Nietzsche editors were attracted to it. But Elisabeth hesitated because she secretly hoped that Koegel would come back. "Frau Förster still cannot calm down about Koegel," Kessler noted in his diary in October 1897, "I believe she would really like to have him back but cannot bring herself to ask him." It was not until the first of October 1898, more than a year after Koegel's departure, before Elisabeth appointed a new editor. She chose Dr. Arthur Seidl, a little-known writer on musical subjects and a contributor to anti-Semitic journals, upon whose loyalty she could count. As it turned out, Seidl stayed only a year and left when he found a more permanent position in Munich. His successors were the brothers Horneffer, Ernst and August, who faced the formidable task of deciphering the hieroglyphic aphorisms Nietzsche had jotted down in the fall of 1888. Since they were much less familiar with Nietzsche's handwriting than Koegel, who had wrestled in vain to make sense of many passages, it was a slow and tedious process—much too slow for Elisabeth, who wanted to see quick results in the form of publishable manuscripts. Gast had warned her, before she had dismissed him, that these "volcanic eruptions of genius" were thrust upon the paper with feverish up-and-down strokes of the pen and could not be deciphered by anyone except himself: "I am not saying this in vanity but rather in sadness that you will need me for their publication." As Elisabeth watched the two Horneffers wrestling with her brother's handwriting, she became more and more convinced that Gast had been right. It would take years before they produced any acceptable manuscripts. And time was of the essence. Her brother's readers clamored for more books, and each new volume added to the royalties she so badly needed for the upkeep of her large establishment.

Villa Silberblick was rapidly becoming a meeting place of Germany's most promising artists, writers, and poets. Even Carl-August, the ruling grand duke of Sachsen-Weimar, paid the sister of the mad philosopher an unexpected visit because, as he admitted grudgingly, "you cannot open a newspaper these days without seeing the name of Nietzsche." A pilgrimage to Weimar became de rigueur for many fervent German Nietzscheans, and an increasing number of foreign scholars walked up the hill to pay their respects to the sister of Zarathustra.

While the object of this idolization was totally unaware of it, Elisabeth basked in his glory and considered it her duty to represent him in a royal manner. This meant that she had to spend large amounts for entertainment, in addition to the considerable sums required to run her household and carry on the editorial work of the archives. There were times when she had a staff of ten people on her payroll: She employed a cook, a maid, a coachman, a private secretary, gardeners, and occasionally four editors. Her total expenses amounted to five or six times the annual salary of a university professor. Since royalties from her own and her brother's books were her sole source of income, she was constantly hard pressed for money. Hence her impatience with editors like the brothers Horneffer, who took more than a year to bring out two *Transvaluation* volumes. She remembered that Gast had told her five years ago that the material he was sorting out would certainly amount to from five to six volumes of four hundred pages each and that "all of it would correspond to the planned major work *Will to Power.*"

Elisabeth had never forgotten this sentence. It expressed all those aspects of her brother's philosophy that evoked a very positive response in her. She sensed that it reflected a rapidly growing mood in German society. For centuries Germany had been a sleeping giant, but now he had awakened and was stretching his muscles. It was Germany's turn to have a place in the sun, the Emperor declared. He would understand the *Will to Power.* He might even read the book. Her efforts to bring Nietzsche and Wilhelm II together had failed so far. But with the publication of *Will to Power* she might gain the ear and the patronage of the All Highest. The book had to be published now. Unfortunately, Gast seemed the only one who could decipher her brother's manuscript. She realized that she had made a mistake when she dismissed him five years ago. He had been right when he had told her: "Only somebody who is intimately familiar with Nietzsche's way of thinking and vocabulary can raise these treasures." To all others they remained hidden beneath a sea of scribbles. She had to find a way to entice Gast back to the archives; but would he come back after the humiliating manner in which she had dismissed him?

There was one ray of hope. Naumann had told her that Gast had liked the first volume of her brother's biography. To express her appreciation, she had sent him an inscribed copy of her brother's poems. Gast had accepted it

with—Elisabeth hoped—silent gratitude. She did not know he wrote Overbeck that he had almost laughed about Elisabeth's cordial handwritten inscription because

> this angelic lady is just now once again suing Naumann. She knows
> nothing better than to unsettle, torment, and torture people. I am glad I
> gave the Llama such short shrift when she returned from America. I felt at
> once that we would not get on together, despite my good nature. For
> Nietzsche's cause it was unfortunately a mistake that I became alienated,
> for I would have planted a different picture of him and his teachings into
> the hearts of people.

Such was Gast's opinion of Elisabeth when he received a formal invitation
to visit her in Weimar. She told him that she would like to discuss with him
the possibility of his becoming the editor of Nietzsche's musical compositions. Gast had to be in Weimar on other business, and since he was curious
to see his sick friend again and the new home of the archives, he accepted
Elisabeth's invitation. He was royally received at Silberblick and spent three
days talking with Elisabeth, who went out of her way to make him feel at
home, told him that she regretted the unfortunate differences of opinion that
had led to their estrangement, and expressed the hope that he would seriously consider her proposal. Charmed by Elisabeth's cordiality, Gast agreed to
enter her service once more. Since he knew that Overbeck would wonder
what had made him change his mind, he wrote rather cryptically that he could
not even begin to enumerate all the reasons for his decision.

Actually, the reasons for Gast's change of heart are simple enough. He
had for years tried to establish himself as a musician and he had failed. His
opera *The Lion of Venice,* which Nietzsche at one time hoped would rival
Wagner's operas, had been rejected by every conductor to whom he had submitted it. His numerous symphonies suffered the same fate. Try as hard as he
might, rejection slips were his only reward for his musical labors. But while
he failed to arouse attention as a musician, his friendship with Nietzsche became widely known. He received frequent requests from editors to con-
tribute articles on Nietzsche or write critical reviews of the flood of books on
his friend's philosophy that were running off the presses. And indeed, who
was better qualified to interpret the famous philosopher than Nietzsche's
most faithful disciple? Gast had been following Nietzsche's rising fame from
the obscurity of his Annaberg home for the last five years. They had been
years of disappointed hopes to him. He was forty-five years old, but he was
still dependent on his father for his livelihood. He had been in love with a
young woman for almost ten years and wanted to marry her. But as long as he
could not support himself, let alone a wife and family, marriage was out of
the question. Now Elisabeth offered him a well-paid position, a chance to
marry and to step out of the obscurity of his humdrum existence in Annaberg
into the limelight that surrounded his venerated teacher.

"As things stand now," Gast informed Overbeck on August 4, 1900, "I

shall stay in Weimar for the next few years. On September 3, I intend to marry Elise Wagner of Leipzig, who is twenty-six years old and has been my
sweetheart for the last ten years." He urged Overbeck to come through
Weimar on his annual visit to relatives in Dresden. Knowing Overbeck's
aversion to meeting Elisabeth, he assured him that there was no danger of
that at all because "Frau Förster does not go downtown anymore. She only
rides in her carriage accompanied by her coachman and a liveried servant.
She has become a real court lady and is in great demand in aristocratic circles
as a conversationalist."

The condescending tone in which Gast refers to Elisabeth is deceptive. He
was writing to Overbeck and did not want to give Overbeck the impression
that he was making common cause with Elisabeth, although this is precisely
what he was doing. He was impressed by the role she was playing in Weimar
society and moved by the way she treated her brother. Nietzsche had always
been to Gast the prophet of a new religion that was proclaimed in
Zarathustra, "a sacred book," Gast called it, "a modern bible." He was
pleased to notice that Elisabeth fostered this belief, for he found his sick
friend dressed in the long-flowing, white robe of a Brahmin, his "Christlike
hands" folded in his lap. Nietzsche gave no sign that he recognized his
former famulus and disciple, but Gast was sure he sensed his presence. He
spent a few minutes of quiet meditation in his sick friend's room and, when
he tiptoed out of it, was more convinced than ever that Nietzsche was a saint.

The occasion to proclaim Nietzsche's sainthood to the world came three
weeks after Gast had told Overbeck that he had moved to Weimar. On Saturday, August 25, 1900, a stroke snuffed out the flicker of life that for eleven
years had remained in Nietzsche's mindless body. Count Kessler was in his
Berlin club when his attention was drawn to a special bulletin of the Wolff
press agency, announcing Nietzsche's death. At home he found a telegram
from Elisabeth: "At noon today my ardently beloved brother passed away.
The funeral service will be on Monday afternoon at five o'clock in the
Nietzsche Archives. Please come on Monday morning if possible."

Kessler did not wait till Monday. He arrived in Weimar on Sunday afternoon and immediately went to see Elisabeth. He found her in deep mourning
but determined that nothing should go wrong with the funeral ceremony that
she and Gast had arranged. Her brother's body had been laid out on white
linen and damask in a heavy oak coffin in the archives room amid potted
palms and a forest of flowers. Kessler noted that Nietzsche's face seemed
woefully emaciated and small, like that of a child. His huge frost-gray
mustache hid the pained expression of his mouth. Elisabeth wanted a death
mask taken, but since there was no time to get a professional sculptor,
Kessler offered to do it with the aid of an apprentice plasterer. The result was
less than perfect. Elisabeth later complained that her brother's face had not
been as lopsided as it appeared in his death mask.

Concerning the ceremony itself, Elisabeth had invited the well-known
Berlin art historian Kurt Breysig to give the funeral oration and Ernst Hor-

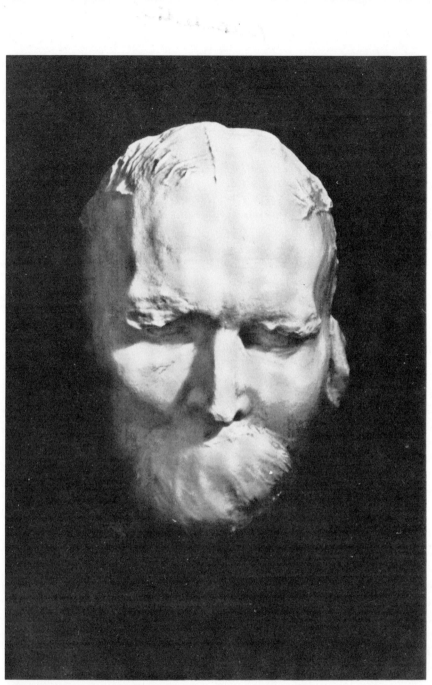

Nietzsche's death mask, August 1900.

neffer the valediction. For the opening of the ceremony, a female choir would sing a Brahms song and for the closing, a motet from Palestrina. There would only be a small group of invited mourners, close friends, and members of the family. A larger public could attend Nietzsche's burial, which was planned for the following Tuesday at his birthplace in Röcken. With Gast's help she had prepared press releases and drawn up a list of mourners. Overbeck had been invited by telegram to attend, but he did not do so despite Gast's urgent pleas.

The ceremony began punctually at five o'clock. Lighted candles surrounded the open coffin. The archives room was so crowded that

> one had to stand quite close to the coffin, almost touching the deceased. I felt awe and shame. For then the Berlin art historian Kurt Breysig leaning at the windowsill, began to deliver a lecture. The solemnity of the hour demanded but a few words spoken from the heart. Instead, the lecturer pulled a large manuscript out of his pocket and began to read it. Since he felt awkward at the windowsill a lectern was improvised with Frau Förster's sewing box. On and on, mercilessly, Breysig read a learned paper on the cultural significance of Nietzsche's work. I have seldom experienced grimmer moments. The same sterile scholasticism against which Nietzsche had fought all his life followed him into the grave. If he had arisen, he would have thrown the lecturer out of the window and chased the rest of us out of his temple.

It was not Kessler who wrote this account, but the architect Fritz Schumacher, a genuine admirer of Nietzsche, although not a member of the inner circle. Kessler merely noted that Breysig's oration had been far too long and uninspiring. What struck him more forcefully was the middle-class mentality of most of the mourners: "Stöving, Heinze, Gersdorff, Gast, etc. are all good but entirely mediocre people. There is not one outstanding character among them."

This impression was even more pronounced the following day, when the entire Nietzsche and Oehler clans assembled at Röcken for Nietzsche's burial. They were all solid citizens, pastors, lawyers, civil servants, with not one remarkable face among them. Elisabeth had given instructions that her brother be buried next to his father's grave at the edge of the churchyard near the parsonage, where he had been born fifty-six years ago, and that the ceremony follow the traditional Lutheran style. Thus the self-proclaimed Antichrist was put to rest amid the accompaniment of pealing church bells, hymns sung by the church choir, and solemn gestures of farewell offered by each of the mourners, who stepped to the edge of the grave and threw three handfuls of earth on the coffin, which was decorated with a shiny silver cross. As a sign of special reverence, some mourners recited passages from *Zarathustra.*

Gast stepped forward and gave the benediction. He praised Nietzsche as one of the gentlest beings that ever lived, the creator of new values, the har-

binger of glad tidings, and ended with the exhortation: "Hallowed be thy
name to all future generations."

In his last letter to Jakob Burckhardt, written just after his breakdown,
Nietzsche had said that he would far rather be a professor in Basel than God,
but that he could not permit his egoism to interfere with his duty to create the
world. And he had ended with the Italian phrase *son dio ho fatto questa
caricatura*—"I am God, I have made this caricature." While Nietzsche was
sane, he said that he was afraid he might be canonized someday, but the
moment the restraints of reason were gone he played the role of God. He
would have chuckled or, more likely, burst into Homeric laughter had he witnessed how well his loyal little Llama, aided and abetted by maestro Pietro
Gasti, had staged what he both feared and hoped.

PART V
1900-1935

20·The Missing Manuscript

*T*HE SOLEMN RITUAL at Nietzsche's graveside had an unexpected sequel. Upon Elisabeth's request, the village inn at Röcken had provided refreshments for the mourners and their retinue of footmen and coachmen. Many of the latter did not attend the funeral service; instead they made ample use of the free food and drink available at the inn. Elisabeth was horrified when she received a bill for four hundred fifty-six marks for refreshments consumed. She demanded an itemized statement. The innkeeper reported that he had served one hundred fourteen people and that each had consumed four marks' worth of food and drink. Both figures, Elisabeth declared indignantly, were totally fictitious. She refused payment and threatened to sue the innkeeper for overcharging her. After lengthy negotiations, which did not endear her to the villagers, a compromise was reached. The innkeeper settled for two hundred fifty marks but swore that he would never again provide refreshments for a Nietzsche funeral.

After her brother's death Elisabeth inherited his small fortune of thirty-six thousand marks and was able to pay back the thirty thousand marks she had borrowed from the Berlin banker Mendelssohn. Since she was also receiving substantial royalties from her brother's works and her own writing, her financial future seemed at last secure. But her life-style was not geared to modest living. "I may possess some virtues, but also one great vice: I need much money," she had told Gustav Naumann in a moment of candor. It was her ambition not only to move as an equal among the court circle of Weimar but to bring about a cultural renaissance in the Thuringian capital.

The times seemed propitious for this design, for a new ruler, Grand Duke

Wilhelm Ernst, had just ascended the throne of Sachsen-Weimar. He was a young man of unknown qualities who might be persuaded, if properly guided, to pursue the cultural traditions of his famous ancestors, Karl August and Karl Alexander. The former had transformed an insignificant provincial capital into the "Athens of Germany" by bringing Goethe to Weimar. Under Karl Alexander's liberal and benign rule, the arts, especially music, had flourished, with Franz Liszt as the most famous star.

Elisabeth dreamed of a "third era" of Weimar greatness, centered upon herself and the Nietzsche Archives. She had long envied Cosima Wagner's role in Bayreuth and was determined to make her home in Weimar an equally renowned meeting place of distinguished men and women. To make her dream come true, she needed the support of promising young artists. She had met a number of them, in Caroline Richter's elegant salon in Berlin, who paid homage to her as the sister of the philosopher they revered. One of them was the young Belgian architect and designer Henry van de Velde. Elisabeth invited him to visit her in Weimar and took him on a sentimental journey to her brother's grave in Röcken, an honor reserved for very special friends. Like most ambitious young men, van de Velde was captivated by Elisabeth's charm and was flattered when she suggested that the cultural climate of Weimar was a far more fertile soil for his genius than Berlin, where people were mainly interested in business and politics. Van de Velde assured her that he would gladly come to Weimar if he received an invitation from the grand duke.

Enlisting the support of Count Kessler, who was well acquainted with many important personages at the Weimar Court, Elisabeth began a very determined campaign among her own aristocratic friends to persuade Grand Duke Wilhelm Ernst that van de Velde's presence in Weimar would add luster to his reign. She gave teas and dinner parties for the grand duke's ministers and praised van de Velde as the recognized leader of a "new style" in the field of arts and crafts. His furniture, draperies, book covers, pottery, and metal work had been shown in widely acclaimed exhibitions in Berlin and Paris. His presence in Weimar would be not only a feather in the cap of the young grand duke, but also a boon to the struggling home industries of the duchy. Van de Velde would teach native craftsmen new designs, new methods of construction, and a more functional use of materials. She clinched her arguments by saying that she herself planned to employ van de Velde to remodel Villa Silberblick and make it a worthy home for her brother's books and manuscripts.

Although neither the grand duke, whose main interests were hunting and Prussian parade-ground drill, nor his ministers, who were fully occupied with court intrigues, had any understanding of van de Velde's artistic endeavors, they could not resist Elisabeth's ardent advocacy of the Belgian artist. After a series of high-level meetings the grand duke appointed van de Velde in December 1901 as his artistic consultant and the director of the Weimar Art School. A few months later he also invited Count Kessler to come to Weimar

*Count Harry Kessler, portrait by
Edvard Munch, 1906.*

and assume the directorship of the Weimar Art Museum. Elisabeth rejoiced. The presence of her two talented friends augured well for her own role in the cultural life of Weimar.

Van de Velde had no sooner arrived in the Thuringian capital than Elisabeth put him to work on preparing the architectural drawings of an extensive remodeling of her home. She demanded that the entire ground floor, which consisted of a number of small rooms, be converted into a spacious library and reception room, large enough to accommodate sixty people. The dining room, adjoining it, was to provide room for twenty guests. And van de Velde should personally design all the interior decors.

While this work, which took more than a year to complete, was going on, Elisabeth spent most of her time traveling. She had her brother's manuscripts moved into a rented apartment next door, and left Peter Gast in charge of editing Nietzsche's notebooks. In collaboration with the brothers Horneffer, Gast had just brought out *The Will to Power*, which, Elisabeth insisted, was her brother's major work. Although she had little to do with the laborious work of compiling the chaos of aphorisms her brother had jotted down during the last years of his life and which he had planned to publish either under the title *Transvaluation of All Values* or *The Will to Power*, she wrote a lengthy introduction. The purpose of her introduction was to declare that, unfortunately, her brother had not been able to complete *Will to Power* or rather that he may have completed the work but that the manuscript had disappeared at the time of his breakdown "when nobody of those who had been charged with taking care of the sick man's manuscripts had paid any attention to them." This was a thinly veiled accusation that through Overbeck's carelessness—for it was Overbeck who had rushed to Nietzsche's aid in Turin—a priceless manuscript had been lost.

After having installed the Nietzsche Archives in temporary quarters Elisabeth retired to Tautenburg to work on the third volume of her brother's biography. It dealt with the last and most productive period of Nietzsche's life but also the one with which Elisabeth was least familiar because she had been in Paraguay. With the help of Gast, who had been close to her brother then, she could reconstruct many events. But Overbeck, who had even been closer, refused to let her see her brother's letters. This infuriated Elisabeth. She suspected that her brother had said uncomplimentary things about her to Overbeck, for she had come across some drafts of letters in her brother's notebooks that were so compromising that she decided to suppress them. The trouble was that Koegel had copied them, and there were mysterious allusions in the press about "Koegel's secret excerpts," which supposedly showed what Nietzsche really had thought about his sister. To prevent their publication, Elisabeth took legal steps against Koegel and, after his untimely death in 1904, against his young children. She declared that any excerpts that Koegel had copied, while he was editing Nietzsche's notebooks, were her property and must be returned to her. She felt entirely justified in suppressing any passage in her brother's works or letters that, in her opinion, was in bad taste or reflected poorly on their relationship or on her interpretation of his philosophy.

While she was in Rapallo in search of material for the third volume of her brother's biography, she remembered that her brother had made a derogatory remark about the House of Hohenzollern. She wrote Gast, who was editing the notebook in question: "I cannot find a passage that we had better omit and which reads about as follows: 'What do I care whether Hohenzollern exist.' Let us leave it out." Elisabeth shuddered when she thought of a piece of paper on which her brother had scribbled in the large handwriting of his demented state that he had decided "to have the Emperor shot." She revered the Emperor and hoped to be presented to him someday. She was sure Wilhelm II would understand the concept of *Will to Power* and she said so in her biography.

Elisabeth returned to Weimar in the summer of 1903 and was pleased with the new look of Villa Silberblick. Its whole appearance had changed. Gone was the drab bourgeois face of the front entrance. It now featured a solid oak door with a heavy bronze door handle, specially designed by van de Velde to reflect the letter *N*. The visitor who was admitted through the massive door passed through a small vestibule into a large library and reception room that presented a dazzling array of colors and forms. Reddish yellow beechwood paneling gave the room a warm glow, in strong contrast to the bright whiteness of the ceiling. Built-in bookshelves and curvaceous couches in strawberry-colored upholstery combined simplicity with elegance. Grouped around a large bronze fireplace were specially designed, handcrafted chairs. A grand piano at the far end of the room directed the glance to the massive Nietzsche bust of white marble, made for the occasion by the sculptor Klinger and placed on a pedestal between the rear windows.

The total effect of the new Nietzsche Archives was stunning, but so was the cost. When all the bills were in, Elisabeth learned that the remodeling had cost fifty thousand marks, or ten thousand marks more than what she had paid for Villa Silberblick. Since she did not have anywhere near that amount, she was forced to take on a large mortgage and was burdened with very high-interest payments. Once again the financial condition of the Nietzsche Archives had become precarious.

However, Elisabeth was undaunted. As the representative of the greatest genius of modern times, she felt she was entitled to a dignified home, particularly since her poor brother had been forced to spend much of his life in very dreary quarters. When she needed money, she demanded advance royalties from her publisher or she borrowed from relatives and friends. Count Kessler gave her twelve thousand marks to pay for her brother's bust. In addition, she worked hard. She wrote articles, essays, reviews, and she finished the third volume of her brother's life. The book appeared in 1904 and sold well, although some critics pointed out that she had not treated some of her brother's friends fairly. Her account of Nietzsche's friendship with Lou Salomé was criticized widely. But since Lou, who had become a

Elisabeth Förster-Nietzsche, the mistress of the Nietzsche Archives, standing in the doorway of Villa Silberblick after its renovation by Henry van de Velde; ca. 1904.

writer and was much admired among the avant-garde in Berlin, did not deign to take public issue with Elisabeth, and since only a few insiders knew the true story of her encounter with Nietzsche, the general public was not influenced by these adverse criticisms. Elisabeth's three-volume *Life of Friedrich Nietzsche* attracted many readers to her brother's books and shaped the "seer-saint" image that henceforth enveloped the dead philosopher like a mythical shroud. Her account of her brother's illness—she says that his sudden collapse in Turin was the result of overdoses of chloride taken in despair because his countrymen had so cruelly neglected him—induced a sense of guilt in many Germans. They felt that Germany had once again betrayed a national hero who, like Siegfried, had fallen victim, stabbed in the back by an invisible foe.

Elisabeth was particularly determined to leave no doubt about the cause of her brother's illness, since it had become a topic of controversy after the appearance in 1902 of a detailed report on Nietzsche's medical history by Dr. P. J. Möbius, a respected Leipzig physician, who had received permission from Elisabeth herself to inspect the clinical records kept in Basel and Jena while her brother was institutionalized, and to subject them to a scientific analysis. She had supplied Möbius with much information about Nietzsche's background, stressing the physical and mental health of both branches of the family and insisting that there was no trace of any mental disease that her brother might have inherited. Their father, she insisted, had died of a brain tumor that had developed as the result of a fall. It was malicious gossip that he had suffered from fainting spells. Her brother had been a very healthy child, and, apart from being very nearsighted and occasionally suffering from migraine headaches, he had enjoyed excellent health all his life. He had ruined his health by overwork, which had caused insomnia and started a tragic train of events. For to combat his insomnia her brother had taken large doses of chloride as well as a mysterious brown liquid from Java that a Dutch captain had given him as a sleeping draft. She had often warned him against the use of these drugs and he had promised to be careful. But, alas, she had not been with him during the last critical years of his life when he was working at superhuman speed and needed love and companionship. Instead, he had met with derision and neglect. The combination of overwork, drugs, and despair had ruined this great mind.

Möbius listened to Elisabeth's explanations, but after a careful study of Nietzsche's medical history, he dismissed them. He found much evidence in Nietzsche's letters to his friends, in reminiscences of people who had known him, and in reports by doctors who had treated him that health had been Nietzsche's major problem most of his life. On more than one occasion Nietzsche had told his friends that he feared he was suffering from a brain disease. After consulting other physicians Möbius diagnosed Nietzsche's illness as "progressive paralysis" and hinted that it was caused by syphilis. The mere mention of the word *syphilis*, a disease that was unacceptable in any stratum of society and unmentionable among Elisabeth's genteel friends, made her see red. She declared that Möbius's "pamphlet"—that is how she referred to Möbius's study *Concerning the Pathologic Traits in Nietzsche*—was beneath contempt. What worried her most was Möbius's conclusion that the poison that caused Nietzsche's paralytic stroke in 1889 had been in his body for years and had affected all his writings from *Zarathustra* on. Möbius warned his countrymen that they should beware of Nietzsche, for his works were the products of a diseased brain.

Elisabeth countered these vile insinuations by enlisting the support of relatives and friends. Everybody agreed it was preposterous to suggest that Nietzsche had ever touched a prostitute from whom he might have contracted the disease. He was a man of great delicacy and chaste by nature. The numerous lewd passages in *Zarathustra* IV, to which Möbius had drawn attention, had no other significance than that Nietzsche was well aware of what went on between the sexes. Thus Möbius's warning fell on deaf ears, his report went unread, and Elisabeth's picture of her saintly brother prevailed.

However, there was one reader who had been closer to Nietzsche than anyone else during the years dealt with in Elisabeth's biography who registered a protest. "One often hears that the world wants to be deceived," Overbeck noted,

> and yet rarely has the reading public been so duped as in Förster's book. It reads sometimes as though Frau Förster wants to prove that she is far wiser than her brother. She is often praised now as a saint among sisters. But this will change. The time may come when she will be considered a prime example of the type: dangerous sisters.

Overbeck added that he was in possession of a comprehensive correspondence that someday would clarify what Nietzsche himself would say about the publicity-seeking activities of the Nietzsche Archives in Weimar.

These words started an increasingly bitter controversy, which was carried on in newspapers and literary journals for years and which pitted Overbeck's friends against Elisabeth and her supporters. Among the latter, Gast played the least enviable role. He had been Overbeck's friend and a bitter critic of Elisabeth until he had joined the archives' staff. Now he was forced to side with her against Overbeck. Upon her insistence, Gast wrote Overbeck that the story of Nietzsche's syphilitic infection, which Möbius had published after inspecting the medical records of the asylum for the insane in Jena, was based on a confidential remark Overbeck is said to have made to Professor Binswanger, the director of the institution, when he committed Nietzsche. Overbeck received Gast's letter in May 1905, about a month before his death and although he was extremely weak, he answered it at once. He denied ever having made such a remark. If it occurs in the official medical records kept in Jena by the psychiatrists in whose care Nietzsche had been, either they or Nietzsche himself were responsible for it. In a postscript, Overbeck added that Binswanger had told him in February 1890, after swearing him to secrecy, that there was no doubt in his mind about the syphilitic origin of Nietzsche's paralysis. "I have kept Binswanger's confidence, except in your case, Mr. Gast. Don't you remember a walk in the Grosse Garten in Dresden?''

Perhaps Gast remembered, perhaps he did not. In any case, whatever he told Elisabeth, his explanation did not satisfy her. She demanded a written declaration from Overbeck that he had not made the remark in question. When she heard that Overbeck was dying, she requested that Mrs. Overbeck have her husband sign a denial on his deathbed. She was furious when Mrs. Overbeck refused.

She was even more furious when the newspapers reported that in his will Overbeck had left his Nietzsche letters to the University of Basel with instructions that his friend, the writer C. A. Bernoulli, was to publish them. To prevent that, Elisabeth brought suit against Bernoulli and his publisher Eugen Diederichs, claiming that Nietzsche's letters to Overbeck were literary documents and were protected under the copyright laws. She owned the copyright to all her brother's works, including his personal letters. She requested that the court prohibit any publication without her consent during the thirty-year copyright period, that any letters already published be destroyed, and that the two defendants pay the costs of the suit.

Bernoulli and Diederichs countered that since Nietzsche's letters to Overbeck were private communications between friends, the copyright law did not apply and they were entitled to publish them. After lengthy deliberations the Weimar court rejected Elisabeth's suit and found her liable for the costs. Her appeal to a higher court in Jena was also rejected. But she obtained a temporary injunction against publication of her brother's letters until an appeal to the highest German court, the Reichsgericht in Leipzig, could be heard.

While Elisabeth was embroiled in this lengthy and costly legal dispute and had to employ five lawyers at times, she was sued for libel by Overbeck's widow because she had said in an article in the *Literarische Echo* that "through the negligence of the late Professor Franz Overbeck in Basel some manuscripts of my brother have been lost at the time of his illness in January 1889 in Turin as well as in Sils Maria." The basis for this accusation was a mysterious manuscript, said to be by Nietzsche and presumably the missing part of *Will to Power*, which in the late 1890s had been offered for sale at a considerable price to a number of people, including the wife of the poet Richard Dehmel. However, nobody had seen the manuscript or its present owner, although Elisabeth herself and Koegel, who was then still her close friend, had spared no efforts to find it. It had remained invisible. Elisabeth had finally concluded that she had been the victim of a hoax and that no such manuscript existed. During her meeting with Overbeck in Leipzig she had made no mention of it.

Her charge after Overbeck's death that through his negligence a valuable manuscript had been lost not only outraged Overbeck's widow, who demanded a public retraction, but angered his colleagues and friends. They considered it an unwarranted reflection on Overbeck's character both as a friend and a scholar. Even the brothers Horneffer, who had helped to compile *Will*

The Nietzsche Archives, Weimar.

to Power and knew that it was incomplete, resented Elisabeth's accusation. Ernst Horneffer wrote a long article in which he categorically rejected Elisabeth's charges. He stated that at the time when he was working on *Will to Power* and noticed serious gaps, he had asked Elisabeth if part of the manuscript might have been lost in Turin after Nietzsche's collapse. But "she had denied emphatically that anything could have been lost in Turin." Horneffer surmised that Elisabeth's change of mind was the result of her frustrated anger with Overbeck whose refusal to let her have his Nietzsche letters represented a potential threat to her position as the sole legitimate representative of Nietzsche's philosophy.

Elisabeth answered her critics by publishing a pamphlet entitled *The Nietzsche Archives: Its Friends and Its Foes*, in which she flails her male opponents mercilessly. They attacked her, a single unprotected woman, because they were jealous of her achievements. She had implored Overbeck and the University of Basel to take charge of her beloved brother's notebooks and manuscripts when she had returned from Paraguay, a widow in mourning. But Overbeck had turned her down scornfully; nor was Basel or any German university interested in Nietzsche at that time, although some foreign universities were. An American millionaire had offered her two hundred thousand dollars for her brother's literary estate, which he wanted to present as a gift to Harvard. She had rejected this lucrative offer because she thought Nietzsche's manuscripts should remain in Germany. In the face of obstacles that would have taxed the strength of any man, she had succeeded in building a worthy memorial for her beloved brother. She was determined to carry on her task as the keeper of the sacred flame undeterred by the spite of little men.

The net result of this prolonged and acrimonious public controversy was an increase in Nietzsche's fame and in Elisabeth's notoriety. She was clearly a woman to be reckoned with. On the occasion of her sixtieth birthday in 1906 hundreds of greetings by well-wishers, private and public, poured into the Nietzsche Archives, which was transformed into a veritable garden by the abundance of floral offerings. It made no difference at all that there were also some caustic comments, such as Alfred Kerr's poem in a Berlin paper. Elisabeth and her Weimar friends read it with amused delight:

The Superwoman

Nietzsche's sister's sixtieth
birthday party. Hold your breath.
Grand old lady's portrait tall
now adorns the archives' wall.

Downstairs in the dining room
gala Nietzsche dinner—cum
Friedrich near the chandelier:
Brother! if he could be here.

Compliments, magnificent
floral gifts. Telegrams,
toasts and speeches. Verbal fudge
Superwoman kaffeeklatsch.

21 · A Swedish Angel

I N FEBRUARY 1905 Elisabeth received a letter from an unknown Swedish Nietzsche enthusiast who told her how deeply her account of her brother's life had moved him. Nietzsche had been the lodestar of his life for years; he wanted to translate some of his works into Swedish and asked for Elisabeth's permission.

"I hear many pleasant things and get many compliments about the biography," Elisabeth replied, "but your words have made me particularly happy." When she wrote this sentence, Elisabeth knew nothing about her Swedish admirer except his name and address: Ernest Thiel, Blockhusudden, Stockholm. She did not know that Thiel was a very wealthy Swedish banker and industrialist who had been brought up in the strict faith of an Orthodox Jew. Thiel, in turn, did not know the anti-Semitic past of Nietzsche's sister. He revered Nietzsche as the model of a "good European" to whom he owed a great debt of gratitude because Nietzsche's writings had liberated him from the taboos of Swedish Victorian society.

By background and tradition, Thiel was a good European. His father Jacques, a French-speaking Catholic Walloon, born in Eupen in 1827, had moved to Stockholm in his late teens and become a control technician of the leading clothing factory in Sweden. His mother, Fanny Stiebel, was of German-Jewish descent. She was born in Bockenheim near Frankfurt in 1837 and had also moved to Stockholm, where she was employed as a maid in the family of a successful Jewish merchant. Jacques had met Fanny at a boat landing in Stockholm and was so struck by the beauty of *la belle juive* that he proposed marriage. Fanny was quite willing to marry her handsome Catholic suitor, but her parents, who were Orthodox Jews, refused their consent unless Jacques promised to have his children brought up in their mother's faith. Jacques was far too much in love with Fanny to be deterred by such a condition, but since marriages between Christians and Jews were prohibited by law in Sweden, the couple had to be married in a country where mixed marriages were legal. They traveled to Copenhagen and were married there in July 1858.

In August 1859 their son Ernest was born and a year later their second son and last child, Arthur. Both boys were registered in the Jewish congregation in Stockholm and attended the synagogue regularly. At home they spoke German with their mother and French with their father. During their first years in a public school their worst grades were in Swedish. So close were the ties of the Thiel family with the Jewish community in Stockholm that when Jacques died, he was buried in the Jewish—not the Catholic—cemetery of Stockholm.

Ernest Thiel was a brilliant young man, self-disciplined and determined to make his way in the world. His portrait, painted by Edvard Munch, shows his inner strength, both by his proud bearing and by the fearless glance of his dark, penetrating eyes. He decided to become a banker, joined the banking firm of Wallenberg, and had made a considerable fortune before he was thirty by successful operations in international banking. He owned his own bank in Stockholm and actively promoted the rapidly growing Swedish industries.

In the spring of 1884 he married Anna Josephson, the daughter of a prominent Jewish family in Stockholm. His reputation as a financial genius attracted the attention of the Swedish government, and he was under consideration for the post of Minister of Finance when an event occurred that shocked his family and friends, caused indignation among Swedish society, and changed the course of his life completely. While his wife, Anna, was pregnant with their fifth child, Thiel fell in love with his wife's companion, Signe Hansen, a beautiful, blonde widow, and decided, in the face of universal condemnation, to divorce his wife and marry Signe. What outraged the Victorian morality of Swedish society was not that Ernest Thiel fell in love with a young woman—he was a handsome and vital man and entitled to a discreet liaison since his wife was frequently pregnant—his crime was that he was not content with having a mistress but that he divorced his wife. That was unforgivable. To make matters worse, rumor had it that Ernest's brother, Arthur, had also been in love with Signe while she was his wife's companion and that Anna Thiel had taken Signe into her home to protect her sister-in-law's marriage.

Signe Hansen, née Peters, the not-so-innocent perpetrator of these upheavals, was the daughter of a German sea captain who had deserted his Swedish wife soon after the birth of their daughter, had gone to America, and was never heard of again. Signe's mother and her Swedish relatives took care of the child, who grew up to become a striking blonde, sensitive, moody, and much interested in the arts. When she was barely eighteen, she married a

Ernest Thiel, Elisabeth's Swedish angel, ca. 1908.

well-to-do merchant and devoted herself to the pursuit of beauty. She be-friended artists, painters, and poets, and inspired romantic dreams in the hearts of many a young man. But before she was twenty-five years old a dou-ble tragedy had shattered her happiness. Her husband suffered a serious reverse of his fortunes, went bankrupt, and died, leaving her destitute. And a few months later she mourned the death of her beloved infant son. Her mar-riage to Ernest Thiel introduced her into a world of opulence that she had not known before, and yet a shadow of melancholy remained with her all her life. It grew stronger during the years of her marriage and caused her tragic end.

In an autobiographical poem Thiel confessed that it was Nietzsche's chapter on child and marriage in *Zarathustra* that gave him the courage to brave the opprobrium and the social ostracism he knew he would meet with if he divorced his wife. Nietzsche had said: "That which the many-too-many call marriage, those superfluous ones—alas what shall I call it? Alas, the poverty of the soul in pair! Alas, the filth of the soul in pair! Alas, the pitiful complacency of the soul in pair!" As Thiel reflected on his own ten years of marriage, he felt it was the truth. He took Zarathustra's advice, broke a mar-riage that had been meaningless from the start, and married the woman he loved, whose ideals he shared. In 1900, when he was little more than forty years old, he gave up his position as director of his bank and proceeded to devote himself exclusively to cultural and philanthropic concerns. It was his ambition to assemble a representative collection of contemporary Swedish art and to house it in a gallery that combined the features of an early Swedish manor house with those of a modern art museum. With his young wife's en-thusiastic participation, Thiel supervised the design and construction of a palatial building, which was ready for occupancy by Christmas, 1905.

It was during these years that Thiel translated into Swedish Nietzsche's *On the Genealogy of Morals*, a pamphlet that asserts that there are two kinds of morality: the morality of the strong and the morality of the weak—a master and a slave morality. The actions of superior men—Nietzsche cites Napo-leon—cannot be judged by the moral yardstick of the many-too-many. Thiel embraced this concept because it reflected his own deep convictions. As a su-perior man, he was not subject to the moral code of Swedish society. Zarathustra preached that "superior men" were the goal of the earth and issued the stern command: Have the will to become superior men! It evoked a responsive echo in Thiel, whose life's passion had been to transcend the limitations of his origin and to surpass his contemporaries. He felt an im-mediate kinship with the author of *Zarathustra*.

In the spring of 1905, soon after his first letter to Elisabeth, Thiel made a pilgrimage to Weimar to pay his respects to the sister of his idol. Elisabeth received him with open arms. Her only regret was that because of the many social activities she was engaged in on that particular day she did not have much time for Thiel. She invited him to join in the festivities and presented him with the following program:

I invite you to come to the Nietzsche Archives at one o'clock and have breakfast with me and a small circle of friends. We shall only be six.

Count Harry Kessler invites you most cordially to attend a concert in his home at three thirty. Konrad Ansorge will be there with a local string orchestra.

At eight o'clock I hope you will dine with me and a fairly large company. You will meet Mr. & Mrs. Hugo von Hofmannsthal, Mr. & Mrs. Ludwig von Hoffman, Mr. van de Velde, Count Harry Kessler, Baron and Baroness von Nostiz-Wallwitz, Professor & Mrs. Roual Richter, Mr. Alfred Heymel and a few others.

Thiel was captivated by Elisabeth's charm and her social graces. During the dinner she put everyone in her large company at ease by skillfully directing the conversation to a great variety of topics. Besides art and politics, music and philosophy, she talked about child rearing, education, German colonies, and her experiences in Paraguay. Dressed in a long, black silk gown, her graying hair swept upward and held in place by a pert lace cap, she supervised her servants with the self-assurance of a born hostess.

Before Thiel left the mistress of the Nietzsche Archives he told her that having admired her brother for years, he now realized how fortunate Nietzsche had been in having a sister like her. Elisabeth returned the compliment by saying that it was a pity Thiel had not met her brother. She was sure they would have been friends. With such expressions of mutual admiration, a friendship started that endured for thirty years and survived such vicissitudes as the First World War, the rise and fall of the Weimar Republic, and the advent of Hitler. It ended only with Elisabeth's death in 1935.

The letters Thiel and Elisabeth exchanged in the course of their long friendship document their joint resolution to establish the Nietzsche Archives as a center for the promotion and dissemination of Nietzsche's ideas. Thiel supported this activity with substantial sums of money because he saw in Nietzsche's doctrine of excellence a salutary counterforce to the modern trend of mediocrity. Elisabeth accepted Thiel's generous gifts with expressions of profound gratitude, calling him her "good angel who had come just in time to save her and her brother's work from the envy of their enemies."

In the first letter Thiel received from Elisabeth after his return to Stockholm, she told him that the Norwegian painter Edvard Munch had recently also been in Weimar and had aroused much interest among artist and court circles. They would like to see him come back.

Van de Velde wants his portrait painted by Munch, but since one commission is not enough, it has occurred to me that you might like to commission Munch to paint a portrait of my brother and, if worst comes to worst, a portrait of me, too. I cannot imagine that any painter could paint a passable picture of me (I have no paintable face), but I would sacrifice myself to give our local artists the pleasure of seeing Munch again.

Elisabeth Förster-Nietzsche, portrait by Edvard Munch, 1906.
Copyright, Thielska Galleriet, Stockholm

After briefly touching on the current political differences that existed between Norway and Sweden, which she hoped would not affect artists—Munch being Norwegian and Thiel Swedish—she advised Thiel to get in touch with Munch as though the idea of having him paint portraits of Nietzsche and his sister had been his own "which in fact it has." This concluding sentence must have puzzled Thiel, for it had certainly not been his idea to commission Munch to paint Nietzsche and Elisabeth, but he did what she asked him to do. Both Elisabeth's request and Thiel's response are symptomatic of their relationship.

A few months later Elisabeth wrote Thiel that Munch was in Weimar and was making sketches in preparation for a portrait of her brother. "But dear Mr. Thiel, Munch insists that you have also commissioned him to paint my portrait. Surely, this must be an error. But Munch remains adamant despite my protests and has already made several sketches of me." She congratulated Thiel on his good fortune at having the means to support struggling artists. She wished she could do it, too. Alas, her modest means did not allow it. Having thus introduced the subject of her "modest means," which came as a surprise to Thiel, for her life-style in Weimar was anything but modest, she approached him a few months later with the urgent request for a loan of eleven thousand marks. She needed that sum to pay back a loan of sixteen thousand marks to her publisher. Naumann was making a fortune on Nietzsche, but he refused to extend credit to her. She had hoped to pay back the loan over a period of years from royalties due to her. However, Naumann would agree to that only if they renegotiated a publishing contract recently signed for the ten-volume paperback edition of her brother's works, which she had edited. Naumann had agreed to pay her royalties in the amount of ninety-six thousand marks. But he had second thoughts and wanted to change that sum. His demand for immediate repayment of an old loan of sixteen thousand marks was sheer harassment. He knew that she did not have that much money; all she could spare at the moment was five thousand marks. She urgently needed eleven thousand more, and since Thiel was the only wealthy man among the true friends of Nietzsche—all the others were scholars or artists without capital—she turned to him for help.

Thiel responded promptly by sending her a check for eleven thousand marks, which, he told her, was not a loan but a gift to the Nietzsche Archives. "Now everything is in good order," Elisabeth wrote jubilantly, "and with a bittersweet face Naumann will have to give up his plan of tying my hands." From then on she turned to her Swedish angel whenever she was in financial difficulties, and Thiel always came to her rescue. His initial gift of eleven thousand marks multiplied many times over the years and had reached the half million mark at the time of Elisabeth's death.

Elisabeth considered the fact that Thiel was Swedish a particularly fortunate omen, for it was her secret ambition to be awarded the Nobel prize. She hoped that Thiel's connections with the Swedish Academy could pave the way for that. Much to Thiel's surprise, he was approached in June 1907 by

Elisabeth's cousin, Dr. Richard Oehler, who informed him that a group of leading German university professors—he mentioned Hans Vaihinger, Alois Riehl, Richard Heinze—had proposed Elisabeth for the Nobel prize for literature in 1908.

But since Nietzsche is still a somewhat controversial figure, the three gentlemen fear that their nominee may be rejected and think it would be helpful if another party would intercede in this matter. I am, therefore, taking the liberty of asking you, most honored Mr. Thiel, if you could exert your personal influence in Stockholm in support of the Nobel prize for Frau Elisabeth Förster-Nietzsche.

Thiel replied that any intercession on his part would be useless, and, in fact, it would be resented by the Nobel committee. Instead he asked Oehler to enlighten him about the financial condition of the Nietzsche Archives. Oehler explained that although he was not familiar with all the details, he knew that Villa Silberblick was heavily mortgaged. Elisabeth had incurred these debts because she had to pay high salaries to the various editors of her brother's works and had spent considerable sums for the purchase of Nietzsche's letters. He knew she was worried about the future of the Nietzsche Archives. She hoped to leave it after her death either to the city of Weimar or to the University of Jena. But it was doubtful that any public institution would accept a heavily mortgaged property. Hence, a number of her friends and admirers of her brother were considering the establishment of an endowment with a board of directors as curators. Oehler doubted that this plan was practical because it would require a capital of from two to three hundred thousand marks. "To obtain this sum from private donors seems to me a very difficult undertaking. It is much more likely that the contents of the Nietzsche Archives will be sold to an American and thus lost to Europe forever." Oehler's reference to an "American buyer" of Nietzsche's literary estate is interesting. Elisabeth regularly mentioned this possibility when she was in financial difficulties.

Thiel pondered the endowment proposal for some time, talked it over with his wife, and informed Elisabeth early in September 1907 that he had willed the Nietzsche Archives a donation of three hundred thousand marks, payable after his or Elisabeth's death. The continued existence of her lifework was thus assured. Overwhelmed by Thiel's generosity, Elisabeth wrote her "dear and excellent friend" that her feet had trembled as she was reading his wonderful letter: "I sat down and wept and wept. The worry about the future of the archives has been taken from me and from the top of a mountain I am looking down upon a wide world of happiness."

A few days later, after she had recovered from her shock of happiness, she wrote Thiel a long letter of lament. She told him she was deeply worried that his generous donation after her death would come too late. She was hard pressed for money now. A group of envious men, bent on the destruction of the Nietzsche Archives, had joined forces and embroiled her in six lawsuits.

She already owed three thousand marks to her four lawyers, and God alone knew how much more she would have to pay before all the lawsuits were settled. Moreover, her house—the death house of her beloved brother—was so heavily mortgaged that she was afraid it would be foreclosed and sold after her death. One of the mortgages, a sum of nine thousand marks, was due next year. Could Thiel not assume the entire mortgage debt of sixty thousand marks, or could he lend her nine thousand marks now and put down another twenty-one thousand as a first installment on the endowment so that it could be established now? If that were done, she would not have to face these troubles unaided. "It is very hard for a defenseless woman if a group of envious enemies make common cause against her."

Thiel again responded favorably to her request. "I needed two days before I could recover from the emotion caused by your magnificent words and your magnanimous proposal. What a tragedy that my brother is not alive to appreciate your wonderful donation." When Thiel told her that his wife, Signe, was part-donor, she wrote a special letter of thanks to her "dear friend, her beloved Signe, embracing her with a grateful heart."

As a token of her gratitude she sent Thiel the original manuscript of her brother's *Twilight of the Idols*, a book that Thiel had translated, with the inscription "the best deserve the best." She also informed Thiel that her friends interpreted his donation as a reward for her "courage in meeting the enemy." Her enemies, who had wanted to ruin her, were now livid with rage. She had written a newspaper story and told the world that her creation, the Nietzsche Archives, was now safe from any attack and secure for all eternity.

Thiel's answers to Elisabeth's effusions were shorter but equally heartfelt. "But dearest friend," he wrote her, "you are thanking me far too much. I feel like hiding myself in a corner. I am ashamed, for after all, it is only money."

When Elisabeth suggested that he give her an annual pension of ten thousand marks, he raised the question: "Concerning the ten thousand marks I would like to know if I have to commit myself to pay them annually? It was my understanding that I had to provide only that amount which was lacking from the ten thousand marks in royalties as long as you were alive. Is that not so?"

It was so, but Elisabeth needed a guaranteed annual income and Thiel provided it. In April 1908, while Elisabeth was in the midst of her court battles and almost at the end of her rope, Thiel and his wife, Signe, visited her and signed the endowment documents, which also included an annual pension for Elisabeth. Like her husband, Signe was captivated by the warmth of Elisabeth's welcome. She was treated like a prodigal daughter who has returned home. Elisabeth called her *Herzenstöchterchen*, sweetheart little daughter of mine, and overwhelmed her with maternal love. Signe, who had never experienced anything like that in her life before, responded by addressing Elisabeth as "darling little grandma," kissed her dear hands, and assured her that she was thinking of her all the time. "I rejoice in the depth of my heart," Elisabeth wrote her, "when you tell me that your hearts belong to me. If one has two such friends, it matters not that the world is full of devils. We shall overcome."

A month later, on May 23, 1908, the minister of state of the grand duchy of Sachsen-Weimar approved the establishment of the Nietzsche Endowment as a nonprofit, scientific, and cultural institution. Its purpose was to maintain the Nietzsche Archives in perpetuity as a center for Nietzsche research and a collecting point for books, essays, and articles dealing with Nietzsche's philosophy. The endowment was governed by a seven-member board who would elect a president. As it turned out, Elisabeth's cousin Dr. Adalbert Oehler was the president of the Nietzsche Endowment for many years. Legally, the Nietzsche Endowment was a separate entity from the Nietzsche Archives, but in reality Elisabeth managed both. Oehler admitted that during Elisabeth's lifetime, no sharp demarcation could be drawn between the expenses and the income of the sister and the endowment. Either Thiel did not know or he did not care how his money was being spent. "That the endowment now has become a fact makes me and my wife extremely happy," he told Elisabeth. "I have the feeling that I have not lived in vain."

22·The Nietzsche Cult and the First World War

*H*URRAY, HURRAY—we have won a brilliant victory!" Elisabeth jubi-lantly wrote Gast when a Jena court ruled in 1908 that quotations from personal letters could not be published without the permission of the letter writer. The letters in question had been written by Gast to Overbeck and were to be published in a long and scholarly study of Overbeck's friendship with Nietzsche by Bernoulli. As a result of this verdict the second volume of *Franz Overbeck and Friedrich Nietzsche: A Friendship* appeared with blank spaces in place of the prohibited quotations.

Elisabeth's jubilation is understandable. The Jena court's decision could affect her own still-pending suit concerning the publication rights to her brother's letters, although in her case the letter writer was dead, while Gast protested that publishing excerpts from his private letters during his lifetime would cause him embarrassment. He had brought suit against Bernoulli and Bernoulli's publisher, Diederichs, on Elisabeth's insistence, but also because he feared the compromising nature of some statements he had made about Elisabeth in his letters to Overbeck. Since he was now her collaborator, it would be embarrassing if she discovered what he thought—or had thought—of her.

When he had entered her service again in 1900, he had not planned to stay more than a year or two, but he had found his work interesting and life in Weimar pleasant. He was happily married, had a young daughter, and had the chance to meet many illustrious men and women. And yet he had never felt entirely at ease with Elisabeth. She was a hard taskmaster, always urging him to work faster than he liked. And she demanded absolute loyalty from her employees in her numerous legal battles with publishers and her "Basel enemies." Gast was by nature easygoing and conciliatory. Elisabeth's pugnaciousness and her sharp tongue and pen irritated him. He had stayed with her eight years chiefly because she offered him a steady income and because he felt obligated to assist with the publication of his friend's posthumous works. As long as he was in charge of deciphering and editing Nietzsche's notebooks, he could correct some of the errors of former editors.

Gast's faith in Nietzsche was badly shaken when he discovered by accident that Nietzsche—his revered friend and teacher—had contemptuously referred to him in letters to Elisabeth as "a bore, a clumsy clod, lacking in learning and tact," whose vulgar habits he detested. Gast had come across these unkind words in a brief prepared by Mrs. Overbeck's lawyer in her libel suit against Elisabeth. According to the lawyer, Elisabeth had told Overbeck in a letter in 1894, when she was about to dismiss Gast as editor of her brother's works, that Nietzsche had made these derogatory remarks about Gast in letters to her. Since Elisabeth had no scruples about "editing" her brother's letters whenever it suited her, as Gast knew very well, it is of course possible that Nietzsche never spoke about his "maestro Pietro Gasti" in such unflattering terms. On the other hand, Nietzsche was not above using sarcastic, indeed offensive, language about his friends when he was irritated. This trait he shared with his sister.

Deeply hurt by what he felt was Nietzsche's disloyalty, Gast wrote Elisabeth: "I had no idea what Nietzsche thought of me, otherwise I would have withdrawn from him at once instead of sacrificing to him more time and effort than to anyone else in my life." He left Weimar in 1909, taking with him his letters to Nietzsche. Elisabeth was not unhappy that he left. He had finished his work, and she wanted to offer his position to her favorite cousin, Max Oehler. But she was furious when she learned that Gast had taken his letters to Nietzsche. She insisted that when she paid him for her brother's letters to him, it was understood that his letters to Nietzsche would remain in the archives. She demanded the letters back and threatened to sue him if he refused. But Gast refused to be intimidated. As long as he was alive, the verdict of the Jena court protected his right to his letters. Elisabeth felt outmaneuvered and complained to her cousin, Dr. Adalbert Oehler, the head of the Nietzsche Endowment, that "the most unpleasant aspect of this whole affair is how Gast now talks about Nietzsche. After all, the only great event in his life was that he has known Nietzsche and could be of service to him."

Gast's departure and Overbeck's death strengthened Elisabeth's position as her brother's sole legitimate representative. Once again she had triumphed over her male adversaries. Since she was no longer entirely dependent on income from royalties, she could concentrate on her self-appointed task of promoting the "Nietzsche movement," as she began to refer to it, among a steadily growing number of devotees in Germany and in other parts of the world. Every Saturday afternoon she held an open house and gave audiences to visiting Nietzscheans. She received Persian grandees, who expressed gratitude that Nietzsche had chosen a Persian sage to be the prophet of a new and superior race of men; French and Italian intellectuals who praised her brother's advocacy of the "good European"; American professors and Japanese scholars, Indian students, and Germans from all walks of life. Every German writer of note made a pilgrimage to Zarathustra's sister. The guest book of Villa Silberblick contained such names as Stefan George, Hugo von Hofmannsthal, Richard Dehmel, Detlev von Liliencron, Paul Ernst, Ernst Hart, Gerhart Hauptmann, Graf Hermann Keyserling, Thomas Mann, Oswald Spengler, to mention only a few. In the first decade of the twentieth century Nietzsche's gospel attracted a larger following and more attention than any other cultural movement. Even English Fabians, like Bernard Shaw, saw no contradiction between Nietzsche's concept of a master race and their vision of a socialist utopia. With the publication in 1908 of a limited, deluxe edition of *Ecce Homo*, designed by van de Velde and so expensive that only wealthy connoisseurs could afford it, Nietzsche's disciples learned from their master's own mouth that he was not a man but dynamite, that a new chapter had begun in the history of mankind that would bring "wars, the like of which had never before been seen on earth."

Instead of being alarmed by such dire prophecies, young and old Nietzscheans rejoiced. The time was ripe for a reordering of society. A new race of rulers was needed to stop the decline of the West caused by the stalemated struggle for power between the vulgar rich and the vulgar poor.

To provide a shrine where Nietzsche's disciples could worship their messiah, Count Kessler proposed the building of a Nietzsche memorial temple on a hillside overlooking Weimar. He envisaged a monument designed by van de Velde in the style of a classical vault with statues of Apollo and Dionysos, which the French sculptor Aristide Maillol was commissioned to carve. An international committee was to supervise the construction of this edifice and raise the necessary funds. But no sooner had this plan been accepted by all concerned—Elisabeth agreed to it reluctantly because she felt that the money spent on a temple could be put to far better use at the Nietzsche Archives—when Count Kessler's fertile imagination decided that it needed enlarging. A Nietzsche temple was not enough. What was needed was a stadium where the youth of Europe could compete in athletic events in the spirit of ancient Greece. Nietzsche was more than a thinker who deserved a place for meditation, he was an activist; his call to arms was a challenge meant to spur the young on to intellectual and physical contests.

Kessler was under no illusion that it would cost millions to realize this ambitious project. But he was so deeply convinced that a temple alone would not do justice to Nietzsche's philosophy that he went ahead with his plan even when Elisabeth opposed it. Elisabeth's opposition was aroused by a group of German patriots who resented the cosmopolitan concept of Kessler and his international committee and pointed out that Nietzsche would be appalled to have a stadium built in his name. They showed Elisabeth a letter in which her brother speaks with utmost contempt of "the idle rich mob of

Europe who ape Greek customs without having the slightest understanding of how deep the religious and political roots were that gave birth to Greek festivals.''

Undeterred by Elisabeth's opposition, Kessler promoted his project among his influential friends in France, Italy, and England. He gained the support of André Gide, Anatole France, Gabriele D'Annunzio, Gilbert Murray, and H. G. Wells. But opposition to Kessler's "ambitious scheme,'' as it was called in the German press, grew among the populace. The good people of Weimar feared that their peaceful town would be invaded by hordes of foreign athletes and demanded that the city fathers take action against such a calamity. Nor could Kessler hope to get support from the Grand Duke. Wilhelm Ernst was no friend of his. He had humiliated Kessler in front of his whole court and forced him to resign his position as director of the Weimar Museum. In the face of this formidable opposition Kessler called a meeting of the International Nietzsche Memorial Committee on June 9, 1912, and received a vote of confidence. It was decided that the Nietzsche temple and stadium be built in Weimar as planned and that the German chancellor, Prince Bernhard von Bülow, be invited to assume the honorary presidency of the project. A subscription list, limited to three hundred names, was drawn up and the fund raising begun.

Soon rumor had it that Kessler had collected millions for his project. It caused Elisabeth and the Grand Duke to reconsider their objections and to join the ranks of those who hoped to profit from Kessler's golden bounty. Elisabeth insisted that she had never been really opposed to Kessler's plan; however, he should remember that the Nietzsche Archives also needed financial support. She hoped that any funds not needed would be transferred to the Nietzsche Endowment. The Grand Duke approached van de Velde and indicated that he had no objections to Kessler's millions coming to Weimar, "but was it really necessary that the money be so obviously linked with the name of Nietzsche?''

Agreement was finally reached that to mark the occasion of the seventieth anniversary of Nietzsche's birth, October 15, 1914, the cornerstone would be laid for the Nietzsche memorial temple and stadium in the presence of an invited international elite of Nietzscheans at solemn ceremonies in Weimar. Dr. Oscar Levy, the editor-in-chief of Nietzsche's works in England, announced in May 1914 that

> a considerable fund has already been collected for that purpose and that any surplus that may accrue will be used for the support of the Nietzsche Archives, which under the guidance of Nietzsche's sister has done and is doing so much good work for the study of Nietzsche. It is likewise proposed that the latter institution shall be constituted an intellectual center for securing that cultural unity of Europe which must precede its political and commercial union.

Nine weeks after that announcement, the first of the great wars that Nietzsche had prophesied had broken out and the good Europeans who had planned to worship in Weimar in his name were at one another's throats.

In the years leading up to this climactic event, Elisabeth was hard at work writing a new and shorter version of her brother's life. There was a great demand for a popular account of Nietzsche's personal history, and who was better equipped to tell it than she? Although her active social life did not leave her much time for writing, she finished the first volume of her new biography—*The Young Nietzsche*—by the end of 1911. It was to appear simultaneously in Germany, France, and England. She was confident it would sell well because "it reads like a novel, although every word is literally true." And she was right in her expectations. "You have once again wrought a miracle," her Swedish friend wrote her. "I shall use your little book as a manual for the education of my young son."

Elisabeth was elated. Thiel and his wife, Signe, were her most valuable allies in her continuing struggle to secure the survival of her lifework. In her letters to them she constantly lamented the still-precarious financial condition of the Nietzsche Archives. Her new publisher, Alfred Kröner, was just as stingy and unreliable as Naumann had been about royalty payments. And Insel, who had published *Ecce Homo*, insisted that she pay back at once a thirty-thousand-mark mortgage loan on Villa Silberblick, which she wanted to amortize over a period of years. Cautiously, she inquired whether Thiel could assume that mortgage in addition to his other bequests. To show her gratitude for Thiel's unstinting generosity, she sent her "loyal and beloved friends" numerous gifts. When they announced the birth of their son, Tage, she insisted on becoming his godmother and sent a jewelry box containing her brother's serpent ring and a few strands of his hair. To her "beloved darling daughter Signe" she sent a piece of Paraguayan lace, telling her at the same time that she would be overjoyed if Signe would translate her book into Swedish because "the account of my brother's noble life would counteract the many prejudices against him and his philosophy that still exist in Sweden. I wish the gentlemen of the academy could read it in their own language."

Although expressed in veiled language, this was an important request, for Elisabeth had just again been nominated for the Nobel prize by a group of distinguished German professors. Again Elisabeth protested that the nomination had not been her idea and that she would not pursue it if Thiel felt she had no chance of getting the award. It would, of course, be an honor to receive the Nobel prize, and the money would greatly enrich the Nietzsche Archives. But she was not counting on it. She had overcome the worst difficulties with Thiel's support. All she would like to find now was a trustworthy archivist. She had asked her beloved cousin Max Oehler, but he was an officer and had chosen a military career.

Thiel did not discourage her from trying for the Nobel prize, although he repeated that he could not exert any influence on the academy. Her work must be her witness. And Thiel loved her book:

> It is so simple, so natural and bright as sunlight. I have lived through every day of your brother's life. . . . This man, whom I have never known,

is closer to my heart, my instinct, than any living person. For the last six-teen years I have not been able to read any books other than his—and now yours: you are as one in my heart. I kiss your blessed little hands.

In October 1913, when the Thiels had another child, a daughter, they christened her Inge Maria Elisabeth. They made plans to visit Weimar in the summer of 1914 and show "grandma Elisabeth" her new and very own grandchild. But peaceful travel was the first victim of the war that engulfed all Europe that summer. To be sure, Sweden was neutral, but many Swedes were not neutral in their hearts. The Thiels did not hide their strongly pro-German sentiments. As for Elisabeth, her old patriotic heart rejoiced at the spectacle of her people in arms. "If my brother were alive today," she wrote Thiel, "he would go to war at once despite his seventy years." Germany's mobilization was a work of art. "Our troops are rolling over France and Belgium like a tidal wave. This war shows the force of my brother's words— 'become hard.' " The secret source of Germany's strength was Nietzsche's doctrine: Will to Power. Thiel, who had read Nietzsche's caustic remarks about the Germans, replied, "I often reflect what your brother would have said if he had been privileged to live in this glorious time. I am sure he would have corrected some of his views about Germany and her heroic sons."

Like most of her countrymen, Elisabeth confidently expected that Ger-many's "invincible armies" would crush their enemies in a few weeks. When they failed, she informed Thiel that the euphoria of the first weeks had given way to grim determination. "Our troops will not surrender one piece of the conquered territories." The British would get the shock of their lives when they discovered that Germany had become hard, and was no longer a land of poets and dreamers but a people in arms, a land of warriors.

To show that she too had become hard, Elisabeth dismissed her extrav-agant cook and hired a young peasant girl whom she taught to prepare simple meals. This meant more work for her and delayed the completion of a new book that she had started, dealing with Nietzsche and Wagner at the time of their friendship. She loved writing it because it brought back many pleasant memories of her own visits to Triebschen and Bayreuth. Wagner's letters to her brother were so cordial, it was a joy to read them. That Cosima had burned the more than hundred letters her brother had written to Wagner was a crime, for "these letters were cultural documents of the first order."

In the fall of 1915 it had become evident that there would be no early vic-tory. The rapid German advance in the West had been halted, a costly and embittered trench warfare begun, and the British blockade brought about the first food shortages in Germany. At this melancholic time Elisabeth received the incredible, the dreadful, news of the death of her beloved, "adopted daughter" Signe Thiel. For undisclosed reasons Signe had put an end to her life by taking an overdose of opium. Bitterly lamenting this "incomprehensi-ble deed," Elisabeth begged Thiel for an explanation of this tragedy. At the same time she assured him that she would understand if he did not want to write about it. And Thiel never did. Instead, he began to pay off the donation of three hundred thousand marks, which he had promised the Nietzsche Endowment after his death, in varying installments all through the war.

In 1917 he informed Elisabeth that he had instructed his second eldest son to deposit for the Endowment a series of Japanese bonds he had bought in 1905 that had just matured. They would yield one hundred twenty-five thousand marks. Elisabeth was stunned by this unexpected gift and called Thiel "the pillar of the Nietzsche Archives in these difficult times." She told him she was investing some of his money in German war bonds, an action that Thiel applauded. In January 1918 Thiel sent her sixty thousand marks as a New Year's present, saying that he was particularly happy because he had received that sum from an English firm. Hence "these sixty thousand marks represent the first payment of war reparations from England to Germany."

Both Thiel and Elisabeth believed in a German victory to the end. When the news reached Weimar that in some English publications, her brother—called "the mad German philosopher"—was held responsible for the war, Elisabeth became indignant. Only imbeciles or Englishmen could mistake her brother's "Will to Power" for "Will to Violence." It was quite true that the German people had faith in strong leaders and had not been poisoned by the pernicious doctrine that all men are equal. It was also true that eleven thousand copies of *Zarathustra* had been sold in less than six weeks, but that did not mean that her brother or Zarathustra's disciples were war criminals. The real culprits were French and British politicians who had plunged the world into war because they were envious of Germany's rise to power. They were responsible for the terrible suffering that the war had inflicted on the world.

Large segments of the German people shared these views and celebrated Zarathustra's sister "almost to death" on her seventieth birthday. More than five hundred greetings and telegrams and hundreds of floral gifts poured into the Nietzsche Archives. Elisabeth marked the occasion by being hostess to a group of wounded war veterans. "We are living in terrible times," she wrote Thiel, "but even after a thousand years people will sing the heroic song of Germany's victory over a world of enemies." She started to compile a booklet of Nietzsche sayings about war and victory. What worried her was the rise of social democracy. She could not understand why any German would support a party that advocated mob rule. Did not Germany's victories prove that "a people attains the greatest power within the framework of a firm monarchical order"? Her brother had been right when he declared that democracy was a sign of decadence, a product of slave mentality.

As the war dragged on and the majority parties of the German Reichstag presented a peace resolution, Elisabeth became alarmed and assured Thiel that the majority of the German people did not share these peace sentiments. They wanted victory. The British would have a rude awakening if they thought they could starve Germany into surrender. German U-boats would teach them a lesson. Thank God Sweden kept out of the war, despite the machinations of perfidious Albion. The will of the German people to bring the war to a successful conclusion had been strengthened by the founding of a new political party—the *deutsche Vaterlandspartei*—to which she and all of her friends belonged.

The Russian revolution confirmed Elisabeth's conviction that a weak government meant disaster. If the Czar had been a resolute leader, he would have nipped the revolt in the bud. For Germany, Russia's collapse proved a godsend because there would soon be a surplus of food from the Ukraine. Not that Elisabeth herself had suffered any serious food shortages. Remembering her peasant life in Paraguay, she had started growing her own vegetables, and she kept chickens and even had a pig. And she was better off financially than ever before. More and more people were buying her brother's books. More than forty thousand copies of *Zarathustra* were sold in 1917, and there was no reason to doubt that the Nietzsche movement would continue to grow. What troubled her was the more distant future. The copyright law protected Nietzsche's works until 1930. After that she could not count on any royalty income from her brother's books. If she were alive, she would be over eighty years old by that time, and it was possible that she would be without sufficient means of support. The income from the Nietzsche Endowment covered little more than half of her expenses. Hence she proposed the establishment of a special "old age fund" for herself. In January 1918 her cousin, Dr. Adalbert Oehler, the president of the Nietzsche Endowment, informed Thiel that such a fund had been started and invested in German war bonds—"the safest investment in the world today." Thiel responded by sending a check for two thousand marks. Elisabeth acknowledged it, "deeply moved," and told her friend that she was preparing a deluxe edition of Nietzsche's works because she was confident that the war would soon be over. "Our enemies must recognize that they cannot defeat us."

But she was mistaken. The war dragged on all through the spring and summer of 1918. In September, Elisabeth admitted that Germany's situation had worsened.

> Our victorious troops, used to advancing, find it difficult to make strategic withdrawals. However, our triumphant enemies should not forget that these battles are fought on French soil, far from the German borders. We firmly believe in our final victory, and if our enemies demand that we surrender the conquered territories of France and Belgium, we just laugh and shout: "come and get them."

Two months later, Germany, engulfed in revolution, had to sue for peace. In a mood of utter despair, Elisabeth, quoting from one of her brother's poems, wrote Thiel:

> "This is the fall and it will break my heart." That the German people themselves are destroying their magnificent fatherland is the most terrible tragedy. I cannot bear it. Our armies at the front were undefeated but our stupid home guards, fools and children, have stabbed our brave soldiers in the back. The social democratic parties are behaving disgracefully and are throwing dirt on our best and greatest leaders. Germany offers a dreadful spectacle. Every day I wish I would die.

23·The Fight against the Weimar Republic

*E*LISABETH'S DEATH WISH at the sight of her beloved fatherland convulsed in a revolution that forced the Emperor to abdicate and toppled all thrones, including that of Sachsen-Weimar's unpopular ruler, Grand Duke Wilhelm Ernst, soon gave way to her strong will to live. With horrified fascination she watched the birth of a new political and social order against which all her beliefs, convictions, and instincts rebelled. Nobody could convince her that a people could govern themselves. Government of the people by the people was pernicious nonsense. Without leaders peoples were lost, and it was absurd to think that out of a squabbling mob of politicians a leader could arise. She had a chance to observe that first hand in Weimar, which had been chosen as the meeting place of the German National Assembly because Berlin was threatened by Spartacist uprisings and was not considered a suitable location for an assembly called into session to write a constitution for the newly proclaimed German Republic.

From a reserved seat in the visitor's gallery, Elisabeth watched some of the sessions and was appalled by the sight of the fanatic expressions on the faces of some members of the assembly. They seemed determined to tear down the very fabric of Germany's traditional order and to replace it with a Socialist utopia. She shuddered as she listened to their revolutionary oratory, and was afraid that she might be personally attacked someday because it was no secret that the Nietzsche Archives was the center of a powerful counter-revolutionary current. Nor was it a secret that her brother's influence was growing by leaps and bounds. "Last autumn, when the revolution broke out—I call it the revolt of the masses—twenty-five thousand copies of the cheap edition of *Zarathustra* were sold in four weeks.''

In her fight against the Weimar Republic, Elisabeth was not alone. The Nietzsche movement began to attract German patriots from all segments of society. To stimulate it, the wealthy Hamburg merchant Consul Christian Lassen donated in 1919 a five-thousand-mark prize for the best book written in Nietzsche's spirit. The recipient of the ''Nietzsche prize'' was Thomas Mann for his just-published *Reflections of a Nonpolitical Man*, a scathing attack on the Western democracies. Elisabeth congratulated Mann on his timely warning against the vulgar trends of the times. She hoped that his book would attract many readers to her brother's writings. Mann accepted the prize with an expression of gratitude and pride, assuring Elisabeth that her kind words of praise ''had moved him more than he could say.''

During the uneasy spring of 1919, when many parts of Germany were being terrorized by Spartacist uprisings, the Nietzsche Archives became a besieged fortress. Elisabeth's cousin, Dr. Adalbert Oehler, the mayor of Düsseldorf, who had been arrested by the Spartacists and driven from office, sought refuge there, as did her two second cousins, Major Max Oehler, a professional soldier now unemployed, and Richard Oehler, the librarian. The whole of Weimar was a besieged city in those months, for to protect the National Assembly a ring of government troops had been thrown around it. Unhappily, these soldiers, mostly young men, consumed a great deal of food and caused resentment among the populace because they compounded the serious food shortage that plagued Germany after the cessation of hostilities. The ghost of famine that had threatened Germany during the war began to stalk her streets in earnest now. ''Germany is paralyzed,'' Elisabeth wrote Thiel, ''because people are undernourished and because fanatical agitators are spreading the Russian poison . . . shall we ever rise again from the dust? I am very depressed.''

While Elisabeth was harboring such melancholic thoughts, the terms of the peace treaty, which the Allies had drawn up in Versailles without consulting the German delegation, were being discussed in the National Assembly. They were harsh and vindictive. Elisabeth was outraged when she heard them, and echoing the feelings of many of her countrymen, demanded that they be rejected. To make sure that her point of view would be heard, she invited the leading members of the assembly to a ''diplomatic tea'' at the Nietzsche Archives. It turned out better than she had expected. Even the Social Democrats were against the treaty and assured her that they would never accept a ''dictated peace.''

It soon became evident, however, that they had no choice but to accept it. When they did so, albeit under protest, Elisabeth felt personally insulted. The *Versailles Diktat* was the second nail in the coffin of the Weimar Republic. The ''stab in the back'' of Germany's victorious armies by a mob of traitors at home had been the first. ''The sight of such miserable creatures as

Erzberger, who is now playing a big part, makes me sick," Elisabeth wrote Thiel; "his rise to power is a national tragedy." While Matthias Erzberger and his party were betraying Germany to her enemies, the country was rapidly sinking into an economic morass. Prices were rising sharply. A pound of tea, which had cost ten marks in 1918, was costing seventy-five marks a year later, and sugar was unobtainable. Books, too, had become very expensive, and yet there had never been as great a demand for Nietzsche's works as during and after the war. Between 1914 and 1919 more than one hundred sixty-five thousand copies of *Zarathustra* were sold, compared with one hundred thousand in the preceding twenty-two years. If these figures meant anything, the time would come when a new generation of Germans would rise up in Nietzsche's name against the decadent spirit of their present leaders.

Elisabeth's main consolation during the difficult postwar years was her Swedish friend's constant and generous support. "How shall I find words to thank you?" she wrote Thiel in December 1919 when she received, quite unexpectedly, a check for one hundred thousand marks as a Christmas present. And Dr. Oehler added, "Seldom have glad tidings come at a time of such dire need. We were both overwhelmed. It was a miraculous ray of light in these dark hours."

Like all her conservative friends, Elisabeth was terrified by the rise of the "red menace" in the towns and villages of Thuringia. "Our workers are bloodthirsty and can barely be held in check by our few troops." She was convinced that the Allies had made a terrible mistake in not allowing Germany sufficient soldiers to put down the revolution because it was bound to spread beyond Germany's borders. At that time some of Germany's former enemies had begun to understand the danger that Bolshevism posed for the entire Western world. She had heard that the British ambassador in Berlin had approached "our magnificent Field Marshal Ludendorff" and asked him to "take command of Allied and German troops in the fight against Russian Bolshevism."

It was a fight she was waging in her brother's name with growing success, if judged by the mail from former enemy countries that began to arrive at the Nietzsche Archives. The Nietzsche movement was obviously gaining ground abroad too, largely, Elisabeth thought, as the result of her biography, which was attracting many new readers to her brother's works. Even in England, where Nietzsche had been so maligned during the war, he now found disciples again. Proudly, Elisabeth sent Thiel a letter she had just received from an Englishman who wanted

> to pay respectful homage to one of the best sisters a man ever had. I have recently been reading your two volumes of the life of your now *very* famous brother and was profoundly impressed by the love and devotion you so unswervingly showed toward your brother. Henceforth, I think that you ought to be remembered among the famous women of history.

It was comforting to Elisabeth to read such words while she sat shivering in her Weimar home, deprived, like everybody else, of fuel, light, and water because of the general strike that the government had declared to prevent a military take-over by rightist extremists. "Our government uses this incredible method to remain in power. I have the feeling that we are standing at the beginning of the end of German culture. If the Nietzsche Archives did not have you, dearest and most loyal friend, we would have to close its doors this year," Elisabeth wrote Thiel in March 1920. A Swedish colonel, who was on a much-discussed lecture tour in Germany, had recently visited her and told her he was trying to arouse public support for a new political order in Europe based on the unification of all Germanic peoples into one great Germanic empire. Elisabeth was afraid that the harsh realities of life in Germany, at present, prevented people from paying much attention to such a grand concept. Thiel had no idea how rapidly prices were rising. It had become almost impossible for people on fixed incomes to buy enough food. The other day two old Weimar ladies, who were living alone and feared that they would starve to death, had taken their own lives. Tragedies wherever you looked. And the government was paralyzed because the political parties were more interested in fighting each other than in joining forces to fight for the resurrection of their fatherland.

On the occasion of the twentieth anniversary of her brother's death, Elisabeth publicly raised her voice once again in defense of Germany's ancient virtues. She wrote an article for the *Vossische Zeitung* on "Goethe, Nietzsche and the Pursuit of Happiness." Her brother had been right when he said that men do not pursue happiness—only Englishmen and Americans do that—they pursue greatness. It was time for the German people to remember their great past and give up chasing after cheap ideals. Self-discipline, order, obedience, and hard work—these were the qualities that had made Germany great and these were the qualities she needed to recover from her defeat and regain the respect of her former enemies.

Although Elisabeth never made any secret of her contempt for the Weimar Republic, she was the recipient of many public honors on her seventy-fifth birthday, July 15, 1921. Delegations from the city of Weimar, the state of Thuringia, and the German Reich offered her good wishes and complimented her on her patriotic work. The dean of the philosophy faculty at the University of Jena, dressed in his official red and purple robe and accompanied by four senior professors, personally presented her an honorary doctorate. He emphasized the fact that Elisabeth was the first woman ever to be awarded this high honor. She accepted it with a few gracefully spoken words of thanks, but a few minutes later she whispered to an old aristocratic lady friend of hers that while she was pleased to have the title of "doctor *honoris causa*," she would far rather have that of "excellency."

But no title and no honors could protect her from the tidal wave of inflation that was sweeping over Germany. Prices were rising astronomically and the value of the mark declined from day to day. Politically, too, the situation was getting worse; a Socialist government had come to power in Weimar. "Should our red rulers discover how hostile Nietzsche's ideas are to theirs, life for me could become extremely unpleasant," Elisabeth confided to Thiel. She was hard at work preparing an anthology of her brother's sayings about peoples and states.

My brother wished us dangerous times. Well, we are now living dangerously enough. Let us hope that a great star will arise out of this chaos, a truly great man and leader like Napoleon after the French Revolution. Our young people want to worship, venerate and love someone, but there is nobody loveable among our present leaders.

In September 1922 Elisabeth was for the third time proposed for the Nobel rize in literature by a group of German university professors whose friendship she had cultivated. She asked her cousin, Max Oehler, to inform Thiel and to point out that according to the statutes of the Nobel Foundation she was well qualified for the prize. It was to be awarded to the author of works "that have great cultural significance." Oehler mentioned Elisabeth's various versions of her brother's biography, which had been translated into many languages, her work as editor of the ten-volume pocket-book edition of Nietzsche's works; and, in particular, her founding of the Nietzsche Archives, "one of the leading cultural centers in Europe." He also mentioned that she was currently finishing work on an anthology of her brother's sayings about peoples and states, and asked Thiel whether "it would be wise to tell the Swedish Academy that this book, which stresses the value of the individual, was directed against socialism, communism, and bolshevism." Would Thiel be willing to review the draft proposal before it was submitted? The Nobel prize would be particularly welcome now because it was paid in Swedish crowns, the German mark having lost practically all its value.

In her own letter to Thiel, Elisabeth emphasized that, although she would feel greatly honored to receive the Nobel prize, it had not been her idea to submit another proposal to the Swedish Academy on her behalf. "However, the gentlemen who are preparing the proposal maintain that my accomplishments for the works of my brother are so meritorious, and the Nietzsche Archives such a unique institution, that they are perfectly justified in proposing me to the Nobel committee." To clinch her point, she added that, as the first woman ever to receive an honorary doctorate from the University of Jena, her fame had risen "phenomenally." The Swedish Academy took notice of the achievements of Nietzsche's sister but decided to award the Nobel prize for literature in 1923 to the Irish poet William Butler Yeats, who was a great admirer of the German philosopher and called him "a strong enchanter."

Undeterred by her third rejection from the Nobel committee, and although the galloping inflation threatened to wipe out the entire capital of the Nietzsche Endowment and "makes us feel as though we are living on a volcano," Elisabeth continued her Saturday open-house receptions. Sometimes as many as sixty people showed up for lectures and music—"grateful that I am carrying on normal social activities as in the good old times." The tea, coffee, and chocolate she served on those occasions she had received either from her Swedish friend, who kept her supplied with food that was unobtainable in Germany, or from her servants, who had bought them on the black market with Swedish crowns.

The only ray of light in those dark months was that her brother's books, although now costing millions of marks, were still selling well, and her royalty income from her own books was also considerable. Her booklet *Nietzsche's Words on States and Peoples* sold thousands of copies within a few months. Her only complaint was that her income would be even higher if her publisher was less greedy. She was once again involved in a bitter quarrel with Kröner, which even her cousin, Dr. Adalbert Oehler, the president of the Nietzsche Endowment, found so capricious that it caused him to resign from his position. Elisabeth felt that he had betrayed her in a time of need and told him that, although she did not understand much about money, she knew "how much a publisher, who has the good fortune to publish the works of Nietzsche, owes to my brother's great name." And, without waiting to give her cousin a chance to reconsider his resignation, she invited her old friend Dr. Paulssen, a former minister in Grand Duke Wilhelm Ernst's cabinet, to assume the presidency of the Nietzsche Endowment.

In August 1923 the capital of the Endowment amounted to one hundred million marks. At the same time a pound of butter cost one hundred eighty thousand marks. "My poor old head, which has been accustomed for so many years to our good old mark, cannot get used to these figures. I am crying all the time." Elisabeth was crying even more bitterly when she learned at the end of 1923 that her entire capital had been wiped out. The German government had declared the old mark bankrupt and had replaced it with a new currency, the Rentenmark. Since the convertibility of old marks into Rentenmarks was practically nil, all savings disappeared overnight. The impact of this financial catastrophe on Germany's notoriously frugal and industrious middle class was traumatic. They never forgave their government for having robbed them of their life's savings, and they were ready to join any man or movement that promised to overthrow a hated regime. Uncontrolled inflation and currency collapse drove the third nail into the coffin of the Weimar Republic.

It took some time before Elisabeth realized that the fortune her Swedish angel had given her through the years to ensure the survival of the Nietzsche Archives in perpetuity was gone and that once again she was entirely dependent on income from royalties. And even that would end in 1930 when the copyright expired. A government capable of such an infamous betrayal of its own people deserved to be overthrown. Elisabeth rejoiced when she heard that a movement of national resurrection was growing in Bavaria, led by Ludendorff, whom she greatly admired, and Hitler, the revered leader of a small band of patriots. If she had been younger, she would have gone to Munich and joined the march on Berlin, even at the risk that it might fail and that she would be arrested for treason.

She envied the Italian people, who had found a strong leader and had succeeded in putting an end to Bolshevist threats and democratic anarchy. To express her admiration for the new Caesar, she sent him a note of congratulations enclosing a picture of her brother. She was thrilled when Mussolini personally acknowledged her gift by telegram and letter, telling her that he had been an admirer of her brother's philosophy for years and would expound Nietzsche's ideas about breeding, order, and discipline in his speech to the forthcoming Fascist congress in Rome. Elisabeth's cousin, Max Oehler, who served as her personal assistant and archivist, shared her enthusiasm for the Fascist leader. He sent Thiel an essay he had written on "Mussolini and Nietzsche," and asked him to submit it to a large Swedish newspaper, although he feared that the leftist Swedish press might not be interested in such a topic. In the Nietzsche Archives Mussolini's name was on everybody's lips, and there was jubilation when the Italian ambassador, accompanied by two attachés, made a special trip from Berlin to Weimar to bring personal greetings from the Duce. He told Elisabeth that Mussolini had read all of Nietzsche's books.

The fame of my beloved brother is spreading all over the world. I am getting flattering mail from Tiflis, Chile, North and South America, and from Paris. And many visitors. Romain Rolland has been here with Madame Rolland, Marquis de Brion, Count and Countess Pourtalès. They all have literary wishes. I must write two new books in spite of my advanced age, otherwise the Nietzsche Archives cannot exist. Money seems to be in short supply everywhere. People complain even in France, England, and Italy.

As the twenties were drawing to a close, Elisabeth's paramount worry was what would happen to her and the Nietzsche Archives after 1930. She decided that a way must be found to extend the copyright for her brother's books from thirty to fifty years, and she began a vigorous campaign to achieve this objective. She wrote articles, submitted petitions, and prepared legal briefs. For the rest she still depended on her Swedish friend's help, although Thiel himself was in financial difficulties. In February 1926 when she urgently needed several thousand marks, she sent him the following SOS: "Once again the waves of worry are rising over my head. Ship in distress!" And Thiel came to her rescue once again.

But it was evident that Elisabeth needed a steady source of income. She was in her late seventies and, although still surprisingly energetic, not able to work such long hours as before. After lengthy discussions in the Nietzsche Archives it was decided to submit a petition, signed by prominent people, to President Hindenburg requesting that he award Elisabeth an honorary pension on the occasion of her eightieth birthday in July 1926. The matter was delicate because Hindenburg was a very pious man and might object to honoring the sister of the author of *Antichrist.* Although it was unlikely that Hindenburg had heard the title of that book, let alone read it, the name was enough to upset him, hence it was not to be mentioned.

The text of the petition that was submitted to Hindenburg stressed the great morale-building qualities of Nietzsche's works. "His major work *Thus Spoke Zarathustra* was the book which—together with the Bible and Goethe's *Faust*—had been taken most often to the front by German soldiers." It glorified the martial virtues: obedience to commands, discipline, and hardness. As to Nietzsche's sister, it was she who had propagated her brother's ideas and made possible the "profoundly ethical impact of Nietzsche's works." Her detailed account of her brother's noble life served as an inspiration to Germany's youth. By collecting, editing, and publishing Nietzsche's notebooks, she had saved his great work *Will to Power* from oblivion. But her crowning achievement was the establishment in Weimar of the Nietzsche Archives, which had become under her direction a cultural center of the first rank. Her energy, her courage, and her patriotism were universally admired. Since the Endowment that she had accumulated through the years for the Nietzsche Archives had been wiped out by the inflation and the currency collapse, she deserved to be supported in her old age.

Drawn up by the president of the Nietzsche Endowment, the petition was signed by a number of prominent people; among them were Rudolf Eucken, winner of the Nobel prize for literature in 1908, Count Harry Kessler, Oswald Spengler, and Professor Hans Vaihinger. It had the desired effect. "Our excellent President Hindenburg awards me an honorary pension for the rest of my life. It is a modest pension, but the Reich will add three hundred marks a month so that I now have four hundred fifty marks monthly— just enough to pay my staff's salaries."

After telling her Swedish friend this good news, Elisabeth described the festivities of her eightieth birthday. Fifty-two people had dined with her, representatives of the Reich, the state of Thuringia, and the city of Weimar. She had personally received one hundred fifty well-wishers and had seen clippings of ninety newspaper articles about herself. "What nonsense some people write! I was celebrated as 'The First Lady of Europe.' "

But Thiel did not think that it was nonsense.

So you have been celebrated as the First Lady of Europe and you object to this honor? Well, let me ask you which other woman deserves it more? . . . I often have a kind of vision: the figures of a brother and a sister carved at the portal of a new age and above them the one word—honesty. This new age ought to make amends to you out of gratitude for the sins it committed against your brother . . . for you represent today the cultural pinnacle of our universe.

This kind of language would have turned the head of any woman. It was poison for Elisabeth's inflated ego. She began to see herself more and more as the executor of her brother's political will. Nietzsche had said that Europe wanted to become one and called for a new breed of "good Europeans." And Elisabeth echoed, "The Nietzsche Archives is now considered the center for European unification. Prince Karl Anton Rohan gave a very interesting lecture about the cultural unity of Europe, and two weeks ago I gave a diplomatic breakfast for Professor Henry Lichtenberger of the Sorbonne, who is pursuing the same objective." She was particularly pleased that French intellectuals considered her brother the fountainhead of European unity and hastened to inform Thiel that a young Frenchman had just published a book called *The Divinity of Friedrich Nietzsche: Germ of a European Religion.*

At long last her brother's prophecies were coming true: a Europe united in his name and through his ideas. To provide political leadership, an "order of superior men" would be founded. It would inspire a sense of sacrifice and self-discipline in the young and oppose the debilitating egalitarian trend of the times. Based on Zarathustra's gospel, it would preach toughness and the overcoming of pity. It would be an expression of the will to power of a new aristocracy, the future lords of the earth.

Despite her advanced age, Elisabeth actively promoted these ideas. She presided over an international congress on "Nietzsche and the Twentieth Century"; gave audiences to supporters of her cause, reserving a particularly warm welcome for those who attacked the infamous Treaty of Versailles, such as Professor Harry Elmer Barnes—"the courageous American fighter against the lie of Germany's war guilt"; and wrote a new introduction to a one-volume India paper edition of *Will to Power.*

Ripeness is all. The time was getting ripe for a leader to arise and forge all these germinal ideas into one great political movement.

24·Elisabeth and Hitler

*O*N NEW YEAR'S EVE 1929 millions of champagne corks popped in Germany to salute the entrance of the third decade of the twentieth century. In Berlin and other cities, people indulged themselves in hectic rounds of festivities—eat, drink, and be merry for tomorrow you will be poor and out of work. A mood of desperate gaiety filled the air. Everybody wanted to have one last fling before the ticking time bomb would go off and blow the fragile postwar order to pieces. Right- and left-wing revolutionaries roamed the streets, fought pitched battles with one another or joined forces against the government. The ghost of the Great Depression loomed like a giant in the background, waiting to drive the fourth and final nail into the coffin of the Weimar Republic.

For the Nietzsche Archives 1930 was the year of decision. Could it be kept open after the Reichsrat had rejected Elisabeth's petition to have the copyright on her brother's works extended for twenty years? The thought that she would have to close it preyed on her mind. She bombarded high government officials in Berlin and Weimar with requests for help. The Reich was under an obligation to support her after having robbed the archives of its endowment. Financial support was particularly needed now that work had started on the definitive, historical-critical edition of Nietzsche's works, which was planned in forty volumes. Her monthly expenses for salaries alone amounted to more than one thousand marks, a considerable drain on her resources, which caused her many a sleepless night worrying about the future.

The loss of royalties from her brother's works at the end of 1930 presented a real threat, the more so since the archives' uncertain future coincided with the uncertain future of the Weimar Republic. Unable to cope with the rapid rise in unemployment and the growing militancy of Hitler's storm troops and the Communist red front, the German government was forced to govern by decree. The only unifying element in the midst of this undeclared civil war was President Hindenburg, and his term of office was coming to an end in 1932. He was eighty-five years old and showed his age both mentally and physically. But unless he could be prevailed upon to run for a second term, there would be such a mad scramble for power that the politically moderate feared that the result would be chaos. To prevent it, they persuaded Hindenburg to run again. In a radio address to the German people Hindenburg said that he was willing to be a candidate again despite his age because he wanted to prevent the election of a partisan extremist whose radical views he abhorred. He meant Hitler, who had been nominated by his party for the presidency.

The staff of the Nietzsche Archives, in particular Dr. Emge, a professor of law of the University of Jena who had been appointed editor of the historical-critical edition, and Elisabeth's cousin, Major Max Oehler, actively supported Hitler. Elisabeth herself said she favored Hindenburg, who had awarded her a pension, but she became deeply distraught when the monetary crisis forced the closure of all banks and she was informed by her own bank in Weimar that she could no longer count on any credit. "You have no idea of the catastrophic effect the great economic crisis has on all of us in Germany," she wrote Thiel. "I find it hard to believe that my life's work should end so tragically." Unless a miracle occurred she would be forced to close the archives at the end of 1931.

Elisabeth's eighty-fifth birthday in July 1931 fell in the midst of the economic and political crisis. A mood of fear and despair gripped the country, but once again Nietzsche's sister was the recipient of many public honors and private good wishes. Mussolini telegraphed birthday greetings and sent a check for twenty thousand lire. She received more than three hundred telegrams from all corners of the earth. The one she cherished most was from Empress Hermine, the wife of the former German Emperor, who had become a close friend of hers.

When Kessler heard of this friendship, he called it "grotesque, considering His Majesty's attitude toward Nietzsche in pre-1914 days. At that time Nietzsche was reckoned as revolutionary and almost as unpatriotic a fellow as the Socialists." Kessler was rapidly becoming disenchanted with Elisabeth. He revered Nietzsche as the advocate of "the good European" and felt—like many others—that Elisabeth, as Nietzsche's sister, deserved to be treated with respect. Her patriotic flag-waving had always irritated him, but when she told him of her friendship with the Empress, he realized that she was misrepresenting her brother. Kessler then felt that he had been mistaken in supporting her all these years. Elisabeth was impervious to such criticism. If the Emperor had not liked her brother it was only because he had not known his work. The Empress did know his work, and that is why she had become Elisabeth's friend.

The most valuable birthday gifts Elisabeth received were laudatory letters from Karl Severing, the Socialist minister in Berlin, and from Dr. Wilhelm Frick, the Nazi minister in Weimar, each promising official subsidies for the Nietzsche Archives. But, alas, promises made in July could not be kept in November because neither the Reich nor the state of Thuringia had money for cultural purposes. They needed all available funds to ameliorate the plight of the unemployed. By the end of the year the situation had become so hopeless that Elisabeth informed Thiel that she would have to close the archives in February 1932. Like the Reich, she was at the end of her financial rope. She said it would break her heart to close the archives, for it was like burying her beloved child, but she could see no way out.

Thiel was saddened to hear this news. He wished he could once again come to the rescue, as he had so often in the past, but his own finances had been so adversely affected by the worldwide depression that he could not invest any more money in the Nietzsche Archives. He was therefore relieved when Elisabeth told him jubilantly a few weeks later that she had just experienced "the most miraculous Christmas of my life."

Six days before Christmas she had won her second suit against her publisher. This meant that Kröner would have to continue paying her royalties for all those works that her brother had not completed, such as *Will to Power*. The court had upheld her contention that, since her brother had not written those books, the copyright belonged to her and not to him. As long as she lived and for thirty years after her death, the archives could count on royalties from all of Nietzsche's works that she had helped to compile and edit. This was an important decision with long-ranging, financial implications.

Her second piece of good luck was that both the Reich and the state of Thuringia had made good on some of the pledges given her on her eighty-fifth birthday. This too augured well for the future.

But most important of all a "wonderful, anonymous donor," who had made large contributions to the archives in the past, had sent her one day before Christmas a check for twenty thousand marks in recognition of her patriotic work. It was like a fairy tale, except that for some time the Prince Charming remained invisible. When his identity was finally revealed, Elisabeth learned that he was the wealthy cigarette manufacturer Philipp Reemtsma. She did not know that Reemtsma also contributed large sums to the Nazis, and was later tried in connection with allegations made at the Nuremberg trials of Nazi war criminals that he had bribed Field Marshal Hermann Göring. In Elisabeth's estimation, Reemtsma joined Thiel as a patron saint of the Nietzsche Archives.

After her financial situation had improved so miraculously, Elisabeth threw herself with renewed vigor into her work. She supervised the two young scholars Karl Schlechta and Friedrich Mette, who were working on the

critical edition, and explained to them the difficulties she had had to overcome when she began to edit her brother's notebooks. She implied that any
textual variants were caused by the illegibility of many passages. Some
former editors had misread Nietzsche's manuscripts. But there had never
been any attempt on her part to change her brother's texts.

A tense situation developed when she was asked to produce the originals
of her brother's letters to herself and her mother. She explained that some
had been lost in Paraguay and that her pious mother had burned others. However, she could vouch for the accuracy of the published version. This answer
did not satisfy the two researchers who had been delegated by the official
German scholars fund, *Notgemeinschaft der deutschen Wissenschaft,* to work
on the critical edition. They scrutinized Nietzsche's notebooks carefully and
discovered numerous cases in which Elisabeth had used letters her brother
had drafted for others but which she had published as though he had written
them to her. Schlechta reports that when he confronted Nietzsche's sister
with this evidence—she was almost ninety years old at the time—she became
furious, uttered a cry of indignation, and threw her heavy oak cane at him. "I
felt she wanted to kill me."

In the face of all criticism Elisabeth continued to rule her realm with undiminished authority. Even her cousin, Major Max Oehler, complained
about the way she treated him, and threatened to resign—a threat that left
her completely unmoved. On the contrary, she told him he should look for
another position. She would not permit any criticism of her handling of the
affairs of the archives. In her mind, criticism was insubordination, and the
punishment for insubordination was dismissal. Major Oehler accepted the
reprimand and decided to bide his time. Elisabeth could not live much
longer, although she was still amazingly energetic. She carried on a large correspondence, participated in editorial conferences, and was writing a book on
Nietzsche and the Women of His Time in which she wanted to show her
brother's contempt for the "intellectual woman." And every Saturday afternoon she still received guests, Weimar friends and prominent visitors, gave
dinner parties, and organized lectures and musicals. In addition, she kept in
close touch with the rapidly changing political situation in Germany. It was
largely because of her behind-the-scenes influence that a play on Napoleon,
coauthored by Mussolini, had its first German performance at the Weimar
National Theater in February 1932.

It was quite a coup for a small provincial stage to premiere a play more
noteworthy for its ideological content than its literary value at a time when
the struggle between fascism and democracy was at its height in Germany.
"We are curious," commented a reviewer in the *Völkischer Beobachter,*
"whether other German theaters, dependent as they are on the good graces
of parliaments and anti-Fascists, will have the courage to perform the Italian
drama." What impressed Elisabeth was Mussolini's treatment of Napoleon.
Like her brother, she had been all her life a great admirer of the Corsican military genius, whose downfall she regretted.

Mussolini's play *Campo di Maggio*, entitled in German *Hundert Tage* [Hundred Days], covers the period between Napoleon's escape from Elba and his final defeat. It represents Napoleon as a blameless hero who goes down to defeat through his own tragic error of divesting himself of absolute power by granting France a constitution. He is not defeated on the battlefield of Waterloo; he is stabbed in the back by intrigants in Paris, led by Fouché, the villain of the piece. As Elisabeth watched the plot unfold, she was reminded of the events that led to the downfall of Germany's invincible armies in the First World War—treason at home. How convincingly Mussolini had depicted a tragic truth.

Elisabeth was not alone in her admiration of the Duce's dramatic skill. The large audience, which filled the theater to the last seat, shared her emotion, which was heightened by the rumor, confirmed just as the curtain went up, that Adolf Hitler was present. He had taken time out from his campaign for the presidency and come to Weimar accompanied by a phalanx of storm troopers. When he heard that Nietzsche's sister was in the theater, he came to her box carrying an enormous bouquet of red roses. Elisabeth, who was talking with a group of Italian newspaper correspondents, was flushed and excited. She was not quite sure whether to consider this unexpected visit an honor. Perhaps it compromised her, because Hitler was running against Hindenburg and she did not think he could win. As it turned out, she was right. She was also upset when Hitler started a lively political discussion in the presence of the Italians, talking rather incautiously, she thought, about the relationship between Germany and Austria. Hitler insisted that he was not interested in the economic or political union of the two countries, which some democratic politicians advocated, because Vienna was not a purely German city. Elisabeth felt he should not have said that, for she was a supporter of the *Anschluss* and had been since it was first proposed in 1919. When Kessler asked her what impression Hitler had made on her, she said that she was particularly struck by his eyes, "which are fascinating and stare right through you." But he struck her as a religious rather than a political leader.

Elisabeth made no mention to Thiel, whom she kept informed of all the important events in her life, of her first encounter with Hitler. She merely told him that there was considerable political agitation in the Archives, that all her employees were ardent Nazis, and that she was carefully watching the rapidly changing situation. "As soon as I see more clearly, I shall give you my personal opinion of these events."

The political unrest made it difficult for her to concentrate on her own work. Besides, the editors of the critical edition took much more of her time than she had anticipated by constantly asking her to produce the original manuscripts of passages that she had published years ago. And finally, she was involved in lengthy discussions with state officials and representatives of the University of Jena concerning a merger of the Weimar archives—the Goethe-Schiller Archiv and the Nietzsche Archives—with the university. If that was done, the state of Sachsen-Weimar would assume some of the operating costs, but it would also exercise some control over the running of the archives. Before she agreed to that condition, Elisabeth wanted to know how much control the state would exercise and how much she would retain. To clarify this issue she invited representatives from the state and the university to a number of breakfast meetings, her favorite method of conducting business negotiations. These remained inconclusive and were soon overtaken by the one event that many Germans dreaded and many passionately hoped for: Hitler's advent to power. If Elisabeth had hedged her bets about the Nazi leader until then, she now embraced him fervently. Hitler's struggle from obscurity to fame reminded her of her brother's similar fate. It was not by accident that an Austrian corporal had become chancellor of the Reich; it was his strong will to power. She was sure that if her brother were alive, he would agree with her.

"Last Sunday," she wrote Thiel excitedly on February 17, 1933, "I had the great good fortune of a personal conversation with our wonderful chancellor. It was in the theater during a solemn performance of *Tristan* in honor of the fiftieth anniversary of Wagner's death. Hitler graciously visited me in my box." She did not mention that this had been her second meeting with Hitler in the theater, but she added that from a practical point of view it was important for her and the archives that she had met the Nazi leader. He could provide the financial support she needed. And she was not mistaken. Hitler listened to her requests for help with a sympathetic ear, made private contributions, and ordered official grants to be given to the Nietzsche Archives. Elisabeth felt that at long last the German Napoleon, the "superman" her brother had called for, had arisen and that she had met him.

We are drunk with enthusiasm because at the head of our government stands such a wonderful, indeed phenomenal, personality like our magnificent Chancellor Adolf Hitler. That is why the tremendous upheaval in Germany probably appears quite different to us than to people abroad. They cannot understand how we endure these vast transformations so cheerfully. Well, the reason is that we have suddenly achieved the *one* Germany which for centuries our poets have depicted longingly in their poems and which we have all been waiting for: *Ein Volk, Ein Reich, Ein Führer.*

Yet while she waxed so enthusiastically about Hitler's Germany in her letters to her non-Aryan Swedish friend, Elisabeth realized that she had to explain the virulence of the persecutions of the Jews. She told Thiel that she regretted them and called them excesses of a few misguided minor party members that would soon be stopped. Since she was the widow of one of the first German anti-Semites, many people thought that she was anti-Semitic herself, but that was quite untrue. Indeed, a number of her good friends were Jewish. On the other hand, she understood why there was so much anti-Semitic feeling in Germany at present. The reason was that in some professions, notably in medicine, law, and banking, Jews predominated while non-Jews were unemployed. She added that it still was not right to persecute them and that some of her Jewish friends had turned to her for help, hoping that she would bring this problem to Hitler's personal attention. She was not sure that she could do that, but she trusted that "milder laws would be made so that the best of the alien race can remain in Germany."

Thiel's reply to Elisabeth's long and enthusiastic declaration of faith in the Führer seems to have been very encouraging, for she was overjoyed to receive his "magnificent Hitler letter." She wrote him that it had made her feel good "that such an independent and enlightened man as you judges Hitler with such approval, particularly now when such stupid lies are spread abroad about Germany." She invited Thiel to come to Weimar and see for himself how radiantly happy everybody was. She had had many foreign visitors, American students, Rumanian professors, and young English ladies who spoke as enthusiastically about the new Germany as the Germans.

But Thiel declined. When his letters started to become critical, Elisabeth warned him not to be misled by hostile propaganda. The foreign press painted a completely false picture of conditions in Germany. It was simply not true that the German people had lost their freedom and felt oppressed. On the contrary, they felt liberated from the terror of the Communists and their fellow travelers. At long last Germany had again become a land of law and order. If there had been some excesses in the early months, Thiel must remember that Germany was in the throes of a revolution and revolutions were never bloodless. However, Hitler had personally assured her that he would not tolerate any unnecessary cruelties. "Last year our deeply venerated Führer visited me three times. I wish I could tell you what a powerful impression this magnificent man makes. His simplicity and kindness are overwhelming."

While some of Elisabeth's oldest friends were forced to leave Germany and go into exile—Count Kessler, for example, who noted that "it is enough to make one weep to see what has become Nietzsche and the Nietzsche Archives"—Elisabeth proudly informed Thiel that the Archives, which he had supported all these years, had become a center for the philosophic presentation of the National-Socialist ideology. *Zarathustra*, the bible of the Hitler youth, had been enshrined—together with Hitler's *Mein Kampf* and Alfred Rosenberg's *Myth of the Twentieth Century*—in the vault of the Tannenberg Memorial, which had been erected to commemorate Germany's victory over Russia in the First World War. Elisabeth also told Thiel that there had been an important conference at the Nietzsche Archives, attended by such "great leaders as Dr. Alfred Rosenberg and Dr. Franck," who hailed Nietzsche as the father of National Socialism.

> Dr. Rosenberg's and Dr. Franck's addresses moved me deeply for I felt how strongly my brother had influenced the whole movement. One of the gentlemen said to me: "These hours must seem to you like the glorious resurrection of your brother." . . . Believe me, Fritz would be enchanted by Hitler, who with incredible courage has taken upon himself the entire responsibility for his people.

Since there is no record of Thiel's answer to Elisabeth's effusion he probably thought it best not to get embroiled in a political controversy with his old friend.

As Elisabeth approached her ninetieth year, she began to feel more and more the weight of her age. She suffered from dizzy spells, from attacks of influenza, and she was rapidly going blind. But despite her age she underwent an operation for the removal of a cataract and, while she was recuperating, dictated the last chapters of her book on *Nietzsche and the Women of His Time* in which she took her final revenge on Lou Salomé. She depicted Lou as an adventuress who had never played any significant part in her brother's life and had exploited her brief acquaintance by writing articles and a book on Nietzsche without any understanding of his philosophy. The entire "Lou Affair" was an unhappy episode and best forgotten.

From her hospital bed, Elisabeth also dictated a long letter to Hitler requesting him to intervene in the proposed closing of Schulpforta, which was to become a training school for Nazi leaders. She asked that the four-hundred-year-old tradition of Schulpforta, where her brother had received such an excellent education, be preserved. She ended her letter with a paean to Hitler's "wonderful book *Mein Kampf*," which she had, of course, read when it was first published, but which was being read to her again in the hospital. She was deeply moved by its eloquent passages on Germany's destiny and found it a great consolation amid her suffering. "I advise everybody who is in pain to read this great book and draw from it the strength and courage necessary to meet a difficult fate." She signed her letter to her "most venerated Führer," as his devoted and admiring Elisabeth Förster-Nietzsche. And as further proof of her devotion, she sent Hitler an autographed copy of her new book, which he acknowledged on July 26, 1935, in a personal note with an expression of sincere gratitude.

A few months later, Hitler, accompanied by his architect Albert Speer, paid Elisabeth a surprise visit. He wanted to assure her that he would provide the money for the construction of a Nietzsche memorial auditorium and library adjoining Villa Silberblick. Such a building was needed to provide the necessary space for conferences, seminars, and workshops, where German youth could be taught Nietzsche's doctrine of a master race. Tears of joy ran down Elisabeth's cheeks as she heard this unexpected news. Her lifelong struggle to secure the future of her Archives had finally been won. Whatever happened to her now, her brother's work and her own were under the personal protection of the architect of the Thousand-Year Reich.

With a joyful heart she told Thiel on October 31, 1935, that the Führer, on his own initiative, had declared he would build a Nietzsche memorial. "One cannot but love this great, magnificent man if one knows him as well as I do."

Ten days later Elisabeth was dead. She had died peacefully during a brief bout with influenza. And she was buried with the pomp and circumstance normally reserved for crowned heads of state. Hitler and some of the leading

Elisabeth, eighty-eight years old, receiving Hitler at the entrance of the Nietzsche Archives, Villa Silberblick. G.D.K.L., Weimar

Hitler posing before the bust of Nietzsche in 1934. G.D.K.L., Weimar

members of his cabinet attended the funeral, as did representatives from the state of Thuringia, the city of Weimar, the University of Jena, and numerous professional and scientific organizations. Also present was Winifred Wagner, Cosima's English-born daughter-in-law, who had long since buried the hatchet of the Wagner-Nietzsche feud and become a good friend of Elisabeth.

The funeral of Zarathustra's sister made the front page of the *Völkischer Beobachter* on November 11, 1935. She was eulogized by Reichsstatthalter and Gauleiter Sauckel as an indomitable German woman at whose bier National-Socialist Germany stood in reverence, for she had singlehandedly preserved the work of her great brother, whose ideas had profoundly influenced the rebirth of Germany. At the end of the service, Hitler solemnly walked up to the coffin and covered it with a large laurel wreath.

25 · Angry Ashes:
A Postscript

*A*FTER ELISABETH'S DEATH, her cousin, Major Max Oehler, who had been her assistant for fifteen years, became the custodian of the Nietzsche Archives; being Elisabeth's assistant was an unenviable role, for she was a hard taskmaster and brooked no interference from anyone in running the affairs of the archives. Oehler was thirty years her junior and she had been very fond of him when he was a young man; she had called him her "favorite cousin" and had even proposed adopting him so that he could bear the Nietzsche name. In 1909, after Gast had left the archives, Elisabeth had invited Max to join her staff as an archivist, an offer that he was tempted to accept. He was a scholar by temperament, the author of a two-volume history of the Order of Teutonic Knights, and he preferred the company of books to that of people. But by profession he was a soldier. After careful consideration, he concluded that he could not give up his profession and the economic security it offered for the uncertain position as Elisabeth's archivist, for he was married and had to provide for a wife and young child. He pursued his military career with considerable success and served as an officer at the Prussian general staff during the First World War. Germany's defeat brought Major Oehler's military career to an abrupt end. He gladly accepted Elisabeth's invitation to come to Weimar and assist her with the administration of the Nietzsche Archives, which, under her direction, had become an internationally famous institution.

Oehler's happiness in having found a position that suited him well was short-lived. He realized very soon that Elisabeth treated him much more like her servant than her assistant. She made all the important decisions herself without consulting him, disregarded and even ridiculed his advice, and referred to him in her letters to her friends as "a nice ornament for the archives but not really necessary." When he asked her for an increase in his salary, which he did reluctantly for he was a proud man, she suggested that if he needed more money, he should look for another position, although she knew very well that it was all but impossible for professional soldiers in Weimar Germany to find work. Outwardly the relationship between Elisabeth and Max remained friendly, despite stormy intervals, but inwardly they drifted more and more apart. Max became embittered and reserved; Elisabeth remained aloof and indifferent. But there was one emotion they shared—their mutual admiration for Hitler and the Nazi party. Major Oehler welcomed the military spirit that Hitler had rekindled among Germany's youth and basked in the glory of meeting the Führer in person. He was greatly impressed when Elisabeth told him that Hitler had promised to finance the Nietzsche memorial. Here was a project to which he could devote his energy, if Elisabeth would let him. Her sudden death provided that opportunity.

Among all the mourners at Elisabeth's funeral, Major Oehler was probably the one who felt most relieved that she was gone. At last he could manage the affairs of the Archives without her interference. He did so efficiently and with dispatch. Two years after Elisabeth's death, the impressive contours of the Nietzsche memorial—auditorium, cloisters, and library—had arisen and was dedicated in the presence of high Nazi officials. It took several more years and half a million marks to finish the building. Before it was completely furnished, the war broke out. But work continued even during the war. In a report on the finances of the Archives prepared in 1942, Oehler stated that it would cost another one hundred fifty thousand marks to finish the memorial. Like many Germans at that time, Oehler confidently expected a German victory. Whether he still thought so a year later is doubtful. He received a call from the stationmaster of the Weimar railroad station notifying him that a long-expected statue of Dionysos, the Greek god of orgiastic rites and a major symbol of Nietzsche's philosophy, a present of Mussolini, had just arrived. Before they could finish their conversation, the air-raid sirens sounded and the frightened official told Oehler that the rail yards were under heavy attack. He wanted to know what should be done with the freight car from Italy that contained the huge Greek statue. Oehler ordered the statue to be unloaded, then he jumped into a truck and drove through the deserted streets of Weimar to the freight depot. There the statue was swung onto the truck by crane. "I sat close to the bearded marble head, directing the drive up the hill to the archives while a hail of bombs burst upon us." Under the protection of the Greek god, Oehler escaped unharmed. After that his luck ran out.

The unthinkable happened: Germany lost the war, the Thousand-Year Reich lay in ruins, and Russian soldiers occupied Weimar. The Nietzsche Archives was high on their list as a center of Fascist propaganda, and Major Oehler, its custodian, was listed as a member of the Nazi party. Perhaps Oehler could have fled to the West, as so many of his countrymen did, but his sense of duty prevented him from doing that. He felt that he had to remain in charge of Nietzsche's manuscripts and all the memorabilia that Elisabeth had accumulated through the years until another had been appointed.

The first Russians to appear were officers who spoke German fluently. They seemed well informed, asked Major Oehler politely to show them around, examined some of Nietzsche's notebooks, and exchanged quiet remarks in Russian with one another. When they left, they told Oehler to remain in charge of the Archives for the time being. On December 6, a Russian woman interpreter requested that Major Oehler accompany her to headquarters for interrogation. She did not know how long he would be gone, but there was no need to take any change of clothes. Three days later the Nietzsche Archives was locked and sealed by order of the Russian commanding officer. Major Oehler's wife waited anxiously for her husband's return as the days stretched into weeks and the weeks into months. Finally, she left Weimar and went to West Germany. It was more than a decade later before she heard that, after having been condemned to forced labor in Siberia on the day he was arrested, her husband had fallen sick and had been thrown into the basement of a house close to the Nietzsche Archives and left there to starve to death. During the first anxious days of waiting for his return, Frau Oehler had often walked past the house where her husband lay dying.

"Become hard and show no mercy," Nietzsche taught, "for evil is man's best force." In her grief over her husband's gruesome fate, Frau Oehler forgot that the Nietzsche Archives had been propagating this dangerous doctrine for years. Nietzsche himself had called it dynamite and felt at moments of anxious forebodings that he had visited a curse on mankind. That is why Zarathustra warned his readers not to be deceived by him. But his warnings had fallen on deaf ears. By vulgarizing her brother's ideals, Elisabeth had perverted them into their opposites—superhumans had become subhumans. Oehler, like millions of others, became victims when Hitler and Stalin put into practice their interpretation of Zarathustra's gospel.

The Writings of Elisabeth Förster-Nietzsche

Books

Dr. Bernhard Förster's Kolonie Neu-Germania in Paraguay. Berlin: Commissions-Verlag der Aktien-Gesellschaft "Pionier," 1891.

Das Leben Friedrich Nietzsches. Leipzig: Naumann, vol. I, 1895; vol. II, pt. 1, 1897; vol. II, pt. 2, 1904.

Das Nietzsche-Archiv, seine Freunde und seine Feinde. Berlin: Marquardt, 1907.

Der junge Nietzsche. Leipzig: Kröner, 1912.

Der einsame Nietzsche. Leipzig: Kröner, 1914.

Wagner und Nietzsche zur Zeit ihrer Freundschaft. München: G. Müller, 1915.

Friedrich Nietzsche und die Frauen seiner Zeit. München: C. H. Beck, 1935.

Introductions to Nietzsche's Works

"Uber die Zukunft unserer Bildungsanstalten," Magazin für Literatur (December 1893).

Wille zur Macht. Nietzches Werke, edited by Peter Gast and Ernst and August Horneffer, vol. XV. Leipzig: Naumann, 1901.

Nietzsche gesammelte Briefe, vols. 1 and 2. Berlin: Schuster & Loeffler, 1902.

Nietzsches Werke. Taschenbuch Ausgabe, vols. 1 to 10. Leipzig: Naumann, 1906.

Nietzsche Worte über Staaten und Völker. Leipzig: Kröner, 1922.

Also Sprach Zarathustra. Ein Buch für Alle und Keinen. Leipzig: Kröner, 1922.

Der Werdende Nietzsche; autobiographische Aufzeichnungen Nietzsches. München: Musarion, 1924.

Articles

"Wie der Zarathustra entstand." Zukunft, Berlin, October 2, 1897.

"Nietzsches Ahnen." Zukunft, Berlin, June 25, 1898.

"Einiges von unseren Vorfahren." Pan. V. Jahrg., Heft 4, 1899.

"Jakob Burckhardt und Friedrich Nietzsche." Neue Deutsche Rundschau, February 1899.

"Nietzsche und die Franzosen." Zukunft, Berlin, March 18, 1899.

"Friedrich Nietzsche über Weib, Liebe und Ehe." *Neue Deutsche Rundschau*, October 1899.
"Die Krankheit Friedrich Nietzsches." *Zukunft*, Berlin, January 6, 1900.
"Der Kampf um die Nietzsche-Ausgabe." *Zukunft*, Berlin, April 21, 1900.
"Nietzsche und Heinrich von Stein." *Neue Deutsche Rundschau*, July, 1900.
"Malwida von Meysenbug und Friedrich Nietzsche." *Neue Deutsche Rundschau*, January 1901.
"Genueser Gedankengänge." *Insel*, Leipzig, April 1901.
"DEr Fall Nietzsche contra Wagner." *Neue Deutsche Rundschau*, June 1901.
"Nietzsche und seine Briefwechsel." *Deutsche Revue*, August 1901.
"Friedrich Nietzsche und sein Verkehr." *Der Zeitgeist, Beilage zum Berliner Tageblatt*, October 3, 1904; also in *New Yorker Staatszeitung*, October 3, 1904.
"Nietzsches Tod." *Zukunft*, Berlin, October 15, 1904.
"Lettres inédites de Nietzsche à Hugo v. Senger." *Revue Germaniques*, Paris, January/February 1905.
"Nietzsche Legenden." *Zukunft*, Berlin, January 28, 1905.
"Nietzsches literarischer Nachlass und Franz Overbeck." *Berliner Tageblatt*, July 26, 1905.
"Der unveröffentlichte Briefwechsel Nietzsche-Overbeck." *Neue freie Presse*, September 10, 1905.
"Handschriften und Briefe von Friedrich Nietzsche." *Neue Züricher Zeitung*, October 2/3, 1905.
"Nietzsche und Stirner." March 16, 1907.
"Nietzsches Werke und Briefe." *Zukunft*, Berlin, June 8, 1907.
"Friedrich Nietzsche und die Kritik." *Morgen, Wochenschrift für deutsche Kultur*, Berlin, September 1907; also *Dortmunder Generalanzeiger*, September 1907.
"Erinnerungen." *Zukunft*, Berlin, October 12, 1907.
"Briefe Nietzsches aus dem Jahre 1888." *Die neue Rundschau*, November 1907.
"Die Nietzsche Briefe an Overbeck." *Deutsche Zeitung*, December 7, 1907.
"Die Nietzsche-Stiftung." *Berliner Tageblatt*, December 12, 1907.
"Mitteilungen aus dem Nietzsche-Archiv." Privatdruck, Weimar, May 1908.
"Die Begründung des Nietzsche-Archivs." *Weimarische Zeitung*, July 30, 1908.
"Ariadne und andere Torheiten." *Die Zeit*, Wien, November 17, 1908.
"Ungedruckte Briefe Nietzsches an Mutter und Schwester." *Süddeutsche Monatshefte*, January 1909.
"Zu Professor Andlers Artikel: Nietzsche-Overbeck." *Die Propylaen*, München, March 3, 1909, and April 21, 1909.
"Max Heinze." *Zukunft*, Berlin, December 4, 1909.
"Nietzsches Krankheit." *Der Tag*, Berlin, January 14, 1910.
"Aus dem Nietzsche-Archiv." *Zukunft*, Berlin, July 2, 1910.
"Contra Dr. Olshausen." *Euphorion*, 18. Bd. 2 & 3. Heft, 1911.
"August v. Kotzebue und die Revaler Theaterchronik." *St. Petersburger Zeitung*, December 19, 1911.
"Die Schillerstiftung." *Zukunft*, Berlin, April 1912.
"Zur Parsifalfrage" (persönlicher Erinnerungen). *Der Tag*, Berlin, September 1, 1912.
"Die Freundschaft zwischen Wagner und Nietzsche." *Der Tag*, Berlin, December 14, 1912.
"Friedrich Nietzsches Bibliothek." *Deutscher Bibliophilen Kalender*, 1913.
"Der einsame Nietzsche." *Zukunft*, Berlin, February 28, 1914.
"Wie Friedrich Nietzsche sich kleidete." *Landeszeitung Deutschland*, Weimar, May 7, 1914.
"Nietzsche und der Krieg." *Der Tag*, Berlin, September 10, 1914.

"Der 'echt-preussische' Friedrich Nietzsche." September 16, 1914.

"Eine Erinnerung an 1870" (Erste Veröffentlichung der Komposition Nietzsches 'Ade, ich muss nun gehen'). *Kladderadatsch*, February 1915.

"Nietzsche und Deutschland." *Berliner Tageblatt*, September 5, 1915.

"Die Honorare für Nietzsches Werke." *Das literarische Echo*, Berlin, December 1, 1915.

"Nietzsche, Frankreich und England." *Neue freie Presse*, June 11, 1916.

"Eine kleine Hindenburggeschichte." *Hannoverscher Kurier*, September 1, 1916.

"Cosima Wagner zu ihrem 80. Geburtstag." *Vossische Zeitung*, December 25, 1917.

"Gräfin von Bünaus *Kleist* Roman." *Vossische Zeitung*, March 14, 1918.

"Nietzsche und das Nietzsche-Archiv." *Vossische Zeitung*, June 21, 1918.

"Der Hymnus an das Leben." *Das Inselschiff*, June 1920.

"Der glückliche Nietzsche." *Vossische Zeitung*, August 18, 1920.

"Welche Nietzsche Ausgabe kauft man?" *Vossische Zeitung*, November 21, 1920.

"Mazzini und Nietzsche." *Neue freie Presse*, February 10, 1921.

"Zur Neugestaltung der Goethe-Gesellschaft." *Der Türmer*, Stuttgart, September 1923.

"Nietzsche Erinnerungen." *Deutsche Zeitung*, Berlin, March 23, 1924.

"Wagner und Nietzsche." *Neue Züricher Zeitung*, August 16, 1924.

"Die deutsche Flagge im Urwald" (Eigene Erlebnisse). *Deutsche Allgemeine Zeitung*, June 27, 1926.

"Friedrich Nietzsche im Verkehr." *Der Türmer*, Stuttgart, July 1926.

"Dreissig oder fünfzig Jahre?" (Offener Brief an Herrn Verlagsbuchhändler Dr. Kirstein). *Leipziger Neueste Nachrichten*, October 20, 1926.

"Nietzsche in Sils-Maria." *Der Türmer*, Stuttgart, February 1927.

"August von Kotzebue." *Monatsschrift Thüringen*, 2 Jahrg. 12. Heft, March 1927.

"Cosima Wagner." *Nord und Süd*, Berlin, 50. Jahrg. Heft 8, December 1927.

"Das Paradiesische Weihnachtsfest" (Weihnachten im Nietzsche Haus 1862) *Neues Tageblatt*, Stuttgart, December 22, 1928.

"Mussolinis Italien" (Brief an den italienischen Botschafter in italienischer Sprache). *Piccoli della Sera*, Trieste, May 7, 1929.

"Antwort an Oscar Levy." *Das Tagebuch*, Berlin, June 1, 1929.

"Quirinal und Vatikan." *Kölnische Zeitung*, June 9, 1929.

"Das geheimnisvolle Manuskript." *Naumburger Tageblatt*, December 20, 1929.

"Friedrich Nietzsches Wunschzettel." *Neueste Nachrichten*, Braunschweig, December 22, 1929.

"Cosima Wagner und Friedrich Nietzsche. Wahrheit und Dichtung." *Der Tag*, Berlin, May 15, 1930.

"Die Geschichte von Nietzsches Werk. Bericht einer Lebensarbeit." *Berliner Tageblatt*, June 6, 1930.

"Die Begründung des Nietzsche-Archivs" (zum 30. Todestag des Philosophe *Deutsche Allgemeine Zeitung*, August 22, 1930.

"Das Nietzsche-Archiv und die kritische Ausgabe von Nietzsches Werken." Sonderdruck, December 5, 1930.

"Nietzsche polnischer Abstammung?" *Neue Preussische Kreuzzeitung*, Berlin, September 16, 1931.

"Ausklang" (Nietzsches Zustand in seinen letzten Lebensjahren). *Deutsche Allgemeine Zeitung*, June 5, 1932.

Notes

Introduction

Part I
1. Pastoral Prelude

2. Growing Up in a Cathedral Town

3. We Fools of Fate

15   the impression of a prison rather : *Friedrich Nietzsche: Kindheit und Jugend* by Richard Blunck,
                                        München/Basel, Ernst Reinhardt, 1953, p. 53.
16   uniformed coercion   : *Friedrich Nietzsche*, ed. Karl Schlechta, München, 1960, vol. III,
                                        p. 149.
16   only two more weeks   : *Friedrich Nietzsche Briefe,* Historisch-kritische Gesamtausgabe,
                                        eds. Wilhelm Hoppe and Karl Schlechta, München, C. H. Beck,
                                        1938–1942, vol. I, p. 38.
16   I am sending   : *Ibid.*, vol. I, p. 43.
16   You had to be careful   : *Die Schwester* by Luise Marcelle, Berlin, Brunnen, 1934, p. 50.
16   I don't really like   : *Nietzsche Briefe*, vol. I, p. 177.
17   Imagine that I am having   : *Ibid.*, vol. I, p. 382.
17   But to be reminded   : *Ibid.*, vol. I, p. 182.
17   I am sorry   : *Ibid.*, vol. I, p. 225.
19   she frequently has   : *Ibid.*, vol. I, p. 411.
19   should said chain   : Unpub. letter, Naumburg/S, July 13, 1868.
19   Mama behaves   : Unpub. letter, Naumburg, second half, January 1871.
21   Mama says   : *Nietzsche Briefe*, vol. I, p. 419.
21   . . . nonetheless, it is   : *Ibid.*, vol. I, p. 318.
21   We are now living   : *Ibid.*, vol. II, p. 58.
22   What I fear   : *Friedrich Nietzsche*, ed. Karl Schlechta, vol. III, p. 148.

4. Life with Brother

23   All the Pinders   : Unpub. letter, Naumburg/S, February 13/14, 1869.
23   We are really fools   : *Friedrich Nietzsche Briefe,* Historisch-kritische Gesamtausgabe,
                                        eds. Wilhelm Hoppe and Karl Schlechta, München, C. H. Beck,
                                        1938–1942, vol. II, p. 287.
25   You must admit   : *Ibid.*, vol. II, p. 266.
26   happily played   : *Ibid.*, vol. II, p. 317.
27   most kindly   : *Nietzsche Briefe*, vol. III, p. 3.
28   everything was blue   : *Ibid.*, vol. III, p. 48.
28   Dear Elisabeth   : *Die Schwester* by Luise Marcelle, Berlin, Brunnen, 1934, p. 78.
28   a pink cashmere gown   : *Der junge Nietzsche* by Elisabeth Förster-Nietzsche, Leipzig,
                                        Kröner, 1913, p. 256.
29   I am sad to be a Swiss   : *Nietzsche Briefe*, vol. III, p. 62.
29   Lieschen is happy   : *Ibid.*, vol. III, p. 427.
29   German war of   : *Ibid.*, vol. III, p. 93.
29   surely, you must   : Unpub. letter, Naumburg/S, December 29, 1870.
30   if I may wish   : *Ibid.*
30   I am in no mood   : *Nietzsche Briefe*, vol. III, p. 112.
31   I have set up house   : *Ibid.*, vol. IV, p. 233.
32   deadly fear   : Unpub. letter, Zürich, October 8, 1884.
32   strange fits   : *Ibid.*

5. Discord in Bayreuth

34   great, brave   : *Friedrich Nietzsche*, ed. Karl Schlechta, München, Hanser, 1960,
                                        vol. III, p. 303.
35   a good but wealthy   : *Friedrich Nietzsche Briefe,* Historisch-kritische Gesamtausgabe,
                                        eds. Wilhelm Hoppe and Karl Schlechta, München, C. H. Beck,
                                        1938–1942, vol. IV, p. 339.
36   headaches from noon   : *Ibid.*, vol IV, p. 294.
36   I have now seen   : *Ibid.*, vol. IV, p. 295.
36   Farewell, my good Lisbeth   : *Ibid.*, vol. IV, p. 296.
36   it's hopeless   : *Ibid.*, vol. IV, p. 296.
37   Perhaps we will not   : *Ibid.*, vol. IV, p. 298.

Part II
6. Turning Point

41   the Jewish race   : *The Life of Richard Wagner* by Ernest Newman, New York, Alfred
                                        A. Knopf, 1946, p. 639.
42   The widow of   : *Friedrich Nietzsche Briefe,* Historisch-kritische Gesamtausgabe,
                                        eds. Wilhelm Hoppe and Karl Schlechta, München, C. H. Beck,
                                        1938–1942, vol. IV, p. 467.

Page

42	besides he resembles	: *Ibid.*
42	he returned	: *Ibid.*
43	You are quite right	: *Ibid.*, vol. IV, p. 457.
43	I must tell you	: *Nietzsche Werke*, Kritische Gesamtausgabe, eds. Giorgio Colli and Mazzino Montinari, Berlin, de Gruyter, 1968, IV, 4, p. 37.
44	The school for scholars	: *Nietzsche Briefe*, vol. IV, p. 326
44	Please help and tell me	: *Ibid.*, vol. IV, p. 341.
45	This is the plan	: *Ibid.*, vol. IV, p. 339.
45	If you get to know	: *Ibid.*, vol. IV, p. 474.
45	insane asylum	: *Nietzsche Werke*, IV, 4, p. 36.
46	Is it possible	: *Ibid*, vol. IV, 2, p. 117.
46	a pseudonym	: *Ibid.*, vol. IV, 4, p. 42.
46	much would have been	: *Der einsame Nietzsche* by Elisabeth Förster-Nietzsche, Leipzig, Kröner, 1913, p. 46.
47	illimitable progress	: Newman, *The Life of Richard Wagner*, p. 591.
47	the unusual circumstances	: *Friedrich Nietzsche*, ed. Karl Schlechta, München, Hanser, 1960, vol. III, p. 1148.
48	I feel utterly	: *Nietzsche Werke*, IV, 4, p. 55.
48	I know your brother	: *Ibid.*, IV, 4, p. 62.
49	When I said	: *Ibid.*
49	as marking	: Newman, *The Life of Richard Wagner*, p. 590.
49	the wives of famous men	: *Nietzsche Werke*, IV, 2, p. 289.
49	Pericles, Cromwell	: *Ibid.*, IV, 4, p. 63.
50	I have ten fruit trees	: *Friedrich Nietzsches Briefe an Peter Gast*, Leipzig, Insel, 1924, p. 31.
50	Unless it is absolutely	: *Nietzsche Werke*, IV, 4, p. 81.
50	The most terrible	: *Friedrich Nietzsches Briefe an Mutter und Schwester*, Leipzig, Insel, 1926, p. 271.
51	My name is	: *Gestalten um Nietzsche* by Erich F. Podach, Weimar, Lichtenstein, 1932, p. 138.
51	I remember	: Unpub. letter, Berlin, May 7, 1880.

7. Lou: A Melodrama in Four Acts
Act One

52	How can a drama	: *The Life of Richard Wagner* by Ernest Newman, New York, Alfred A. Knopf, 1946, p. 612.
54	one March evening	: *Lebensrückblick* by Lou Andreas-Salomé, Zürich, Niehans & Wiesbaden, Insel, 1951, p. 93.
56	greet this Russian	: *Friedrich Nietzsche*, ed. Karl Schlechta, München, 1960, vol. III, p. 1179.
56	the great, distant	: *Nietzsche Werke*, Kritische Gesamtausgabe, eds. Giorgio Colli and Mazzino Montinari, Berlin, de Gruyter, 1968, IV, 1, p. 294.
56	I need a young person	: *Friedrich Nietzsches Briefwechsel mit Franz Overbeck*, Leipzig, Insel, 1916, p. 169f.
56	this Messina	: *Ibid.*, p. 171.
57	her desire	: Andreas-Salomé, *Lebensrückblick*, p. 305.
59	you go to women	: *Nietzsche Werke*, VI, 1, p. 82.
59	I was too excited	: *Franz Overbeck und Friedrich Nietzsche: Eine Freundschaft* by Carl Albrecht Bernoulli, Jena, Diederichs, 1908, vol. I., p. 337.

Act Two

60	Don't faint	: *Friedrich Nietzsches Briefe an Mutter und Schwester*, Leipzig, Insel, 1926, p. 308f.
61	Nietzsche thinks it is best	: *Friedrich Nietzsche, Paul Rée, Lou von Salomé: Die Dokumente ihrer Begegnung*, ed. Ernst Pfeiffer, Frankfurt/Main, Insel, 1970, p. 118.
61	I urge you	: *Ibid.*, p. 139.
61	conditions in the Berlin	: *Gestalten um Nietzsche* by Erich F. Podach, Weimar, Lichtenstein, 1932, p. 138.
64	one day a bird	: Pfeiffer, *Nietzsche, Rée, von Salomé*, p. 174.
64	please come	: *Ibid.*, p. 175.

Act Three

65	Don't get the idea	: *Ibid.*, p. 254.
65	madly in love	: *Ibid.*, p. 255.

Page

66	Strangely enough	: *Ibid.*, p. 217.
66	What was a lie	: *Ibid.*, p. 255.
66	I withdrew completely	: *Ibid.*, p. 256
67	my talks with Lou	: *Ibid.*, p. 228f.
67	He either marries	: *Friedrich Nietzsche und Lou Salomé: Ihre Begegnung 1882* by Erich F. Podach, Zürich, Niehans, 1937, p. 73.
67	The Russian doesn't	: Pfeiffer, *Nietzsche, Rée, von Salomé*, p. 258.

Act Four

68	our dear Lou	: *Ibid.*, p. 230.
68	Just as Christian	: Andreas-Salomé, *Lebensrückblick*, p. 315f.
69	a solitary suffers	: Pfeiffer, *Nietzsche, Rée, von Salomé*, p. 250.
69	my dears Lou and Rée	: *Ibid.*, p. 269.
69	I cannot bring myself	: *Ibid.*, p. 277.
70	Is this terrible creature	: *Ibid.*, p. 287.
70	the only thing we want	: *Ibid.*, p. 288.
70	low, sensuous, and cruel	: *Ibid.*, p. 289.
70	that Fritz and Rée had brought	: *Ibid.*, p. 290.
70	The thread of my life	: *Ibid.*, p. 291f.
70	I cannot tell you	: Unpub. letter, Naumburg/S, January 7, 1883.
71	A friend of ours	: *Ibid.*
71	man is a rope	: *Nietzsche Werke*, vol. VI, 1, p. 10.
71	Southern Russia	: *Deutsche Colonien in dem oberen Laplata Gebiete mit besonderer Berücksichtigung von Paraguay* by Dr. Bernhard Förster, Naumburg/S im Selbstverlag des Verfassers, 1886, p. 7.
72	for the road that lies	: Pfeiffer, *Nietzsche, Rée, von Salomé*, p. 303.
72	I don't want	: *Ibid.*, p. 304.
72	I have taken	: *Ibid.*, p. 483.
72	Antichrist	: Unpub. letter, Rome, April 4, 1883.
72	Cosima had indeed violated	: Pfeiffer, *Nietzsche, Rée, von Salomé*, p. 294.
72	my dear sister	: *Ibid.*, p. 312.
73	the typewriter	: *Ibid.*, p. 313.
73	Fritz has been here	: Unpub. letter, Rome, June 10, 1883.
73	her literary masterpiece	: Pfeiffer, *Nietzsche, Rée, von Salomé*, p. 321.
74	hated his sister	: *Ibid.*, p. 344.
74	My brother's goal	: Unpub. letter, Naumburg/S, September 15, 1883.
75	people like my sister	: Pfeiffer, *Nietzsche, Rée, von Salomé*, p. 351.

8. To Catch a Husband

77	As I reflected	: Unpub. letter, Naumburg/S, January 1883.
78	so that your home	: Unpub. letter, Naumburg/S, November 28, 1883.
78	may it convey	: Unpub. letter, San Bernardino, November 30, 1883.
78	you have robbed me	: Unpub. letter, Naumburg/S, January 12, 1884.
79	I feared the power	: *Ibid.*
80	It saddens me	: Unpub. letter, Naumburg/S, January 28, 1884.
80	Please let me tell	: Unpub. letter, San Bernardino, May 15, 1884.
81	beloved friend	: Unpub. letter, Naumburg/S, July 5, 1884.
81	my beloved friend	: Unpub. letter, Naumburg/S, August 2, 1884.
81	I would be enchanted	: Unpub. letter, Naumburg/S, August 20, 1884.
82	I think first of all	: Unpub. letter, Naumburg/S, August 28, 1884.
82	I have read	: *Ibid.*
83	Sometimes a voice	: Unpub. letter, Zürich, Pension Neptun, October 12, 1884.
84	on the last day	: Unpub. letter, Naumburg/S, November 1, 1884.
84	which are meant	: Unpub. letter, Naumburg/S, December 15, 1884.

9. Knight, Death, and Devil

85	Dr. Förster's return	: *Friedrich Nietzsches Briefwechsel mit Franz Overbeck*, Leipzig, Insel, 1916, p. 291.
85	The instinct of	: *Friedrich Nietzsches Briefe an Mutter und Schwester*, Leipzig, Insel, 1926, p. 345.
85	a personal	: *Ibid.*, p. 389.
85	I have been approached	: *Briefwechsel mit Overbeck*, p. 295.
86	My relatives have	: *Ibid.*, p. 297.

Page

86   not because they want   : *Deutsche Colonien in dem oberen Laplata Gebiete mit besonderer*
                                     Berücksichtigung von Paraguay by Bernhard Förster,Naumburg/S
                                     im Selbstverlag des Verfassers, 1886, p. 3.
88   keeping this splendid   : *Briefe an Mutter und Schwester*, p. 379.
88   my God or perhaps   : *Ibid.*, p. 393.
89   You will be surprised   : *Briefwechsel mit Overbeck*, p. 304f.
89   Fritz loves you   : Unpub. letter, Naumburg/S, September 13, 1885.
89   otherwise the idea   : *Briefwechsel mit Overbeck*, p. 305.
90   Fritz thinks   : Unpub. letter, Naumburg/S, September 15, 1885.
90   I am sending you   : Unpub. letter, Naumburg/S, n.d.
90   You could hardly   : Unpub. letter, Naumburg/S, n.d.
90   I have tried to hide   : Unpub. letter, Naumburg/S, September 30, 1885
91   so that we can   : Unpub. letter, Naumburg/S, n.d.
91   if we are to perish   : *Ibid.*
91   I did not find   : *Briefwechsel mit Overbeck*, p. 311.
92   I confess   : *Briefe an Mutter und Schwester*, p. 422.

Part III
10. The Queen of Nueva Germania

98   My relatives have sent me   : *Friedrich Nietzsches Briefwechsel mit Franz Overbeck*, Leipzig, Insel,
                                     1916, p. 346.
98   Concerning my money   : *Friedrich Nietzsches Briefe an Mutter und Schwester*, Leipzig, Insel,
                                     1926, p. 445.
98   particularly because   : Unpub. letter, Asunción, September 12, 1887.
98   that on March 5   : Unpub. letter, Nueva Germania, March 18, 1888.
101 My sister has written   : *Friedrich Nietzsches Briefe an Peter Gast*, Leipzig, Insel, 1924, p.
                                     285.
101 it is possible   : *Ibid.*, p. 222.
102 A few days ago   : *Briefe an Mutter und Schwester*, p. 511.
102 I have just heard   : *Gestalten um Nietzsche* by Erich F. Podach, Weimar, Lichtenstein,
                                     1932, p. 151.
102 What a chance we offer   : *Ibid.*, p. 152f.
103 It is Sunday   : *Bayreuther Blätter*, vol. IX, 1889, p. 285.
104 It seems to us   : *Ibid.*, p. 288.

11. 1889: Drama and Tragedy

105 there were days and nights   : *Friedrich Nietzsches Briefwechsel mit Franz Overbeck*, Leipzig, Insel,
                                     1916, p. 412.
105 I say to myself   : *Friedrich Nietzsches Briefe an Peter Gast*, Leipzig, Insel, 1924, p. 263
105 that princely residence   : *Ibid.*, p. 272.
105 The lecture hall is   : *Briefwechsel mit Overbeck*, p. 421.
105 I, too, have reason   : *Friedrich Nietzsches Briefe an Mutter und Schwester*, Leipzig, Insel,
                                     1926. p. 503.
106 To my own surprise   : *Briefwechsel mit Overbeck*, p. 433f.
106 My publisher tells me   : *Ibid.*, p. 434.
106 In Vienna, St. Petersburg   : *Ibid.*, p. 446.
106 the one great innermost   : *Nietzsche Werke*, Kritische Gesamtausgabe, eds. Giorgio Colli and
                                     Mazzino Montinari, Berlin, de Gruyter, 1968, vol. VI, 3, p. 251.
106 Do you know   : *Ibid.*, vol. VII, 3, p. 338.
106 I know my fate   : *Ibid.*, vol. VI, 3, p. 363.
106 including my peddler   : *Briefe an Mutter und Schwester*, p. 526.
106 I mean to constrict   : *Briefwechsel mit Overbeck*, p. 452.
107 For fame is a sweet   : Unpub. letter, Nueva Germania, September 6, 1888.
107 in Paraguay things   : *Friedrich Nietzsche*, ed Karl Schlechta, München, Hanser, 1960,
                                     vol. III, p. 1345.
108 If I could only get   : Unpub. letter, Nueva Germania, end of March 1889.
109 I know quite well   : Unpub. letter, Nueva Germania, April 9, 1889.
109 if only I had remained   : Unpub. letter to Gast, Neu-Germania, March 24, 1889.
109 I hear that Overbeck   : Unpub. letter, Nueva Germania, February 28, 1890.
110 Nothing was lacking   : *Enthüllungen über die Dr. Bernhard Förstersche Ansiedlung Neu-Ger-*
                                     manien in Paraguay by Julius Klingbeil, Leipzig, Kommis-
                                     sionsverlag Baldamus, 1889, p. 36.
110 the man possessed   : *Ibid.*, p. 37.
110 Finally, she came   : *Ibid.*, p. 40.

Page

110	With much elegance	: *Ibid.*, p. 41.
110	Not one had	: *Ibid.*, p. 40.
111	possessed an incredible	: *Ibid.*, p. 43.
111	What a sad life	: *Ibid.*, p. 43.
111	Dear Mr. Schubert	: *Gestalten um Nietzsche* by Erich F. Podach, Weimar, Lichtenstein, 1932, p. 159.

12. Homecoming

115	a weak, brokenhearted	: *Dr. Bernhard Försters Kolonie Neu-Germania in Paraguay* by Elisabeth Förster-Nietzsche, Berlin Commissionsverlag der Aktien-Gesellschaft "Pionier," 1891, p. 127.
116	an influential woman	: Unpub. letter to Overbeck, November 20, 1893.
118	No other publisher	: *Zur Geschichte des Nietzsche-Archivs* by Adalbert Oehler, unpub. ms., p. 10.
118	one could laugh oneself	: Unpub. letter Gast to Overbeck, April 4, 1891.
120	Do we have the right	: Unpub. letter, Naumburg/S, September 28, 1891.
121	The contract with	: Unpub. letter, Naumburg/S, February 14, 1892.

13. Flight

122	I do not believe	: *Gestalten um Nietzsche* by Erich F. Podach, Weimar, Lichtenstein, 1932, p. 165.
123	it is impossible	: Unpub. letter, Nueva Germania, November 28, 1892.
124	You are perhaps not	: Unpub. letter, Naumburg/S, November 28, 1892.
124	play the role	: Unpub. letter, Naumburg/S, February 2, 1893.
124	German colonial policy	: Podach, *Gestalten um Nietzsche*, p. 171.
125	I must say farewell	: *Bayreuther Blätter*, vol. IV/V, 1894, p. 176.

Part IV
14. My Brother's Keeper

131	but his life	: Unpub. letter, Naumburg/S, September 17, 1893.
131	the high priest	: Unpub. letter, Naumburg/S, September 22, 1893.
131	You must understand	: Unpub. letter, Naumburg/S, September 27, 1893.
131	joyfully undertake	: Unpub. letter, Berlin, October 20, 1893.
132	enveloped in an aura	: *Ibid.*
132	The guardianship has	: Unpub. letter, Naumburg/S, October 5, 1893.
133	by this return	: Unpub. letter, Annaberg, October 6, 1893.
133	I shall, of course	: Unpub. letter, Berlin, October 20, 1893.
133	Don't get the idea	: Unpub. letter, Naumburg/S, November 20, 1893.
133	We must tell nobody	: *Ibid.*
134	seven prologs	: Unpub. letter, Naumberg/S, December 2, 1893.
134	Please do not talk	: Unpub. letter, Naumberg/S, October 24, 1893.
134	I cannot help myself	: Unpub. letter, Berlin, April 24, 1894.
135	Dr. Koegel and his	: Unpub. letter, Annaberg, November 19, 1893.
135	Dr. Koegel has a truly	: *Franz Overbeck und Friedrich Nietzsche: Eine Freundschaft* by Carl Albrecht Bernoulli, Jena, Diederichs, 1908, vol. II, p. 363.
135	I shall never again	: Unpub. letter, Berlin, April 24, 1894.
135	I shall hardly ever	: *Ibid.*

15. Poor Koegel

137	basic changes	: *Der Fall Elisabeth* by Gustav Neumann, unpub. ms., p. 30.
137	if I once indulge	: Unpub. letter, Naumburg/S, August 22, 1895.
137	This is the situation	: *Zur Geschichte des Nietzsche-Archivs, by Adalbert Oehler, unpub. ms., p. 56.*
139	I would be tormented	: Unpub. letter, Naumburg/S, November 21, 1894.
140	follow Dr. Koegel's	: Oehler, *Geschichte des Nietzsche-Archivs*, p. 89.
141	Last September	: *Ibid.*, p. 89.
141	we are very good	: *Ibid.*, p. 90.
141	A very lonely	: Unpub. letter, Naumburg/S, August 11, 1895.

16. Mother and Daughter

142	Lieschen refuses to	: Unpub. letter, Naumburg/S, August 29, 1895.

Page

143 Nobody understands   : Unpub. letter, Naumburg/S, March 9, 1897.
143 a woman without   : Unpub. letter, Naumburg/S, February 14, 1895.
145 she would have driven   : *Ibid.*
145 Imagine the terrible   : *Ibid.*
147 Perhaps you are   : Unpub. letter, Naumburg/S, December 4, 1895.
148 she received me   : Unpub. letter, Leipzig, September 19, 1895.
148 a mental confusion   : *Der Kranke Nietzsche. Briefe seiner Mutter an Franz Overbeck,* ed. Erich F. Podach, Wien, 1937, p. 193.
149 I testify herewith   : *Zur Geschiche des Nietzsche-Archivs* by Adalbert Oehler, unpub. ms., p. 77.

17. The Case of Elisabeth

150 the Jews would then boast : Unpub. letter, Berlin, December 29, 1895.
151 I am terribly afraid   : Unpub. letter, Naumburg/S, January 24, 1896.
151 he is an excellent   : *Ibid.*
151 it makes me sick   : *Ibid.*
151 everything is new   : Unpub. letter, Naumburg/S, February 2, 1896.
152 the gentlemen of   : *Zur Geschichte des Nietzsche-Archivs* by Adalbert Oehler, unpub. ms., p. 88.
152 That my daughter   : *Der Kranke Nietzsche. Briefe seiner Mutter an Franz Overbeck,* ed. Erich F. Podach, Wien, 1937, p. 202.
152 It is unfair of you   : Unpub. letter, München, March 29, 1896.
153 although Dr. Koegel is   : *Der Fall Elisabeth* by Gustav Naumann, unpub. ms., p. 15.
153 You have probably   : *Ibid.,* p. 17.
154 I would very much   : *Ibid.,* p.23.
154 Koegel is not really   : *Ibid.*
154 In these matters   : *Ibid.,* p. 24.
155 the Nietzsche editor   : Unpub. letter, Weimar, December 26, 1897.
155 The scene in the   : Naumann, *Der Fall Elisabeth,* p. 32.
155 both men fell   : *Ibid.,* p. 33.
156 If there is anything   : *Ibid.,* p. 4.
156 Dr. Koegel intends   : Unpub. letter, Leipzig, December 10, 1896.
156 she did not understand   : Naumann, *Der Fall Elisabeth,* p. 1.
157 a defenseless woman   : *Ibid.,* p. 38.
158 Dr. Koegel arrived   : Unpub. letter, Weimar, February 15, 1897.
158 Dr. Koegel has left   : Unpub. letter, Annaberg, October 7, 1897

18. Villa Silberblick

159 had really become   : Unpub. letter, Kiel, March 5, 1897.
159 I am being terribly   : *Ibid.*
160 Who knows if my son's   : *Der Kranke Nietzsche. Briefe seiner Mutter an Franz Overbeck,* ed. Erich F. Podach, Wien, 1937, p. 184.
161 I think of you as   : Unpub. letter, Weimar, August 5, 1897.
161 I have followed   : *Ibid.*
161 Dear Elisabeth   : Unpub. letter, Marschlins, August 16, 1897.
161 *you* love luxury   : *Ibid.*
162 I could not wait   : Unpub. letter, Weimar, August 18, 1897.
162 Unfortunately   : *Ibid.*
162 Please give me   : *Ibid.*
162 I can only smile   : Unpub. letter, Marschlins, August 26, 1897.
164 It is better   : Unpub. letter, Marschlins, January 1, 1898.
164 Believe me   : Unpub. letter, Marschlins, April 4, 1898.
164 I do not know   : Unpub. letter, Marschlins, January 2, 1898.
164 Meta has not the   : Unpub. letter, Weimar, January 8, 1898.
164 I am really sorry   : Unpub. letter, Weimar, July 14, 1898.

19. Staging Nietzsche's Funeral

165 One of the few   : *Der Monat,* vol. 170, nr. 15, 1962, p. 56.
166 Weimar, August 7   : *Sonderdruck aus dem Jahrbuch der deutschen Schiller Geshellschaft,* 1968, vol. XII, p. 72.
167 he was asleep   : *Ibid.,* p. 74.
167 I half got up   : *Ibid.,* p. 75.
168 Frau Förster still   : *Ibid.,* p. 75.
168 I am not saying   : Unpub. letter, Annaberg, October 6, 1893.

Page

169   you cannot open   : *Erinnerungen an Elisabeth Förster-Nietzsche* by Max Kruse, unpub.
                                              ms., Kösen, April 7, 1918.
169   all of it   : Unpub. letter, Annaberg, October 6, 1893.
169   Only somebody who   : *Ibid.*
170   this angelic   : Unpub. letter, Annaberg, April 14, 1898.
170   As things stand   : Unpub. letter, Annaberg, August 4, 1900.
171   Frau Förster does   : *Ibid.*
171   At noon today   : *Sonderdruck*, p. 77f.
173   one had to stand   : *Erinnerungen eines Baumeisters: Stufen des Lebens.* by Fritz
                                              Schumacher, Stuttgart, 1949, p. 201.
173   Stöving, Heinze   : *Sonderdruck*, p. 80.
174   Hallowed by thy   : *Das Leben Friedrich Nietzsches* by Elisabeth Förster-Nietzsche,
                                              Leipzig, Kroner, 1913, vol. II, p. viii.

Part V
20. The Missing Manuscript

177   I may possess   : *Der Fall Elisabeth* by Gustav Naumann, unpub. ms., p. 18.
180   when nobody of   : *Wilie zur Macht*, vol. XV, Leipzig, Naumann, 1901, p. XVII.
181   I cannot find   : Unpub. letter, Rapallo, March 1903.
184   One often hears   : *Franz Overbeck und Friedrich Nietzsche. Eine Freundschaft* by Carl
                                              Albrecht Bernoulli, Jena, Diederichs, 1908, vol. II, p. 431.
184   I have kept   : Unpub. letter, Basel, May 21, 1905.
185   through the negligence   : *Literarisches Echo* 8, vol. 5, December 1, 1905.
186   she had denied   : *Nietzsches Letztes Schaffen* by Ernest Horneffer, Jena, Diedrichs,
                                              1907, p. 28.

21. A Swedish Angel

188   I hear many   : Unpubl. letter, Weimar, February 20, 1905.
191   That which the many   : *Nietzsche Werke*, Kritische Gesamtausgabe, eds. Giorgio Colli and
                                              Mazzino Montinari, Berlin, de Gruyter, 1968, VI, 1, p. 86f.
191   I invite you   : Unpub. letter, Weimar, April 4, 1905.
192   good angel   : Unpub. letter, Weimar, October 2, 1907.
192   Van de Velde wants   : Unpub. letter, Weimar, July 3, 1905.
194   which in fact it has   : Unpub. letter, Weimar, July 3, 1905.
194   But dear Mr. Thiel   : Unpub. letter, Weimar, April 14, 1906.
194   Now everything is   : Unpub. letter, Weimar, November 18, 1906.
195   But since Nietzsche is   : Unpub. letter, Weimar, June 28, 1907.
195   To obtain this sum   : Unpub. letter, Weimar, July 9, 1907.
195   I sat down and wept   : Unpub. letter, Weimar, September 10, 1907.
196   It is very hard for   : Unpub. letter, Weimar, December 5, 1907.
196   I needed two days   : Unpub. letter, Weimar, October 2, 1907.
196   dear friend, her   : Unpub. letter, Weimar, October 23, 1907.
196   the best deserve   : Unpub. letter, Weimar, November 5, 1907.
196   But dearest friend   : Unpub. letter, Blockhusudden, October 10, 1907.
196   Concerning the ten thousand   : Unpub. letter, Blockhusudden, December 23, 1907.
196   I rejoice in the depth   : Unpub. letter, Weimar, April 26, 1908.
197   That the endowment   : Unpub. letter, Blockhusudden, June 19, 1908.

22. The Nietzsche Cult and the First World War

198   Hurray, hurray   : Unpub. letter, Weimar, October 2, 1908.
199   a bore, a clumsy clod   : Unpub. letter, Weimar, April 7, 1894.
199   I had no idea   : Unpub. letter, Annaberg, April 4, 1911.
199   the most unpleasant   : Unpub. letter, Weimar, June 16, 1911.
200   wars, the like of which   : *Nietzsche Werke*, Kritische Gesamtausgabe, eds. Giorgio Colli and
                                              Mazzino Montinari, Berlin, de Gruyter, 1968, vol. VI, 3, p. 364.
200   the idle rich mob   : *Geschichte meines Lebens* by Henry van de Velde, München, Piper,
                                              1962, p. 351.
201   but was it really   : *Ibid.*, p. 354.
201   a considerable fund   : *Nietzsche in England 1890−1914* by David Thatcher, University of
                                              Toronto Press, 1970, p. 268.
202   it reads like a novel   : Unpub. letter, Weimar, March 7, 1911.
202   You have once again wrought   : Unpub. letter, Blockhusudden, April 28, 1912.
202   the account of my   : Unpub. letter, Weimar, July 17, 1911.
202   it is so simple   : Unpub. letter, Blockhusudden, April 28, 1912.

Page

203	If my brother were	: Unpub. letter, Weimar, September 4, 1914.
203	Our troops are rolling	: Unpub. letter, Weimar, February 15, 1915.
203	I often reflect	: Unpub. letter, Blockhusudden, August 25, 1914.
203	Our troops will not	: Unpub. letter, Weimar, February 15, 1915.
203	these letters were	: Unpub. letter, Weimar, July 8, 1914.
204	the pillar of the	: Unpub. letter, Weimar, January 15, 1917.
204	these sixty thousand	: Unpub. letter, Blockhusudden, January 1, 1918.
204	We are living	: Unpub. letter, Weimar, April 5, 1915.
204	a people attains	: Unpub. letter, Weimar, June 22, 1917.
205	the safest investment	: Unpub. letter, Weimar, January 27, 1918.
205	Our enemies must	: Unpub. letter, Weimar, March 2, 1918.
205	Our victorious troops	: Unpub. letter, Weimar, September 19, 1918.
205	This is the fall	: Unpub. letter, December 20, 1918.

23. The Fight Against the Weimar Republic

206	Last autumn	: Unpub. letter, Weimar, February 7, 1919.
207	had moved him more	: Unpub. letter, München, December 19, 1918.
207	Germany is paralyzed	: Unpub. letter, Weimar, April 11, 1919.
208	The sight of such	: Unpub. letter, Weimar, August 12, 1919.
208	How shall I find	: Unpub. letter, Weimar, December 21, 1919.
209	seldom have glad	: Unpub. letter, Weimar, March 15, 1920.
208	Our workers are	: Unpub. letter, Weimar, March 29, 1920.
208	our magnificent	: Unpub. letter, Weimar, March 29, 1920.
208	to pay respectful	: Unpub. letter, Stoke-on-Trent, April 25, 1920.
209	our government uses	: Unpub. letter, Weimar, March 15, 1920.
210	Should our red rulers	: Unpub. letter, Weimar, February 6, 1922.
210	My brother wished	: Unpub. letter, Weimar, June 3, 1922.
210	it would be wise	: Unpub. letter, Weimar, September 7, 1922.
210	However, the gentlemen	: Unpub. letter, Weimar, September 18, 1922.
210	makes us feel as	: Unpub. letter, Weimar, December 13, 1922.
211	grateful that I am	: *Ibid.*
211	how much a publisher	: Unpub. letter, Weimar, June 20, 1923.
211	My poor old head	: Unpub. letter, Weimar, August 3, 1923.
212	The fame of my	: Unpub. letter, Weimar, June 27, 1925.
212	Once again the waves	: Unpub. letter, Weimar, February 12, 1926.
213	His major work	: Unpub. letter, Weimar, July 10, 1926.
213	Our excellent President	: Unpub. letter, Weimar, August 26, 1926.
213	What nonsense some people	: *Ibid.*
213	So you have been	: Unpub. letter, Stockholm, September 9, 1926.
213	I often have a kind	: Unpub. letter, Stockholm, February 24, 1928.
214	the Nietzsche Archives	: Unpub. letter, Weimar, February 10, 1927.
214	the courageous American	: Unpub. letter, Weimar, June 16, 1927.

24. Elisabeth and Hitler

216	You have no idea	: Unpub. letter, Weimar, August 4, 1931.
216	grotesque, considering	: *The Diaries of a Cosmopolitan* by Count Harry Kessler, London, Weidenfeld & Nicholson, 1971, p. 426.
217	the most miraculous	: Unpub. letter, Weimar, January 13, 1932.
218	I felt she wanted	: Oral communication of Karl Schlechta to author.
218	We are curious	: *Völkischer Beobachter*, February 9, 1932.
219	which are fascinating	: Kessler, *Diaries*, p. 426.
219	As soon as I see	: Unpub. letter, Weimar, August 15, 1932.
220	Last Sunday	: Unpub. letter, Weimar, February 17, 1933.
220	We are drunk with	: Unpub. letter, Weimar, May 12, 1933.
221	milder laws	: Unpub. letter, Weimar, May 12, 1933.
221	that such an independent	: Unpub. letter, Weimar, July 28, 1933.
221	Last year our deeply	: Unpub. letter, Weimar, February 14, 1935.
221	it is enough to	: Kessler, *Diaries*, p. 426.
221	these hours must seem	: Unpub. letter, Weimar, May 29, 1934.
221	Believe me, Fritz	: Unpub. letter, Weimar, October 31, 1935.
222	I advise everybody	: Unpub. letter, Jena, June 19, 1935.

25. Angry Ashes: A Postscript

226	a nice ornament	: *Erinnerungen an Elisabeth Förster-Nietzsche* by Margot Boger-Langhammer, unpub. ms., p. 46.
226	I sat close to	: *Ibid.*, p. 69.

Index

240